Sons and Daughters of the Soil

Sons and Daughters of the Soil

Land and Boundary Conflicts in North West Cameroon, 1955-2005

Walter Gam Nkwi

Langaa Research & Publishing CIG
Mankon, Bamenda

Publisher:
***Langaa* RPCIG**
Langaa Research & Publishing Common Initiative Group
P.O. Box 902 Mankon
Bamenda
North West Region
Cameroon
Langaagrp@gmail.com
www.langaa-rpcig.net

Distributed outside N. America by African Books Collective
orders@africanbookscollective.com
www.africanbookscollective.com

Distributed in N. America by Michigan State University Press
msupress@msu.edu
www.msupress.msu.edu

ISBN: 9956-578-92-4

© Walter Gam Nkwi 2011

DISCLAIMER
All views expressed in this publication are those of the author and do not necessarily reflect the views of Langaa RPCIG.

Content

Dedication vii
Acknowledgements ix
Preface xii

Chapter One
Introduction 1
   A) Dancing the Plot and Riding the Past into the Present 1
   B) Understanding inter-community boundary conflicts
       within Homer-Dixon Framework 9

Chapter Two
The Geographical and Ethnographic Survey of Bamenda
Grassfields 11
   A) Staking the Study Area 11
   B) Peoples of the Region 15
   C) Traditional and Socio-Political Organisations 21
   D) Decentralised Societies 22
   E) The contending issues of boundary conflicts in
       the Bamenda Grassfields 23

Chapter Three
A History of Bambili/Babanki-Tungoh and the Genesis
   of the Boundary Conflict 39
   A) Geographical Locations and Daily Activities 41
   B) From Fraternal Friends (up to 1950s) to Fraternal
       Enemies? 43
   C) Contending issues: causes of the boundary conflict
       between Bambili and Babanki-Tungoh 45

D) The Manifestation of the Boundary Conflict
c. 1950-1955: The epoch of Law Suits 53
E) Decision on Land Dispute Between Babanki-tungoh
And Bambili Agreed Upon By The Bafut........................ 57
F) The War Period 65
G) The 1995 War... 79
H) The Wesmacott's myth: a commentary 88

Chapter Four
The "Cold" Years, 1995-2005... 99
A) The Complaints Period 99
B) The Koungo Edima Commission 106

Chapter Five
Consequences of the Bambili and Babanki-Tungoh Boundary
Conflict and Some Suggested Solutions 117
A) Social Consequences 117
B) Economic Consequences 130
C) Political Consequences 131
D) Efforts at Resolving the Boundary Conflict 134
E) Why the attempted solutions failed 145
F) Suggested Solutions 151

Chapter Six
General Conclusion 161

Appendices 169
Notes on Sources... 217

Dedication

To Professor Emeritus, Martin Zachary Njeuma, who rested in the lord on 28 April 2010, without seeing the outcome of this piece of work which we jointly laid the foundation together, way back in 1997 at his residence at Governor's quarters, Buea.

Acknowledgements

In the writing and completing this book inspiration was received from many people whom I would like to acknowledge. My profound gratitude goes to Professors Martin Zachary Njeuma and Victor Julius Ngoh who first accepted to guide me through my Masters thesis thereby getting the academic ball rolling. In a like manner I am indebted to Mr. Kiawi Paul Tuh whom I first came in contact with in 1982 as my history teacher in secondary school and who in 2008 gave me an abundance of primary data which helped me to enlarge and sharpen my views and extend the scope of this study. To him I say "Thank You".

Professor Dr. Francis B. Nyamnjoh; Mr. Justine Cox and Dr. Divine Fuh kept on encouraging me to write. I also want to extend my gratitude to Mr. Epie, who made it possible for me to lay hands on a court judgment which I desperately needed for this book. My immeasurable gratitude goes to the authorities of the Afrika Studie Centrum who granted me two weeks to travel to the Public Record Office (PRO) archives in Kew, London, in November 2007 where I coincidentally got some relevant material.

I am grateful to the entire staff of the PRO archives for the generosity they showed me during my time of stay in that archives. In that direction, I also wish to register my deep appreciation to the African Studies Centre which through my mentor, Professor Mirjam Elizabeth de Bruijn and her collaborators made it possible for me to visit PRO IN November 2007. The staff of the Buea National Archives, Bamenda Provincial Archives is not forgotten. My parents who gave me all the affection are not left out. My elder brother, Rev. Father Oliver Chiatu Gam also helped me with some data; to him I am not ungrateful. To all the informants whose names appear in the bibliography, I am also grateful to all of you. Last but not the least, I am grateful to my «Mona Lisa» (my wife), Felicitas who endured my absence from home and kept it going. She also helped me with some typing technicalities in this volume. My three sons: Ankinimbom, Ajimsimbom and Afuhmbom were very understanding. To them I would remain forever grateful.

Preface

Some eighty years ago, the German Kamerun which had been administered by Germany since July 1884 was divided into British and French spheres following the defeat of Germany in the First World War in 1916. The British and the French administered their respective zones, firstly under the League of Nations Mandate from 1922 to 1946 and later as a United Nations Trust Territory between 1946 and 1960. In 1960, Cameroon under the French Administration gained her independence, and on 1 October 1961, the British Southern Cameroons which was part of the Cameroons under British Administration gained her independence through reunification; while the Northern Cameroons opted to join the Federation of Nigeria. The Southern Cameroons, which was later administered as one of the provinces of the Eastern Region of Nigeria, had as of 1938 a total land surface area of 16,581 square miles and a population of 445,735. It was initially divided into four divisions, namely Victoria, Kumba, Mamfe and Bamenda.

In 1949, the Bamenda Division was split into three divisions viz Bamenda, Wum, and Nkambe to make six divisions. The British justified that split on grounds that they wanted to ease administration of the region. As early as 1950, boundary feuds were becoming a daily occurrence in the region. Although scholars like, Chilver, 1962; Chilver and Kaberry 1960, 1965, 1967b, 1970 and 1972; Warnier and Nkwi, 1982; Nkwi 1976; Diduk, 1993; Chem-Langëe, 2003, have written on several aspects of the Bamenda Grassfields, its history of boundary conflicts between c.1950s and 2005 has remained to the best of the author's knowledge a *terra incognita*.

In 1998, I defended a master thesis at the Department of History, University of Buea, Cameroon, with focus on the history of boundary conflicts in the Bamenda Grassfields. Nine years later (Gam Nkwi, 2007:6-42), I published an article in the *Journal of Applied Social Sciences: A Multidisciplinary Journal of the Faculty of Social and Management Sciences*, University of Buea, Cameroon, vol.6, Numbers 1and 2. These works received positive feedbacks albeit criticisms in other quarters. After many years of drudgery on books and archives, I discovered that the works which I had initially written were however, limited in their circulation to the public, and also limited in scope and content.

It is based on the above, apertures that I have decided to re-embark on the topic with the availability of new data to add to the existing material. This present project covers the history up to 2005 because new data has been uncovered, such as files «downloaded» from the Divisional Archives, Tubah, Public Records Office (PRO) Kew Gardens, London and the archives of Bamenda High Court. The present work attempts to fill this lacuna in the historiography of the Bamenda Grassfields and Cameroon historiography in general by focusing on the internal boundary conflict.

It specifically traces the causes of the boundary conflict, its course and ramifications on the sub region. It is only in giving an historical dimension that the contemporary boundary conflicts in the sub region could be well understood. In the opening words of the preface to his book, Walter Rodney reminds us that: "This (His) book derives from a concern with the contemporary African situation. It delves into the past only because otherwise it would be impossible to understand how the present came into being and what the trends are for the future" (Rodney, 1981: vii). While complimenting Rodney, the celebrated African political scientist, Ali Mazrui (1969:661-676) said: "we study history in order to discover how we have come to be where we are."

It is these words that have further inspired the writing of this book, that to understand the subject of boundary misunderstandings in the Bamenda Grassfields and Bambili/ Babanki Tungoh, we need to take an historical dimension and appreciate why the boundary misunderstanding has been protracted for so long. Within the contemporary political dispensation the work shows the laxity of the administration to handle a pernicious situation like the boundary conflicts which have been eating deep in the political and social fabric of the region.

In writing this book, the major sources have been documents which were garnered in the Public Record Office, Kew, London, the National Archives, Buea, the Provincial Archives Bamenda, and the Bamenda High Court. The District Archives in Tubah sub division were of the utmost importance because they provided relevant information. I also used private archives of individuals. In those archives I found some useful letters which I have used in the project. The importance of an archive to historical reconstruction cannot be over emphasised. According to the Hiatian scholar, Michel-Rolph Trouillot (1995:52), «archives are institutions that organise facts and sources and condition the possibility of existence of historical statements. Archival power determines the difference between an historian, amateur or professional, and a charlatan.» Trouillot continued by saying that,

> ...archives assembly and their assembly work is not limited to a more or less passive act of collecting. Rather, it is an active act of production that prepares facts for historical intelligibility. Archives set up both the substantive and formal elements of the narrative. They are the institutionalized sites of mediation between the socio historical process and the narrative about the process. They enforce the constraints on debatability and convey authority and set the rules of credibility and inter dependence; they help select the stories that matter.

In most of these archives files were consulted which touched directly on the two villages, and some which were not directed but which treated issues pertaining to other areas of the Northwest Region. In most of the archives, colonial reports and assessment reports were coloured. Despite their evident bias and subjectivity, however, the archive sources proved a wealth of useful information, if the bias of the writers and the context within which the documents were compiled are taken into account (Whiteman, 1983). Secondary sources were consulted. Interviews were conducted with some of the actors who were directly involved in the scene and some who just heard the story in the two communities.

The Structure of the Book

The book is divided into six chapters. Chapter One, which is the introduction, defines and justifies the work and also reviews some of the extant literature in the study area as well as defining some of the key concepts. Chapter Two opens with the geographical and ethnographic survey of the Bamenda Grassfields. The chapter focuses amongst other things, on the land, human, traditional and socio-political setting in which the contestants of the boundary conflicts find themselves. It ends up with the general causes of boundary conflicts in the Bamenda Grassfields.

Chapter Three treats the arrival of the Babanki-Tungoh and Bambili people in their respective areas. These two ethnic groups constitute the core of the study. In order to better appreciate the inter- societal relations between these two peoples, this chapter examines the period in their history when they were fraternal friends. This chapter is divided into the remote and immediate causes of the boundary conflict. The chapter ends with the manifestations of the conflict from c. 1955-2005. Chapter Four opens with the introduction and actions of new actors and actresses into the drama stage of the boundary conflict. Because there is no clear cut conflict in the name of war, it has been further captured as «cold years».

The consequences of boundary conflicts on the two communities and their neighbours constitute the crux of Chapter Five. The chapter attempts to explain why conflict resolution within this region has failed. This chapter ends with some suggested solutions. The last chapter (chapter six) which is the conclusion opens with an attempt to pull together all the salient threads of the historical narrative and analysis in the introduction and the preceding five chapters. Some materials which were not used during the write up and which could be useful as a pointer to further researchers have been placed in the appendix just before the bibliography. All together there are fifteen appendices.

I should emphasize, in closing that the views which have been expressed in this book are mine and should not in any way either by accidentally or intentionally be attributed to any of those who assisted me. For the errors of fact and interpretation which must have eluded all efforts to keep them out, I am solely responsible.

Walter Gam Nkwi
Buea, Cameroon 2010

Chapter One

Introduction

A) Dancing the Plot and Riding the Past into the Present
The Berlin West African Conference (1884-1885), apparently signalled the creeping European economic and political dominance in Africa and accelerated its shift from informal to formal involvement in African affairs. This led to the drawing up of artificial boundaries, which more or less authenticated various territorial claims by European powers, but, which also divided historically homogenous, contiguous and closely related, sometimes kinship communities. Since the attainment of political independence by most African countries in the 1960s, few, if any country, have not had cause to worry about the position of its boundaries in relation to its neighbours. Most boundaries resulting from the separation of ethnic groups which hitherto then were considered as one single entity have posed problems to policy makers of African states.

For example, Somalia whose essentially continuous cultural area was severed into the separate colonies of British Somaliland, French Somaliland, Italian Somaliland, the Northern Frontier District of Kenya, and the Ogaaden province of imperial Ethiopia; the Maasai cut nearly in half by the Kenya-Tanzania border; the Bokongo separated by the Gabon-Congo (Democratic Republic of the Congo-DRC) and DRC-Angola boundaries; Lunda astride and DRC-Angola and DRC-Zambia frontiers; the Zande or the Azande cut by boundaries into different parts in the Sudan, Chad, the Central African Republic and DRC (Asiwaju, 1985:176; Goldsmith, 1994:57). The European powers embarked on the separation of these ethnic groups because of greed, egoism and more.

What was upper most in their minds was to get spheres of influence, and this was motivated chiefly by economic, social and political considerations in what became popularly known in the second half of the nineteenth century as colonialism. According to McMichael (1996:17), Colonialism is the subjugation by physical and psychological force of one culture by another - a colonizing power - through military conquest of territory. It predates the era of European expansion (fifteen to twentieth century), extending, for example, to Japanese colonialism in the twentieth century and, more recently, Chinese colonization of Tibet.

Colonialism has two forms: colonies of settlement, which often eliminate indigenous people (such as the Spanish destruction of the Aztec and Inca civilizations in the Americas), and policies of colonial rule, where colonial administrators reorganize existing cultures to facilitate their exploitation (such as the British use of local *zamindars* to rule the Indian Subcontinent). The outcomes are first, the cultural genocide or marginalization of indigenous people; second, the extraction of labour, cultural treasures, and resources to enrich the colonial power, its private interests, and public museums; and third, the elaboration of ideologies justifying colonial rule, including notions of racism and modernity.

Apart from the separation of ethnic groups in Africa, almost all African countries have boundary conflicts with their neighbours which, at times, have resulted in wars. For instance, Morocco resorted to war with Algeria to maintain the integrity of its boundaries over Western Sahara; Somalia claims land from Ethiopia; and Kenya over Ogaaden; while Cameroon has not been in the best terms with Nigeria over the Bakassi Peninsular (Ghali and Asfahany, 1973; Prescott, 1971; Oduntan, 2006; Adepoju, 2007).

It was because of the arbitrary lumping of people and complete ignorance of ethnic composition of people by the Europeans, which differences have occurred in boundary understandings of most of African states with some leading to inter-village or ethnic crisis, as well as crisis between states after attaining political independence. A case in point of inter-ethnic boundaries is the North West Region of Cameroon popularly known in colonial historiography as the Bamenda Grassfields. Since the beginning of the first decade of the twentieth century, inter-ethnic conflicts have become a common currency. For instance, the Bali-Nyonga has been disputing over boundary issues with the Baforchu and Chomba; the Balikumbat have contested with the Bafanji over their common border; the Oku have fought the Mbesa; the Bambui have clashed with the Bambili and Funge (CO 554/1239, Disturbances in the Bamenda Division, 1954-1956, Public Records Office henceforth cited as PRO, Kew, London). One of the key conflict areas would however appear to be the Bambili and Babanki-Tugoh boundary conflict which has pre-occupied the last decade of the twentieth century. Yet, in spite of this creeping malaise, little, if any scholarly attention has been focused on this all important issue, its pernicious effects on the two societies and beyond notwithstanding.

The "roaring" years of the 1990s which was like the peak of boundary conflicts in the North West Region of Cameroon will also be remembered in Cameroon and Africa South of the Sahara by the present generation and generations yet to be born for several reasons. The most important of these reasons, being that in 1990, many parts of Africa South of the Sahara embraced a new political dynamic. There was an unprecedented drive towards political and economic liberalisation, including threats to evict most African dictators, sparked by a general call for democratization and the consequent re-birth of multi-party politics. Political kleptocrats responded by engendering and intensifying the struggle over belonging and forms of exclusion and inclusion among their citizens (Gam Nkwi, 2006: 123).

In Cameroon some people were called sons and daughters of the soil while others were simply called "strangers" by politicians who were threatened to be defeated in elections and who were like surrogates to support the ruling regimes at all cost. These people were branded thus, when they were citizens of the same country. In extreme cases, the children of the same family were questioned. Some became the ones that were given birth to, out of wedlock and so had no right over certain portions of the same family resources which they grew up thinking that they were a part. Although this undermined the very notion of national citizenship and national unity/integration, which most regimes in Africa had upheld in the early 1960s and 1970s, using unity as a precondition for nation building (Geschiere, 2004; Nyamnjoh, 2006), these same authoritarian regimes began encouraging conflict between indigenous groups and strangers which would help them to remain in power. In Cameroon in particular, the ruling government since 1990, under Paul Biya, placed an additional emphasis on ethnicity, making use of political and traditional elites. This effort was borne out of a neopatrimonialistic and clientelistic system in which appointments were made based on one's relation to the government rather than on merit and ability.

In the Bamenda Grassfields whose 80 percent of the population is made up of the Tikars and whose oral tradition maintains that they came from the same original home north of Mbam River in Ndobo, present day Northern Cameroon, the idea of political and philosophical ideology of sons and daughters of the soil back fired. It came to mean a different thing as boundary conflicts flared up in the entire sub region between people whose oral traditions claimed a common ancestry and migratory history. It became very acute between Bambili and Babanki Tungoh who had a lot of things in common. The only difference between the two communities was their common border which had a piece of fertile land that was contested..

The Bamenda Grassfields which is, largely known today as the Northwest Region of Cameroon, has for many years been subjected to different forms of research endeavours-sociologists, anthropologists, historians and ethnographers alike have done work in this region from themes as varied as the researchers themselves. This study is yet another new page in the ongoing scholarship of the region. It sets out to examine the hostile attitudes of inter societal interaction in the Bamenda Grassfields and Babanki-Tungoh and Bambili with its focus being directed on boundary conflicts. The study once more will therefore seek to investigate the causes, course and consequences of the Babanki-Tungoh and Bambili conflict and examine at attempted efforts towards resolving the conflict and proffer suggestions which if implemented could go a long way at solving the boundary feud. It also critically examines the consistencies, inconsistencies and flaws of the Cameroon administration in providing a lasting solution to the conflict misunderstanding in the region.

Boundaries, conventionally, are defined to mark the sharp edges of the territorial limits within which the states exercise their distinct jurisdictions. They are, therefore, the lines of contact, more often for conflict than for harmony, between rival systems of governmental control. A boundary could also be the line of delineation or demarcation between administrative units or between geographical regions of various types (Asiwaju, 1985: 239; Stamp, 1966:75). In ancient Greece and Rome, and during the middle Ages, there were no fixed boundary lines between political communities.

The limits of a state jurisdiction were vague; there were border zones of Western Europe which replaced the Holy Roman Empire. Exact boundaries were not possible, however, until the sciences of Geography and Cartography could furnish data needed for delimitation and demarcation.

Boundaries could be looked at from two dimensions: political and physical. The physical is informed by certain physical (Geographical) features of the land mass which may include hydrography, climatology, topography and vegetation. They always direct human activities and interests, consequently, that desire to own and control territory for developmental purposes either political, economic, social, military or industrial domains. From this stand point, boundaries become geographical expressions of political and economic interests (Mitchell, 1954: 7-12; Hartshorne, 1956:184-185). This might not be new in the history of mankind. For they have taken different shapes, dimensions and intensities, with the correspondent and systematic changes in man's activities in nature largely visible at the level of socio-economic formations.

It is imperative to make a distinction between natural and artificial boundaries. While the issue of carving out boundaries is natural to man, these boundaries are artificial. According to Asiwaju (1985: 340), artificial boundaries are those boundary lines which though not being dependent upon natural features of the surface of the earth for their selection, have been artificially or arbitrarily created by men.

Subsequent writers have chosen to stress the ascendancy of astronomically and mathematically determined lines as evidence of the artificiality of Africa's international boundaries. Saunter (1971) accepted this viewpoint when he stated that, "the artificial character of African boundaries is perfectly demonstrated by the statistical evidence to the effect that forty-four percent are made up of astronomical lines (meridian parallels), thirty percent of mathematical lines (arcs, curves) while only twenty-six percent are of geographical feature" (the so-called 'natural boundaries'). The artificiality of boundaries in Africa has caused a lot of international boundary conflicts, not excluding inter-ethnic boundary problems in the Northwest region of Cameroon (Annual Reports for Bamenda Division, 1920, 1924, 1926 National Archives, Buea). Yet most of the studies around boundaries have always tended to overlook the internal dissentions within the modern African state. Most studies tend to examine this phenomenon in the light of trans-national borders. This study is an attempt to show how internal boundary conflicts in an African state could improve the general understanding of boundary conflicts.

The fundamental concepts underlining the establishment of international boundaries are the definition stage, the delimitation stage and the demarcation stage. These concepts were established by the colonial masters in Africa. As far as the definition stage was concerned, the colonial powers allocated adjacent territories to themselves by defining a common boundary line on paper, using pencils and rulers at a joint meeting summoned for that purpose in one of the European capitals. The allocation of territories and the definition of the region were divided. Delimitation involved the selection of a specific boundary site on the basis of some detailed information. Here the boundary line was determined by treaty or other legal forms usually defined in written and verbal terms. Finally, demarcation involved the physical marking of the boundary on the ground by such means like placement of beacons and pillars, erection of fences and cutting of vitas through woodlands or forests. It is important to note that all three concepts are processes in boundary-making. Prescott, however, argues that not all boundaries go through the three processes, as some allocated lines are directly without being demarcated (Fanso, 1989: 31; Prescott, 1971: 10; Oyone, 1982: 6-7).

Nonetheless, there is a difference between a boundary and a frontier. The important difference is that while a boundary denotes exact limits separating areas of administration, jurisdiction and sovereignty, a frontier is merely a zone that does not fix exact limits, and it is usually found on each side of the boundary. Border and frontier refer to the dividing line between two countries or states or the land near that line. Border is more often used when there is a natural division such as a river (Gam Nkwi, 2006).

Much has been written on boundaries (see Asiwaju, 1984; Adepoju 2007; Oduntan, 2006), but from the international boundaries perspectives. As far as internal boundary conflicts in the Bamenda Grassfields are concerned, scholarly works are amazingly lacking. The title of the work shows that the study would be limited to the Bamenda Grassfields which is today known as the North West region of Cameroon with its headquarters at Bamenda. The work will take as a case study the Bambili and Babanki-Tungoh in the North West Region. During the British administration (1922-61), these ethnic groups, the Bambili and the Babanki, were under the Bafut Native Authority. When the Bamenda Division was created and reorganized in 1949 these two areas were administered as part of the South East Federation whose headquarters was in Bamunka, Ndop. Today they are under Tubah Sub Division. Despite these commonalities, the fifty years or so which the conflict has been going on has attracted a lot of attention in the way the two communities has been reacting towards their common boundary. The number of peaceful attempts to finally solve the boundary conflict and the copious correspondences of material has been fascinating.

The year c.1955 does not imply the beginning of boundary conflicts in the region. Before then there were border conflicts. The boundary conflicts in the Bamenda Grassfields began in the early 1820s when the disciples of Uthman Dan Fodio, raiding the Adamawa Plateau of North Cameroon, forced the Chamba and other indigenous groups to migrate south into the Bamenda Grassfields s and during the process captured and subdued aboriginal people.

The year c.1955 as the starting point has been chosen because that was when the Babanki-Tungoh and the Bambili boundary feud sparked off. This does not mean that before 1955 nothing was heard about the boundary conflict. It was precisely in the 1950s that the first colonial arbitrator attempted a demarcation of the boundary. What had existed before was a border zone. A. B. Westmacott, the British Colonial Administrator, the Resident, was the last amongst the three British Officers to attempt a demarcation of this boundary. Today, the two rival neighbours attached justification to this demarcation. This study ends in 2005 because it was in that year that the last significant letter was written by the Fon of Bambili to the Senior Divisional Officer of Mezam asking the administration to implement Ministerial Arrete No.00210/A/MINAT/DOT/SDOA/SCA of 16/8/00.

It will be an over-statement to maintain that something has not been written on boundaries. As a matter of fact much has been written on the subject of boundaries from many perspectives. Broadly speaking, the work of these scholars can be categorized into five themes which correspond to their focus. Some scholars have worked on the theories and concepts of boundaries from a global perspective. (See Boggs, 1940; Gottmann, 1952; Henderson, 1974; Johnson, 1976; Jones, 1945; Moodie, 1945; Prescott, 1965; Samora, 1971etc). Others have studied boundaries from a historico-geographical perspective. (See Akakpo, 1974; Anene, 1970; Barbour, 1961; Cornevin, 1966; Diallo, 1972; Hargreaves, 1963 and 1974; Person, 1972; and Prescott, 1971). Others have researched on boundaries with focus on law. (See Boutros-Ghali,1973; Brownlie, 1979; El-Gaali, 1975; Hertslet, 1909; Quenendec, 1970; and Yakeintchouk,1970).Still, others have focused on international boundaries from a political science perspective. (Ayela, 1969; Bouvier, 1972; Hamilton, 1974; Rezette, 1975; Touval, 1972, 1967 and 1966; Widstrand, 1969; and Zartman, 1965). Similarly a good number of scholars have focused on local frontier economies and societies. (For scholars in this category, see Abir, 1967; Thom, 1970 and 1975; Mills, 1973; Fanso, 1983; Collins, 1974 and 1976; Asiwaju, 1976, 1977, 1978, 1979, 1970; and 1983; Al-Nur,1971).

The work therefore has focused on the following issues: It is an attempt to show how numerous boundary conflicts in the Bamenda Grassfields can be considered as a product of fast degenerating arable land against the background of fast growing population, and that the area is characterised by the ever growing centralised state formation in the sub-region, characterised by ambitions, expansionist and hegemonistic rulers. It has further attempted to show that the Bambili/Babanki-Tungoh conflict was the product of the on-going centralised state-formation process in the Bamenda Grassfields, and that this on-going phenomenon has been fostered by economic imperatives. It finally examines the in/consistencies and flaws of the Cameroon administration in solving the boundary conflict.

The study, therefore, handles the following questions: why is the Bamenda Grassfields rife with many boundary conflicts in general and Bambili/Babanki-Tungoh in particular? What makes the two ethnic groups different, so much so that they fight each other over a piece of land? Who are behind the boundary conflicts in the area? Of what importance is the disputed land between the two contestants under study? Finally the study will envisage filling a lacuna in the historiography of boundary conflicts in the Bamenda.

B) Understanding inter-community boundary conflicts within Homer-Dixon Framework

After carrying out research in the sub-region I was tempted to interpret it in the prism of Hommer-Dixon Scarcity Models (1994:5-40 and 1996:45-46). Thomas Hommer-Dixon worked in Rwanda, South Africa, Chiapas and Pakistan. In these areas he investigated the relationship between population growth, renewable land scarcities and violent conflicts. He contented that rapid population growth with scarce resources, which in our case is land, resulted in large numbers of people competing for a smaller share of resources. Consequently during such competition over scarce resources, the results are often conflicts. A careful look at Hommer-Dixon model shows that the inter-community conflicts in the North-West Region of Cameroon can best be explained in the scarcity of fertile land resources. The scarcity of fertile land is made more challenging because of the ever growing population of the region. This would however be the main issue, but there are also tangential issues which are linked to the conflict.

Hommer-Dixon defined environmental scarcities in terms of three factors. These were: degradation and depletion of renewable resources; the increased consumption of those resources; and/or their uneven distribution. The increased consumption of resources is directly linked to resource growth; hence it is prominent in the said models. The concept of environmental scarcity as posit by Hommer-Dixon thus blends together the generation renewable resources, environmental degradation, population growth and the social distribution of resources into what Fairhead James (1977) called "analytical obfuscation". In this case, environmental degradation is usually confused with renewable resource scarcity, although there is no necessary link between the two. Land shortages, for example, can serve as a catalyst to boost productivity through better agricultural techniques and land husbandry. By adding the social distribution of resources into the definition of environmental scarcity, Hommer-Dixon created a relationship which contended that conflict, often revolves around issues of resource control.

Environmental processes react with such a variety of social processes such as rapid demographic growth, indigenous farming systems, social structure, land tenure regimes, communal land use rights, ethnicity and community organisation and market-oriented agriculture to generate violence. The only missing link in the above model was a serious discussion of economic inequalities. Combined with population growth, Hommer-Dixon argued that resource scarcity encourages powerful groups within a society to shift distribution in their favour, and this is what he referred to as "resource capture". Hommer-Dixon model notwithstanding its flaws will be used to understand the boundary situation in the North West Region of Cameroon.

Chapter Two
The Geographical and Ethnographic Survey of Bamenda Grassfields

Introduction

If we are to study the boundary misunderstandings in Bamenda it will be imperative for us to situate the region and the people of the region. This chapter therefore attempts to describe the geographical and ethnographic survey of the Bamenda Grassfields. It focuses on the land, the peoples, and the traditional and socio-political organisations in which the boundary contestants of the boundary conflicts find themselves. It ends with the general causes of boundary conflicts in the Bamenda Grassfields. The socio-political systems of the Bamenda Grassfields could be conveniently divided into two types: decentralized and centralized systems. The decentralized system includes the Widikum, the Mbembe, the Aghem and Meta while the centralised groups include the Tikar Fondoms of Kom, Nso and Bafut and the Chamba (Bali). Fondom or Fondoms refer to a large traditional administrative area of about 250 square miles under the administration of one powerful person known as the Fon. Most of the time these Fondoms came into being by subjugating weaker neighbours. (For more on the centralized and decentralised systems see, Ajayi and Crowder,1976). The political and social organizations of these fondoms are related directly and indirectly to the boundary and ethnic cleavages that have been eating deep into the region.

A) Staking the Study Area

The Bamenda Grassfields was an important political and economic zone in British Southern Cameroons. As part of the British Southern Cameroons, it was located at the point where the long West African coastline turns sharply south, to run down to the Congo and Cape. It is found east of Greenwich, approximately between longitudes 5° E', 8° 5' and latitudes 9° 5', 11° 0' north of the equator. According to Chilver and Kaberry (1967:1) the Bamenda Grassfields covered the former administrative divisions of Bamenda, Wum and Nkambe which in 1953 had a total population of 429,000 including c. 10,000 nomadic Fulani. (See The Population of West Cameroon, main findings for 1965: 59 and map for the location of the Bamenda Grassfields).

The boundaries of the Bamenda Grassfields were not static during the colonial era. Under the British administration, the boundaries underwent successive modulation. On August 15, 1920, the Bagam area was handed over to the French Cameroons. On January 1, 1924, the Kaka-Ntem area which was formerly administered under the Gashaka Division of the Yola province of Nigeria was transferred to the Bamenda Grassfields. In return for this lost territory, Captain Pollock, the British administrator of Bamenda, handed over the Kentu District to the Noun Division in November 1926 (Annual Reports for Bamenda 1924 and 1926).

The dominant geographical feature of this area is the Bamenda High Plateau. It stretches from the North East and East of the Bamenda Grassfields over the centre of the area at an average height of 4,500 feet above sea level (Ritzenthaler and Ritzenthaler, 1962:10). It is studded with peaks, the highest and most spectacular of them being the Akuofo Mountains between the Bamenda station and former French Cameroon frontier, and the Oku Mountain which is 7,357 feet above sea level (Ngwa, 1976: 5). The Bamenda plateau falls suddenly from Bafut into the former Menchum Valley which is about 2,000 feet above sea level. (See map 1 on page 22 showing the map of Cameroon and Bamenda Grassfields on the shaded area)

According to Tamura (1986) the vegetation of the area has been described as a sub-montane domestic landscape derived from evergreen montane forest under intensive anthropogenic degradation since the mid-Holocene period. The long history, ranging over 4,000 years, of changing cultivation practices, which are sometimes associated with the raising of small ruminants which include goats and pigs accounts for the landscape degradation (Nkwi and Warnier, 1982).

The region is well drained: The Nun and the Mbam in the East flow into the River Sanaga in the former French Cameroons. The Donga, Katsina-Ala and Menchum flow west to join the Benue in Nigeria, while the Momo flows into the tributaries of the Cross River in Manyu Division. There are two main seasons: the rainy season which begins about mid March and ends early in November

Map 1 Showing Cameroon and Bamenda Grassfields (shaded area)

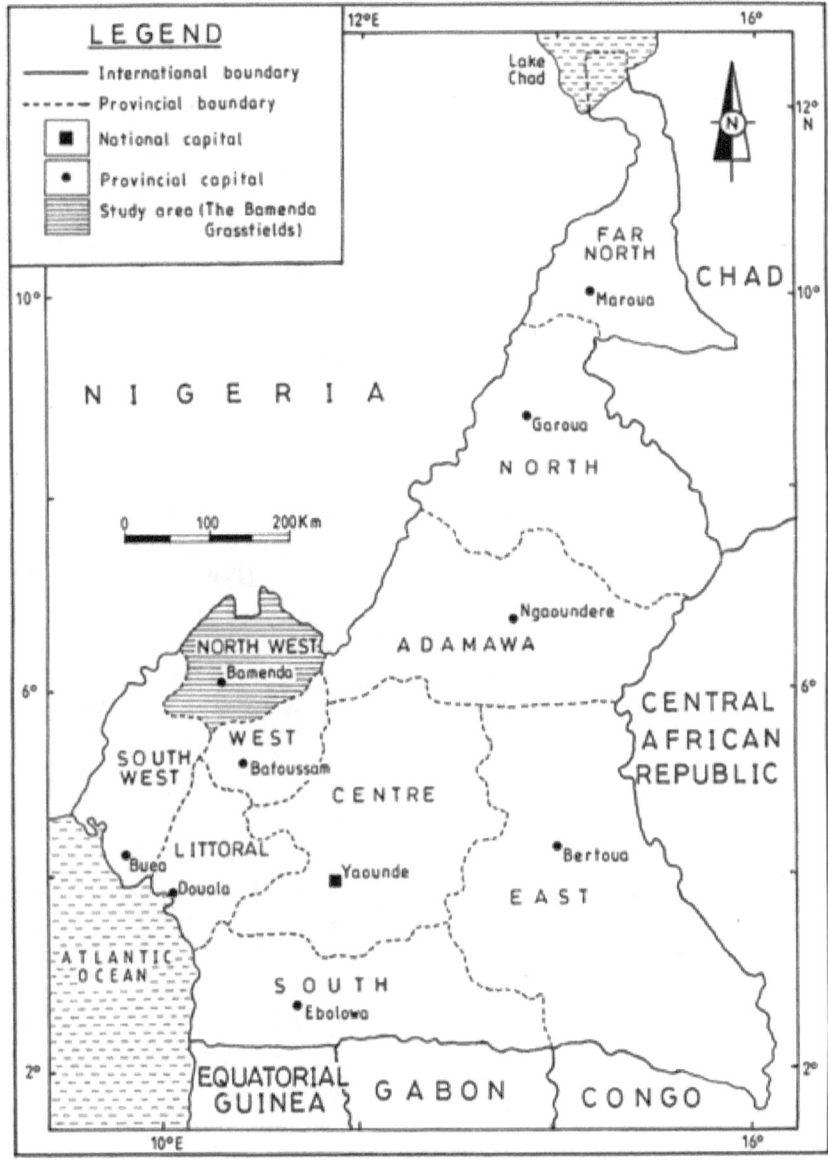

and the dry season which lasts from October to March. Rainfall varies from 65 inches to 125 inches with the heaviest precipitation being concentrated between August and mid-October. Temperatures rise during the day to over 84°c, during the rains it often drops to 65°C and much lower at night.

The traditional economy of the region is based on subsistence agriculture, animal breeding and handicraft. The existence of fertile volcanic soils permits the cultivation of a variety of crops. The cultivation of these crops is mostly done by women while men clear the farms and help in the transportation of the crops. Some of the crops cultivated include: Maize *(Zea Mays)* which is grown in most parts of the region as a staple food except in Ngie, Moghamo and Meta where cocoyam *(Colocasia Antiquorum)* are the main staples. Another staple food-stuff of the region is plantains *(Musa paradisiacal)*. Guinea Corn *(Sorghum Vulgare)* is widely cultivated in the Kom and Nkambe areas. Bulrush millet *(Penninsetun Typhoideum)* is cultivated at Mbembe, while ringer millet *(Eleusine Corocaria)* is cultivated predominantly in Nso and Nsungli areas. Yams *(Dioscorea Dumetorum* and native white carrot *(Coleus Dazo)*, Sweet Potatoes *(Impomoea Batatas)*, manioc *(Manihot Esculenta)*, Bambara nuts *(Voandzeia Subterr anea)* are also widely grown (For more on these, see Purseglove, 1968; Fronlich and Rodewald, 1970).

The German colonial administration introduced potatoes into the region which today is cultivated in increasing quantity by almost all ethnic groups in the area except the forest areas. According to Che-Mfombong (1980:3), the indigenes, of recent, have also begun growing grape fruit, pawpaw, oranges, guavas, soya beans, cabbages, tomatoes and pineapples. While in the Menchum Valley, Bikom and Ndop plain various species of rice are cultivated with the help of the Upper Noun Valley Development Authority (U.N.V.D.A.). The U.N.V.D.A. was created in 1970 and was charged with the development of rice cultivation in the headquarters of Noun above the Bamendjin dam, in order to supplement the incomes of local populations of the region (Neba, 1987: 166).

A lot of importance is also attached to the production of cash crops especially Arabica coffee, groundnuts and tobacco. However, the attractive climate and open grassfields attracted many people to settle in this region in the nineteenth century. Following the Presidential Decree No.92/186 of 1st September 1992 recarving administrative divisions in Cameroon, Bamenda Grassfields was once more reorganised. For instance, Menchum was split into Boyo Division with its Capital at Fundong and Belo as a sub division, while Wum remained the administrative headquarters of Menchum division proper.

B) Peoples of the Region

The indigenous people of the area fall into five main groups based on their oral traditions of origin, and broad linguistic and cultural similarities. These groups are: Tikar who constitute the largest ethnic group of the region; the Widekum who occupy the South Western area; the Mbembe (Mambila ethnic group) in the Northeastern area; the Chamba; and the Aghem (Nkwi, 1976:15). Their relative numerical strength in 1948 as estimated by Chilver and Kaberry (1967:13) was as follows: Tikar 175,000, Widekum 83,000, Mbembe 22,000, Chamba 14,000, Aghem, 7,000. The official 1953 census gives different figures: Tikar had 59,914, Widekum 110,125, Bali-Chamba 29,000, and the other ethnic groups 2,976. To these might be added the Hausas, Bororo and Ibo who entered the area in small but increasing numbers during the British colonial administration (Che-Mfombong, 1980:10). According to the 1953 census, there were 9,931 Fulanis and 3,451 Hausas in the region. As of 1980, the North West Province, the former Bamenda Division, had an estimated population of 809,000 inhabitants over an area of 6,996 square miles (Che-Mfombong, 1980: 11).

The most populous of these peoples are the Tikars. The Tikar were the first to settle on the Bamenda region. According to their oral traditions, they lived originally to the North East of their present territory, somewhere between Tibati and Ngaoundere (Nelson, 1974:70-71; Ngoh, 1996:7; Fanso, 1989: 7-9). This group settled to the south of Bamenda Station in the Ndop plain. As a result, politically-autonomous villages were found. Although controversy seems to exist with regard to their migrations to the Ndop plain, it seems that they arrived in the area in two successive waves. Harold D. Nelson *et al*, (1979), maintains that the Tikars began drifting Southward in eighteenth century or earlier in search of new land, a movement that became stronger during the Fulani invasions of the nineteenth century.

The issue of the Tikars of the Grassfields, has of late posed, and even more recent, an historical enigma, conundrum and controversy amongst researchers of the sub-region. For instance, the first person who touched on the question of the Tikar was M.D.W. Jeffreys (1963) and his conclusions were that the cultural unity of the Grassfields was not because its peoples were of a pseudo-Hamitic origin called the Tikar who were claimed to have "civilized" the area. He further maintains that if he were to ask, who the Tikars were, he would say there are no such people. That did not lay the issue to rest. Chilver (1971) still revisited the issue without much difference. She considered the problem as a non problem.

Price (1979) came back to the problem and restricted the appellation to the Tumu of the Upper reaches of the Mbam River on the grounds that the term was a Mbum alias name. A more recent attempt was made by Fowler and Zeitlyn (1996). The authors rationalized the reference to Tikar origins in terms of claims to relations with superior models of political organization said to be characteristic of the Tikar, the Bamum and Banso. Ngwa and Yenshu (2001) came back to the problem of the Tikars to show how the peoples of the Cameroon Grassfields s could be explained in terms of descent and segmentation. As a matter of fact, Yenshu (2006:15) aptly captures the situation in the following words: "we are the same but differ because we are brothers who broke apart from each other at sometime".

The above works suggests that a plausible reason might be because no serious scholar as at now, have actually situated the Tikars at the centre of research. Researchers who have worked in the area have continued to depend on colonial ethnographies. The colonialists themselves gathered their data more for political and administrative reasons than for academic and scientific purposes. But one thing is fundamental-most of the grassfielders have a common history of migration. This illustrates the case we are attempting to establish here, that although the Bamenda Grassfields are the "same" sons and daughters who once moved together from the same source, and really came into the region in waves, they nonetheless differed. They first founded the dynasties of Bafanji, Bamessing, Babessi and Bamali. The later dynasty gave birth to those of Bambalang, Bamunka and Balikumbat. The second wave of immigrants founded Baba, Babungo and Bangolan. As at the time of settlement, none of these villages could dominate the other, but their relations were characterised by conflicts over land and slave raids. According to their oral traditions, even the Fulani and Chamba raids failed to unite them politically.

The only force which threatened the independence of these villages was a band of the Chamba which, after breaking off from the main group somewhere near the right bank of Noun, defeated a group of earlier settlers (apparently not of Tikar origin) and founded the village of Balikumbat (Drummond, 1926). From this base, this band launched attacks on the Ndop villages until the end of the nineteenth century. Baba, Bamessing, Bafanji and Bambalang at the initial stages of settlement paid tribute in the form of Leopard skins to Balikumbat but under the German Administration Babungo was made responsible for collecting taxes from Baba, Bangolan, Bambalang and Oku (Mc Culloch, 1976: 10).

Other areas of early Tikar migrations were Mbaw, Mbem and Nsungli. This group of Tikar settled below the escarpment in the area formerly known as Ntem, but at a later date three main groups whose descendants founded the Tang, Wiya and War groups of Nsungli moved up to the plateau and established a number of small villages. In each of the three groups, one village head claimed the title of Fon and superiority over the others. Unfortunately for them, their authority was challenged even before the arrival of the Germans by some component villages which were asserting their autonomy.

The last people of the Tikar migrations into the Bamenda Grassfields comprised the following: Kom, Nso, Bafut and Fungom. Kom is the second largest of the Tikar Fondoms in the Bamenda Grassfields with a population of 26,625 in 1953. Their origin which is accepted by Chilver and Kaberry (1967:129) and Nkwi (1976:20), is that the three clans came from Ndobo in the present Adamawa province. They migrated and set up a temporal settlement at Bamessi. While at Bamessi the Kom population increased tremendously and began to prosper more than their host. This prosperity was the root cause of the feud that developed between the guest (Kom people) and their host (Babessi). What is interesting to bear in mind about the above authors is that there is no place at the Ndop plain known as Bamessi. Rather there is Bamessing and Babessi and field work in Ndop plain proofed that the Kom came from Babessi which is found at the airport end of that plain.

Another Tikar group to arrive at the Bamenda Grassfields was Nso (Banso). According to their oral traditions, they originated from Rifum known today as Bankim. It is said that owing to a civil war, Banso, Bamum, and Wiya left the banks of the Mbam for an unknown destination. From Bankim the Wiya, under the leadership of Nyakundji, arrived at their present site via Kuchap while the Nso and Bamum travelled together to the Mvi (Hawkesworth, 1922; Fanso, 1989:35).When they arrived at the Mvi, Share, the founder of the Bamum dynasty, crossed the river first and destroyed the bridge by which they had crossed the river (Che-Mfombong, 1980: 144). Unable to surmount this obstacle, Mfo-Mbam went and settled at Nzimbaam while Mfo-Nso followed the left bank of the river towards the mountains of the North West and eventually arrived at Kovifem, some twelve miles to the Northwest of their present capital, Kumbo.

Bafut, another Tikar Chiefdom, had also moved into the Bamenda Grassfields by the end of the 18th century with Bafreng (Nkwen). Her dynasty claims origins from Ndobo, presumably the area of that name in Northern Bamum and the Upper Mbam from which legends bring the ancestors of the kings. The Bafut dynasty claims to be related to those of Nkwen and the Kijem (Big Babanki). Within Bafut there are variant legends concerning the route taken by the founder of the kingdom. This is not surprising since the chiefdom is made of a composite and varying traditions reflect the interests of different groups within it.

However, two schools of thought have emerged as to when they left their point of origin and arrived in Bamenda. The first school led by Mohamadou and closely followed by McCulloch states that the people of Bafut, traditionally considered the oldest and most senior dynasty of the area, were the first to leave Ndobo, followed by Babanki, Bafreng and Bambili. Another school of thought led by Chilver and Kaberry (1967), maintains that Bafut left Ndobo together with Babanki, Bafreng and Bambili to Bafut from where the last three split off to settle at their present sites. Whatever the case, it should be borne in mind that Bafut originated, like other Tikar peoples, from North Cameroon.

Another Tikar group to arrive at the Bamenda Grassfields was Fungom. Fungom is a village chiefdom which became the headquarters for the Native Authority and Court for 21 villages during the British colonial rule. Fungom was the principal chiefdom claiming their origin from the West of the Limbum - speaking area across southern Bum to Nyos and Bensan where they split up in quest of palm stands. These villages fell into six groups: the Chap group (Fungom itself, Mme, Kuk, Nyos and Fang); the Isu-Furu-Mashi Kentu-groups; and the We-Jua-Munkap group (Munken, Mbele, Missong, Mufu, Mashi and Mundabi). Most of these claim to have come from the direction of Banyo while others point to the Kentu region (Smith 1925; Warnier and Nkwi, 1982).

The Aghem area, the smallest of the ethnic groups, is located in what is today known as Menchum Division. According to their oral traditions they came from the Benue lands from the Tiv country in Nigeria and arrive at their present sites in waves. Some travelled eastward through the open Grassfields South of Wum and finally reached Wum. Their arrival forced the original settlers to leave or be integrated into the Aghem Federation. By mid-19th century, the "Federation" had fully developed its military strength, sufficient to harass and make tributaries of the Aghem Federation (Nkwi, 1987). What caused their movements down south is still not clear and to ascertain that wars and internecine disputes motivated the movements would be a matter of much speculation.

The next group to arrive the Bamenda Grassfields was the Mbembe. According to Pollock (1926), the Mbembe originated from a long way to the East and dispersed from Mbia Hill. The village of Abonkwa, Berabi and Mbiribwa also claim eastern origins. In the case of Abonkwa and Berabi Kimi connections, it is not clear whether these traditions are genuinely local or whether they are reflexes of an earlier passage of Limbum-speaking peoples. The other peoples situated in the steep valleys of the Mbembe lowlands includes: Ako, Abongshe, Jevi, Assa and Akweto (Newton, 1926).

Next in importance to the Mbembes were the Widekums, to arrive at the Bamenda Grassfields. According to their oral traditions the term Widekum refers to the name of the place from where the people of Widekum are said to have originated. This place is situated at the confluence of the Momo and Egwell Rivers in the Southern part of Momo Division. It also appears that early British colonialists used the term Widekum to refer to the forest people who migrated northwards from the Mamfe Division into the Bamenda area in order to differentiate them from their neighbours, the Tikars (Neba, 1987: 10).

Small bands originating from Widekum established their villages over the territory and further became politically and economically autonomous. They accept descent from a common origin, after whom the clan is often named: *Ongiekum* for the Ngie, *Kum* meaning lineage head; and *Ungwo* for the *Ngwo*. In each of the clans one village head was recognised as senior to the others and he presided over the sacrifices to the clan's ancestors and the gods of the earth (Chilver, 1963:95-96).

A majority of the clans except Ngemba, part of Ngo and Meta, inhabit the forest because all attempts to settle on the uplands were forestalled by the Tikar and Aghem. The Tikar group of Bafut colonized Bebadji (Beba) and introduced it to Tikar culture before it broke away and migrated to its present site. The arrival of the Germans in the late nineteenth century saw the subjugating of the Widekum by the Balis (Chilver, 1963: 97).

Another stock of people to arrive the Bamenda Grassfields in the nineteenth century was the Bali Chambas. They were warriors who initially inhabited the area east and west of Yola in Northern Nigeria. They left the area as a warring party, raiding through Kontcha, Ngaoundere and Banyo, conquering and absorbing small tribes on their way. At Banyo the raiding party split into two groups: One under Gwando moved westward raiding Katsina and Takum areas. The other group under Gawolbe continued to raid the South and Western areas from Bamumland. They raided the Bamileke highlands and fought with Batie, Bagham, Bamendjinda and Babaju (Nyamndi, 1996; Nyiwatumi, 1995).

Following the death of Gawolbe, the Bali warriors split into small units under rival princes. They divided into six units under rival princes - Bali Gham, Bali Kumbat, Bali Gangsin, Bali Gashu, Bali Muti, Bali Kontan and Bali Nyongha. Two of the six units led by Nyong Pasi and Galanga moved and settled at Tsen and Goksela on the borders of the Bamum country. These two leaders later moved Westwards from the Bamum borders to the present settlement between the late 1850 and early 1900 (Ngoh, 1987: 5; Njeuma, 1978: 34).

To these ethnic groups may be added the arrival of the Fulanis. They migrated to the Bamenda plateau from French Cameroons in search for pastures and salt. According to their oral traditions, the first group of the Fulani arrived in Bamenda from Banyo in 1916 under Ardo Sabga and settled in Babanki Tungoh. They first faced the problem of securing the good faith of the aboriginal inhabitants who could give them settlement and grazing land. The natives strongly opposed their settlement scheme because they suspected their intentions and the eventual damage of their crops by the Fulani cattle. As time went by, the Fulani won the admiration of the natives through persuasion of gifts like cattle. As a result of this, the chief of Babanki-Tungo provided the Fulanis with baskets of maize and demonstrated his wish to cohabit with them by erecting bamboo houses for Ardo Sabga and his followers (Chilver and Kaberry, 1967:1; Ritzenthaler and Ritzenthaler, 1965:12).

It is clear from the foregoing discussion that a lot has been said and written by some anthropologists and colonial administrators about the Bamenda Grassfields. These same issues have attracted some post independent writers (See Ngoh, 1996; Fanso, 1989; Johnson 1970; Le Vine, 1964; Rubin, 1971). In most of these secondary studies about this region, they attempt at reconstructing the past, however, they have been inadequate because of the uncritical acceptance of some colonialist perceptions about the indigenes' material and cultural realities. Even a few of the writers who attempted going more in-depth into that past were at best Eurocentric. The next section will examine the traditional and socio-political structures of these groups.

C) Traditional and Socio-Political Organisations

The socio-political organisations of the ethnic groups discussed above can conveniently fall into two systems, namely, the centralised and "segmentary" or decentralised systems. In order to better appreciate these systems, it is necessary to look at their fundamental characteristics.

The centralised groups of Fondoms of the Bamenda Grassfields include Kom (Bikom), Bafut, Nso and Bali: Centralised states usually arose when the leader of a local group or of immigrant warriors gained control over a number of decentralised village communities and formed a kingdom. But generally, the pre-existing social and political structure of the village was not seriously tampered with, and each lineage retained its role and status in the village. With the spreading influence of the royal family cult, the leader gradually acquired semi-divine authority over the kingdom. They were known as the *A-Fon* (Bali) or *(Foyn* in Kom) (Espie and Ajayi, 1965: 45-65; Nkwi, 1976:41; Douglas, 1964:183; Padon and Soja, 1970:57; Curtin *et. al.*1978:81-84).

What is important to note about centralised polities is that they started as a clan and expanded by subjugating neighbouring states thereby making them their vassals. The empires of Western Sudan expanded through this method (Harris, 1987:53-64; Fage, 1969:18-34; Davidson, 1970: 35-53). It is the attempt by the centralised Fondoms of the Bamenda Grassfields to expand in this manner of state formation that boundary conflicts have become common place.

On the other hand, "segmentary" societies included the Widekum, Munshi, Mbembe, Mesaje and Fulani. In these types of societies there is little concentration of authority. It is difficult to point to any individual or limited group of men as the ruler or rulers of the society. Such authority roles as they exists in their situations, affect a rather limited sector of the lives of those subject to them. The wielding of authority as a specialized unit within which people feel an obligation to settle their disputes according to agreed rules without resort to force tends to be relatively small (Horton, 1976:72-114; Ajayi and Crowder, 1976: 72-114; Davidson,1970:112-135; Mazrui 1986:16-18).

D) Decentralised Societies

By contrast to the centralized societies, there is the segmentary group of Meta found in what Chilver and Kaberry prefer to call the Tadkon fondom. The Meta occupies the South Eastern edge of the Bamenda Grassfields, and its population is divided into some twenty-eight villages which are mostly patrilineal and exogamous. In other segmentary groups the highest political and administrative unit was the village which comprised several hundreds of inhabitants who resides in lineages. This does not mean that each village was autonomous. Commercial and religious activities had a unifying influence on this society. In times of crisis when external threats became eminent, village groups often contracted alliances for mutual defence (Che-Mfombong, 1980:22).

Each of these villages was under the guidance of a village head that had little or no political authority; village government instead of resting on the government, was run by a Council of Elders comprising the constituent lineage heads known as *Meukum si*. This council met at regular intervals and in times of emergency in the village head's compound. These meetings were usually presided over by the village head and matters of social, religious, economic and judicial importance were discussed (Dillon, 1976:288). As concerns how decisions were arrived at, Chilver and Kaberry (1967: 105) said:

> Decisions were usually taken only when consensus had been reached. Matters affecting the village, lineages or individuals were usually thrown open for the councillors to voice their opinions before final decision were taken. Quite often than not, the audience was swayed by the most eloquent speaker who was listened to in silence while an unimpressive speaker was often hushed down. Decisions which were arrived at by the Council of Elders were disseminated in the lineages by the Councillors who also enforced their execution.

The above, evidence points to the fact that 80 percent of the Bamenda Grassfields ethnic groups claim a common descent, or origin. What is more surprising is that despite this claim; these ethnic groups have shown a lot of inter-ethnic boundary confrontations. The rationale behind these numerous conflicts in the Bamenda Grassfields constitutes the next section of this chapter. In other words, what are the causes of boundary conflicts in the Bamenda Grassfields or why is the region rife with several boundary conflicts?

E) The contending issues of boundary conflicts in the Bamenda Grassfields

The general causes of boundary conflicts in the Bamenda Grassfields can be traced under geographical, political social and economic domains. Geographically, the causes of boundary conflicts in this region can be explained in the settlement patterns in which the ethnic groups find themselves. According to Dudley, settlement is the act of peopling or colonizing a new country or of planting a colony. It is also an assemblage of persons settled in a locality: hence a small village or a collection of huts or houses (Stamp, 1966:415).

There are two types of settlement - the nuclear and linear which is dotted all over a geographical region in order to grab land. With the nuclear settlement, the inhabitants leave the hamlets and work somewhere else. This type is more pronounced in the Bamenda Grassfields. When men, women and children arrived in this region in the Eighteenth and Nineteenth Centuries, each nucleated group acquired fertile land. They could derive their basic necessities from this land. Eventually, with the natural increase of population and new arrivals, there was insufficient land within easy reach of the nuclear settlement. Consequently, some people moved out to clear and settle new land; and, in turn this secondary settlement eventually gave rise other "states". Such expansion from founder villages has occurred in most parts of the Bamenda Grassfields leading to boundary conflicts (Money, 1972: 13; Hammond 1984:71-87).

It should be borne in mind that the interactions between human beings and their environment are complex and always changing. Their very presence and the actions they take in order to survive bring out such changes; and the actions themselves are usually, strongly influenced by environmental conditions. They might not always be logical responses, for human beings may act in a wayward manner, but on the whole they tend to create recognisable patterns of occupation. In an attempt to do this, there are always claims and counter claims on land hence leading to disputes.

Politically, the arrival of the Europeans in this region could be seen as a cause of the boundary conflict. The first Europeans to colonise Cameroon were the Germans, in 1884. By 1889 Zintgraff, the celebrated German explorer reached Bali. With the arrival in Bali, there was a change in policy and even a rupture in the traditional administration. Hunt (1929) maintains that before this time (1902) Bali was the mainstay of government. The German arrival signalled the removal of this mainstay to Bamenda known as the *Bezirk*.

Owing to the fact that the Germans had opened plantations and needed labour, orders for labour recruitment were passed down, to the Bali vassal states which had been under Bali. Bali felt at the time that they had been cheated of their hegemony. This shows that there was a change of policy and the vassals of Bali took advantage. These vassals included amongst others, Mbu (Baforchu) and Chomba. Most of these vassal villages, sixteen in number, refused to pay allegiance to Bali in the belief that the government did not desire their continued vassalage. In 1904 Pinyin refused such allegiance to Bali and in 1905 Hauptman Glauning formally installed Fonyonga as paramount chief of thirty-one villages. Nkwen and Mendankwe, who once paid tribute, were dropped from the list.

In 1906 and 1907 various villages were punished for insubordination to Bali, and it must have been in these years that the five villages: Baforchu, Chomba, Widekum, Ngen-Mbo and Mengen, which afterwards became locally famous and notorious in the 1912 - 16 were rounded up by the Germans and Bali, their villages destroyed and the people herded under Bali. Some dozen or more Meta or Moghamo villages were razed and their inhabitants driven into Bali. These drastic measures were taken in the hope that future defection would cease (Hunt, 1925).

The "herding" of these villages under the umbrella of Bali resulted in the vassalage attempts to maintain their autonomy and the Bali determination to carve out an empire by re-subjugating their former vassals. This dream was later realised when the Germans entered an "entente" with the Bali to subdue the Widekum indigenous groups including Ossindinge and Bafut. It is interesting to bear in mind that as early as 1820, the Bali people had started struggling to conquer their neighbours; and therefore if the Germans ally with Bali, it was perhaps a continuum but at the expense of the neighbours.

However, the German occupation lasted less than thirty-five years. The capitulation of Mora in February 1916 led to the final expulsion of the Germans and thus, invited the British to take over the region because the British forces played a prominent role in sending out the Germans. When the British took over the region they set out to establish a policy of *Pax Britannica*. Its administration was organised around the chiefs. Their policy of Indirect Rule which advocated the use of traditional institutions in the administration of the area promoted a very slow and deliberate process of socio-economic development and dependency as well (Lugard, 1922).

British colonial policy was an empirical one in so far as it was never clear-cut; colonial administration relied on experience and expediency and not on dogmas or fixed principles. The policy was developed piecemeal at the insistence of certain individuals as a panacea to specific problems and when this worked well it was applied to similar situations. It was difficult to assess the extent and nature of a chiefs authority in these regions and for this reason the government undertook a systematic series of assessment and intelligent reports to ascertain the authority of traditional rulers, the basis for their power and the role of religious and other social institutions (Eyongetah and Brian, 1974:108-109; Chilver 1963: 89-139; Geschiere, 1993: 151-175).

It was directly because of this type of policy that when the first boundary conflicts erupted during the British administration, they found it difficult if not impossible to demarcate the boundaries. This should not mislead us to the fact that it was only this time that boundary conflicts were heard. Before this time, what existed were borders or buffer zones. The first attempted demarcation by the British colonial administration which the Germans never took note, gave birth to the appellation – boundary in the western sense of it because it was followed by beacons and cairns rather than the traditional boundary stems that had existed before. Today, the inefficiency of post-colonial administration with reference to the boundaries which were legitimised by the British colonial administration cannot be divorced from boundary conflicts in the Bamenda Grassfields.

Another political cause underlying the boundary conflicts in Bamenda Grassfields may aptly be in line with what we could call the conquest aspirations of the people of the area. The existence of an iron industry in the region as early as the nineteenth century in Babungo and Bamenyam brought a new source of military power. Those who first learnt to use the iron attempted to conquer and rule their neighbours. It is also important to note that centralised authority and administrative organisation seem to be necessary to accommodate culturally diverse groups within a single political system, especially if they have different modes of livelihood.

A look at the hot spots of boundary conflicts in the region reveals that they are predominantly carried out by centralised fondom, against segmentary neighbours. A case in point is the Bali and their neighbours. To assert autonomy and show strength, some fondom, not really centralised in a sense, were attempting to go beyond their boundaries and claim land from their neighbours. For instance the

Balikumbat and Bafanji; Bambili-Babanki-Tungoh; Bambili and Nkwen. Closely linked to this, boundary conflicts could be explained in terms of Social Darwinism. This is the belief that societies, like biological species, evolve and advance through competition resulting in the survival of the fittest and the elimination of the weak (Fortes and Evans-Pritchard, 1940: 9-10; Davidson, 1965:16; Warnier and Nkwi 1982:45; Rosen and Jones 1974:242).

Socially, the proximity to contact with one another is another factor that explains boundary conflicts in the region. It is conventional wisdom that there can be no conflict of any kind without contact, consequently, the Bamenda Grassfields though mountainous still permit a very high degree of contact and with this the communities are always converging. Boundary conflicts would have been largely unheard of, if there were natural barriers. Unfortunately, the absence of these barriers have enabled the Oku to make irredentist claims on the Mbesa; the Bambili on the Nkwen and the Babanki-Tungoh; the Bali on their neighbours and the Balikumbat versus the Bafanji (for more on contact as a source of conflict see,Mack,1963:375).

Demographic influence is also another social factor that lies behind boundary conflicts in the region. This is against the background of degenerating arable land. The ramification of this growth is that it might lead to internal crisis which will lead to an outward push to accommodate the increasing population. The increase in population is not compensated by an increase in the size of the land and *ipso facto*, the demand for food will be incompatible with the accommodation of the growing population. The only safety valve for this problem is an outward push which will result in boundary conflicts. This seems to be the principal factor behind boundary conflicts in the Bamenda Grassfields (Malthus, 1958:7-8). According to the 1953 census, this region had a population of 429,000 alone which was "more than one third of the total population of the British Southern Cameroons (see Bamenda Divisional Annual Report for 1953). The table below shows a partial distribution of population growth of the North West Region for the years 1987 and 2000.

Partial Population distribution of The North West Province for 1987 and 2000

Division	Subdivision	Pop. 1987	Pop. 2000	Surface Area km2	Pop. Density 1987	Pop. Density 2000	Density Change
	Belo	45585	46000	253.25	180.00	181.64	1.64
Boyo	Bum	16411	16600	572.27	28.68	29.01	0.33
	Fundong	32974	66500	715.10	46.11	92.99	46.88
	Njinikom	19132	19300	95.38	200.59	202.35	1.76
Subtotal	*4 subdivisions*	*114102*	*148400*	*1636.00*	*69.74*	*90.71*	*20.97*
	Jakiri	36315	59700	470.45	77.19	126.90	49.71
	Kumbo	93884	175500	486.42	193.01	360.80	167.79
Bui	Mbven	11952	14700	702.85	17.01	20.91	3.91
	Noni	20331	24900	319.78	63.58	77.87	14.29
	Oku	55582	87200	372.50	149.21	234.09	84.88
Subtotal	*5 subdivisions*	*218064*	*362000*	*2352.00*	*92.71*	*153.91*	*61.20*
	Misaje	22616	26700	753.40	30.02	35.44	5.42
Donga	Ndu	61717	98000	540.30	144.23	181.38	67.15
Mantung	Ako	28790	40100	1117.60	25.76	35.88	10.12
	Nkambe Central	58219	106400	509.10	114.36	209.00	94.64
	Nwa	55574	62100	1419.60	39.15	43.74	4.60
Subtotal	*5 subdivisions*	*226916*	*333300*	*4340.00*	*52.28*	*76.80*	*24.52*
	Fungom	43372	43800	2034.50	21.32	21.53	0.21
	Furu Awa	6304	6900	1157.60	5.45	5.96	0.51
Menchum	Menchum Valley	25164	25400	1040.50	24.18	24.41	0.23
	Wun Central	30824	54400	256.40	20.22	212.17	91.95
Subtotal	*4 divisions*	*105664*	*130500*	*4489.00*	*21.75*	*28.07*	*7.32*
	Bafut	36421	45400	418.80	86.97	108.40	21.24
	Bali	33915	86600	184.10	184.22	470.40	286.18
Mezam	Bamenda Central	146021	329600	375.60	388.77	877.53	488.76
	Santa	57459	63100	402.25	142.84	156.87	14.02
	Tubah	39227	54000	460.25	85.32	117.33	32.00
Subtotal	*5subdivisions*	*313043*	*578700*	*1841.00*	*170.06*	*314.34*	*144.28*
	Batibo	42914	55000	349.05	122.95	157.57	34.63
	Mbengwi Cental	32111	39000	452.20	71.01	86.25	15.23
Momo	Ngie	28406	31800	164.73	172.44	193.04	20.00
	Njikwa	18527	20300	329.11	56.29	61.68	5.39
	Widikom	21508	23500	439.91	48.89	53.42	4.53
Subtotal	*5 subdivisions*	*143466*	*169600*	*1735.00*	*82.69*	*97.75*	*15.06*

Chapter Two: The Geographical and Ethnographic Survey of Bamenda Grassfields

		Babessi	37839	42200	347.40	108.92	121.47	12.55
Ngoketunjia		Balikumbat	31940	35600	434.50	73.51	81.93	8.42
		Ndop	47314	83900	335.10	141.19	250.37	109.18
Subtotal		*3 subdivisions*	*117093*	*161700*	*1117.00*	*104.83*	*144.76*	*39.93*
Prov.Total		31 subdivisions	1238348	1884200	17510.00	70.72	107.61	36.89

Source: North West Provincial Service of Statistics 1987

From the population of 429,000 in 1953, by 1980 the population had doubled to 809,000. Further population statistics from the North West Provincial (Regional) Service of Statistics shows partial population figures for the years 1987 and 2000. From the table above, the population of the North West Province (Region) in 1987 was 1,238,348 and by 2000 it increased to 1,884,200. These rough statistics shows that the population of the region has ever been on an increase and if one were to make a projection for the year 2005 the population was estimated at 2,843,000. The areas of dense population have a greater number of boundary/land conflicts than the areas with sparse population distribution. In Mezam, for example, where the population density is close to 200 persons per square kilometre, there is a record score of boundary and land conflicts. Next in population is Ngoketunjia where the case study is found (Bambili and Babanki-Tungoh). In populated Boyo Division, mostly composed of rugged highlands, there have been the Kom-Mbesnaku; Mbesnaku-Oku inter-village conflicts; Kedjom Keku-Ndawara Ranch and the Belo-Ndawara Ranch conflicts.

On the other hand, the sparsely populated, namely Menchum, Donga-Mantung and Momo Divisions witnessed mainly the farmer-grazier conflicts. Although a zone of high population density, the Bui Division has known only the Oku-Mbesnaku; Oku-Noni and the farmer-grazier conflicts. Inter-village conflicts are limited perhaps because the majority of Bui is governed and control by a very strong monarchical system in which the rule of law as established by the pontiff monarch is accepted in much the same way as the Christian dogma. The Kingdom of Nso which is the largest traditional polity in the North West Region of Cameroon covers more than 2/3 of the land area of Bui Division. The rest of the communities exist in one kind of dependency relationship or the other to Nso. Conflicts within that kingdom are of the anti-hegemonic, anti-expansonist and anti-state building type as reported for the village of Nseh (Goheen, 1992). The bottom line to be drawn is that an increase in population has a net impact on the pressure of arable land which is very limited in supply. The consequence of this is friction in areas which appear to be fertile.

However, the pressure on arable land was further compounded and complicated by the fact that the Fulanis arrived sometimes in the middle of the 19th Century with their cattle. These cattle were to graze in the arable land which was already fixed and limited to the already growing population. The conditions of grazing cattle and growing cereals in the region were generally good. The vegetation is mostly grass. During the rainy season, the area is covered with green grass which continues to flourish in the lowlands even during the dry season months (November to March). The climate is also suitable for cattle rearing. It makes trypanosomiasis infection practically non-existent or easy to eliminate, and sustains pasture on the highlands for up to eight months of the year (see file No.17 (4)10068, vol.3, Grazing of Cattle Cameroon Province, 1949, National Archives Buea, Cameroon, henceforth cited as NAB,). One of the most important attractions for the Fulani to the Bamenda Grassfields was the presence of natural salt springs, especially those at Sabga Babungo and Bamessing.

The historicity of the cattle industrial complex in the Bamenda Grassfields dates from 1919 when the Fulani started settling in the sub-region. They came principally from Nigeria and former German Adamawa accompanied by herds of cattle (Awasom, 1984:65-85). These Fulanis were distinctly pastoralists because a cattle rearing venture was their principal economic occupation as well as a way of life. Consequent upon this, they continued to migrate into the region because their pastoral needs were being satisfied. Accordingly in the early 1940s the farmer-grazier conflicts became a serious impediment to peaceful coexistence .In the midst of confusion the Senior Divisional Officer for Bamenda, M.D.W. Jeffreys, employed a rather naïve and unsophisticated solution, but at the same time acting under the Inter-Tribal Boundary Settlement Ordinance.

By that Ordinance, he was empowered by the British Colonial Office to maintain Law and Order within his jurisdiction. As a result he went about demarcating the highlands into farming and grazing lands. It would appear that the sense behind that action was that if farmers and graziers carried out their economic activities in separate and specified areas, the possibility of a clash between the two groups would be low, if not completely eliminated. He demonstrated his total commitment to that theory by the speed of unstoppable velocity with which he carried out the exercise. By 1943 he had completed the demarcation of the Wiya Native Authority areas and Sinna, Ndop and Ngulu areas as well as half of the Nso area.

The demarcation greatly reduced the farmer grazier conflicts as evidenced by a drastic reduction in the number of complaints brought to administrative officers. But the success was very temporary. The cattle population continued to increase. A statistical compilation shows that cattle population rose from 10,000 in 1922 to 91,782 in 1940, while the population of Fulani people staggered from a few persons in 1919 to about 10,000 within the same period (see Njeuma and Awasom, 1990:217-233; Annual Reports for Bamenda Division; also File B2838 Provincial Archives Bamenda, Cameroon; "Table of Census figures Bamenda Province 1953"). The number of cattle rose from 74,092 in 1985 to 78,922 in 2006. Between 1994 and 1995 alone there were 244 cases of farmer-grazier conflicts (Anguh, 2008:173-175).

This increase in cattle and Fulanis forced the Fulani to overstep the grazing limits imposed on them by Jeffreys. Moreover, the indigenous farmers were not prepared to cooperate with the scheme for fear that their rights over certain portions of Fulani grazing land might be lost in the long run. So they took the risk to cultivate on land reserved for grazing to remind the Fulani that they had no title over the land. The scarcity of land and the increase of cattle and population led to further conflicts. As a matter of fact, nearly all administrative reports of the 1940s refer to the farmer-grazier conflict. The most comprehensive report on the subject was that given by P.M. Kaberry in his "Report on Farmer- Grazier Relations and Changing Pattern of Agriculture in Nsaw". The report was written in 1958 and based on Minutes of Native Authority meetings, Native Court records and her fieldwork, and covered the period from the late 1930s to the 1950s. The report did not make any mistakes in stating that the grazier-farmer conflicts which were already underway might take a great deal to arrive at a solution given the fact that the numerical strength of cattle was almost proportionate to that of the population. She concluded that the colonial administration should take a lot of caution in nipping the problem on the bud. As to whether the colonial administration ever understood and took precautions to halt the conflicts is a matter of conjecture.

A picture of cows grazing in the Bamenda Grassfields photographed by the author

This picture was taken in Donga Mantung division where the highest numbers of cows are grazed in the Bamenda Grassfields. The graziers are always in need of land which is scarce and the population too needs land for cultivation.

Furthermore, the importance attached to land in the region cannot be separated from the present boundary conflicts. Land rights were and are either patrilineal or matrilineal. Close agnates-brothers, sisters, father's brothers, cousins - comprise an inner lineage in which there is continuous mutual assistance. The importance of land in Africa was long captured by Ross, (1946: 321-323) who maintained that individual ownership of land before European colonisation was one. To the Africans, "Mother Earth" was the producer, the sustainer and the recipient of life, and as such could only rightly be the sacred and inalienable possession of all the people of the whole tribe. The very concept of individual ownership was illogical, impractical, selfish, anti-social and sacrilegious.

That situation in the Bamenda Grassfields was not an exemption. With the advent of European rule in the region; their conceptions of the essential relationship between people and land were fundamentally different. Different colonial masters decided to give the appellation "crown land" (Karp 1975:1-2; Elizabeth 1971:193-215; Bohannan 1964:180-182). By crown land it simply meant that it belonged to the queen of England. The post colonial period did not help the matter as land was reorganised shortly after independence. With all these the basic spiritual ties between the indigenous group and the earth and even the spirits of the departed whose principal home the earth was, was seriously disrupted.

Land Tenure Ordinance Law No.74 of 6th July 1974 was evoked to govern land tenure system in Cameroon. According to the Cameroon Constitution of 1972 and 1996, the President of the Republic of Cameroon was empowered to make laws. Consequent upon this, law No.73-3 of 9th July authorised the President to establish by Ordinance rules governing land tenure and government owned land. That law stipulated and recognised three categories of land ownership through: National, State and Individual categories.

National land was owned by the government. It fell under that category which was unoccupied and exploited by the government. The traditional ruler was the custodian of such land. Such land could be given out to the state or corporate bodies and to individuals. State land was actually owned by the government and has carried out investment and traditional ruler can dispose of it. This kind of land temporarily failed to become national land and neither the chief nor the village head has any right of custody over it. The last category is that owned by the individuals. Private individual land is that occupied and exploited by the individuals having a title over it. The land tenure Ordinances imposes a fee for the establishment of land certificates.

In addition to the above typology of land is the traditional land tenure system. Cameroon represents an ethnic and social pluralism of bewildering complexity. It is estimated that there are more than 200 ethnic groups predominantly of Bantus and Semi-Bantus in the South. Kirdis and Fulbes in the North of Cameroon and the Chambas and Tikars of NorthWest Cameroon. Superimposed on the ethnic diversity is the bilingual system inherited from the colonial days. To talk about one traditional land system could be a bit erroneous. However, in accordance with national law No.74-1 of 6th July 1974 traditional land tenure was seriously recognised. Furthermore, by that law the chief or village head is automatically the custodian of National land. Despite the provision of that law the system of land tenure and acquisition is often defined by each ethnic tradition or customs. In this context the NorthWest Region of Cameroon which is composed of more than 50 ethnic groups and which depicts a traditional African society where land is a communal property with chiefs and communal leaders being the custodians of the land.

Although the land law of 1974, abolished the concept of communal ownership of land and made all land state land, the concept of communal ownership of land appears to be still rife. Claims to land are legitimated most of the time by reference to history through concepts such as precedence in occupation or the sanctions of colonial tools. Most leaders of the indigenous communities in conflict would either point to their rights to land as first occupants. A case in point is the Bambili and Babanki-Tungoh. Others will point to maps and court rulings. German sketch maps are often presented in court cases pitting two neighbourly communities in conflict over an adjoining piece of land or border. Others point to colonial court rulings which gave them rights over land in question. What comes out from our observation is that, at the onset of the colonial administration, the area was only fairly densely inhabited (Chilver 1961:233) and that intercommunity boundaries were not clearly demarcated or even non-existed between some communities. The growth in population and the consequent density, the introduction of the modern concept of fixed boundaries and the growth of distinct notions of communal identity and grandeur have jointly contributed to the multiplication of conflicts all in most parts of the North West Region of Cameroon.

That did not have a direct bearing on the boundary conflict but what was more was the scarcity of arable land against the backdrop of the ever increasing number of the population of the area. That situation was compounded by the fact that the region is quite mountainous and not fertile all around the year. The mountainous nature of the area makes the arable land smaller and limited and therefore the indigenous population is more often than not clashing on the limited arable lands found between them.

Agriculture *per se* in the fertile land areas has been a cause for concern. This is marched with unequal growth in fertility rates. Over the past four decades there has been an explosive increase in fertility rates. The phenomenon has been accompanied by urbanizations. To meet the demands of the food dependent but powerful consumer system, an elaborate system of agricultural production, processing and distribution has emerged in which the local producers and consumers are now linked to the intricate web of sub-regional and continental markets. It is interesting to note that food produced in the North West Region of Cameroon is sold as far as the Gabon and Congo Republics. In 1991 Emmanuel Yenshu did research on rural community and its development in Cameroon with Bafut being the case study. In that study he noted that the integration of food crops into the exchange system derive from four historical periods. According to him:

> The epoch of subsistence...the epoch of intercommunity exchange in the pre-colonial period, the period of a highly monetarised community built into a network whose centre is the town and whose control is managed by the territorial capital, and the epoch of transnational trade.... The national and transnational exchange, which persist in a subtle but sure manner. The former employ both political power and economic advantage in sweeping across different economic structures which continue to sustain life within the community (Yenshu, 1991: 205).

The photo below shows a typical physical feature of the region which is mountain Physical feature which characterised the North West region. Photo was taken by the author.

Sons and Daughters of the Soil

Plate 2

Such features as shown in plate 1 and 2 above are very prominent in the Bamenda Grassfields of Cameroon (mountains and valleys). These features illuminate the fact that the area is not fertile enough to meet the demands of the increasing population over the years.

Economically, the attempt to control trade routes and trade itself provoked keen competition and conflict among several groups in the region. The strategic positions of some chiefdom on the major trade routes placed them in a jealous situation. These groups survived on the trade. For instance, in the 19th century Bambili, Bambui and Nkwen (Bafreng) laid on the trade route that passed through Sabga from the plateau down to the Ndop Plain. The oil trade between the Meta groups and Ndop went through these fondoms. Livestock, salt, cloth, and beads from the northern markets passed through the Bambui, Nkwen and Bambili traders (Warnier, 1978:300-303; Rowlands, 1979).

The Kom trade with other fondoms in the Bamenda plateau was also handled by these groups. The long distance trade through Banyang country and into Calabar formed part of this network. These fondoms survived also on the inflow of goods from the northern markets. As trade fluctuated, some of these fondoms were compelled to develop new alternatives - new alliances and trade friends. For example, Nkwen tried to secure European goods directly from Bali and she entered into an alliance with Bali. In the 1860s when Balikumbat attempted to subdue Bali-Nyonga, Nkwen stood on the side of the latter and the war turned against Balikumbat (Warnier 1978: 304). Boundary conflicts in this region can be deduced from such hostile relations stemming from the 19th century trade.

Conclusion

This background chapter has described the geographical and ethnographic survey of the Bamenda grassfields. This influenced both the distribution of plant and animal life and also determined human occupation especially the settlement patterns which determined the degree of boundary conflict. It has also discussed the origins and migrations of the Tikar, Mambila (Mbembe) Widekum, the Chamba and Aghem/Fungom. Also, an attempt has been made to divide the people into two political systems based on the degree of centralisation of the indigenous political organisation.

The chapter has ended with an attempt to delineate the fundamental causes of boundary conflicts in the Bamenda Grassfields. The causes are geographical, political, social and economic. In looking at the economic cause, it was realised that Bambili/Babanki were once involved in the long distance trade. The next chapter will focus on the origins and migrations of these two groups: the Bambili and the Babanki-Tungo and the genesis of the boundary conflict.

Chapter Three
A History of Bambili/Babanki-Tungoh and the Genesis of the Boundary Conflict

Introduction

This chapter examines the arrival of the two communities -the Bambili and Babanki-Tungoh, in the region. It will look at, amongst other things, their geopolitical setting, their occupations (activities) and their origin/migratory histories. It is obvious that the two neighbours never arrived at their respective areas as enemies. Their relationship was initially cordial. The chapter further focuses on the period when the Bambili and Babanki-Tungoh were living in cordiality. The chapter ends with the manifestations of the boundary conflict and a conclusion.

A) Origin and the Migratory Histories of Bambili and Babanki-Tungoh

Bambili and Babanki Tungoh belong to the Tikar group and speak a language which belongs to the semi-Bantu group[1]. As already mentioned, the Tikar originated from the northern sector of Cameroon-Ndobo, in waves. According to an account given by the Fon of Bambili in 1926, the Bambili people were related to the Bafut at Ndobo, and left with Baba at the same time but instead of following the usual mountain track, the Bambili broke away from the Bafut and went directly to their present site along the Noun plain passing between Babungo and Bambalang in the Ndop plain. According to the Bambili oral traditions it is maintained that the Mbili people never settled in Bafut before proceeding to their present site. The Mbili assert that they migrated from Ndobo to the Ndop plain and from there they moved to their present site[2]

When they migrated from the Ndop plain, they went to Awing and settled at Mumfieh. Their settlement at Mumfieh was caused by the fact that it was the area around Lake Bambili which did not only have fresh water but also provided fish and contributed to the fertility of the area. When the first migrants arrived at Mumfieh, they named their community, *Mbili*, meaning "to sleep", because according to one of their myths, it was during their sleep that they discovered that the area had favourable conditions for settlement. It was from the word *Mbili* that the village later derived its name, Bambili. They were led to this area by a man called Ishahten who became the first ruler or chief and or Fon.

The *Mbili* were not, however, the first settlers at Mumfieh. The aborigines whom they met were a certain clan head called Nchotilem with his people. The origin of Nchotilem has been difficult to trace. However, according to oral traditions, a conflict soon developed between Nchotilem and his family and the *Mbili* newcomers. This conflict stemmed from the fact that Nchotilem wanted to control the dynasty while the *Mbili* wanted to maintain its sovereign authority with Ishahten at the head[3].The conflict was resolved when Nchotilem accepted the supremacy of the *Mbili* dynasty. A consensus was forged between the two factions with Nchotilem condescending to become part of the *Mbili* dynasty. The *Mbili* further moved and settled at Achi which had been discovered by hunters to be another fertile area.

At the time of the settlement, the only neighbouring village was Bambui whose inhabitants had arrived at the Bamenda plateau much earlier. When the *Mbili* arrived, they quickly spotted the Bambui hamlet since it was lower down on a plain. The *Mbili* attempted to launch sporadic attacks to subjugate the Bambui but all ended in futility due to the strength and fighting tactics of the Bambui. When the attempt failed, the *Mbili* became contented with Mumfieh because it was fertile.

Babanki, also called and spelled differently as Babanki-Tungoh (Tungaw, Tungoh or Kidjem-Ketingu), derived its name from gigantic pillars of rock some hundreds of meters in height that tower on each site of the village. Their oral traditions maintain that they are an offshoot of Big-Babanki (Kedjom Keku). They broke away from Big-Babanki because of problems that arose in the royal family. It should be noted that the two Babankis left Ndop together and settled in the present site of Big-Babanki. They lived in peace until a disagreement erupted between them on whether to celebrate the annual cultural festival *Kabenkendong*, or not. This cultural feast coincided with the death of a prince, who just died as the festival was about to begin. This resulted in a split of the people. Wanti, who had succeeded his father, Yufani, as chief declared that the funeral rites must be postponed until the end of the cultural festival. His brothers refused and proceeded to carry out the usual ceremonies. But *Kwifon* was sent to stop them, and they migrated to a site near *Kuwi* and established themselves as an autonomous unit.

Other informants maintained that after the dispute in Big-Babanki, the leaders came to Bambili and begged for land on which to settle. This land was given not only by Bambili alone but was contributed by Bamessing and Bandja. The Babanki-Tungoh became the guests while Bambili played host[4.] Based on this, it could be said that the two communities never came to settle at their respective places at the same time. The information gathered from the informants holds that the Bambili were the first to arrive in this region. However, when land was given to the Babanki-Tungoh, there was peaceful co-existence before relations became strained over the disputed boundary. But before the era of fraternity will be examined, it is imperative to look at the geographical positions and their daily activities.

B) Geographical Locations and Daily Activities

Geographically, the villages of Bambili and Babanki-Tungoh formed the group that made up the Bafut Native Authority Area of the Bamenda Division of the Cameroons Province in the 1920's[5]. These village-group units lived in the fertile valley basin encompassed on the North by the Kom Mountains, on the West by the distant Meta, Ngie and Ngonu mountains and hill ranges, on the East by the Tingeh hill range and in the South by the escarpment on which the Bamenda Station is perched. Bambili is situated on the lower hill-slope of the area and form a small village about 15 kilometres from Bamenda. It shares boundary with Bambui to the North West, Babanki-Tungoh to the South East and Nkwen to the West. It forms part of Tubah Sub-Division of Mezam Division. Babanki-Tungoh is found in the valleys surrounded by hill ranges on the Northern part of the Bambutous Mountains and stretches down to a portion of the Noun plain. It shares common boundaries with Bambili to the North, Bamessing to the East, Sabga to the Northeast and Balikumbat to the South. (See map II)

Map 2: Showing A The Study Area in Bamenda Grassfields

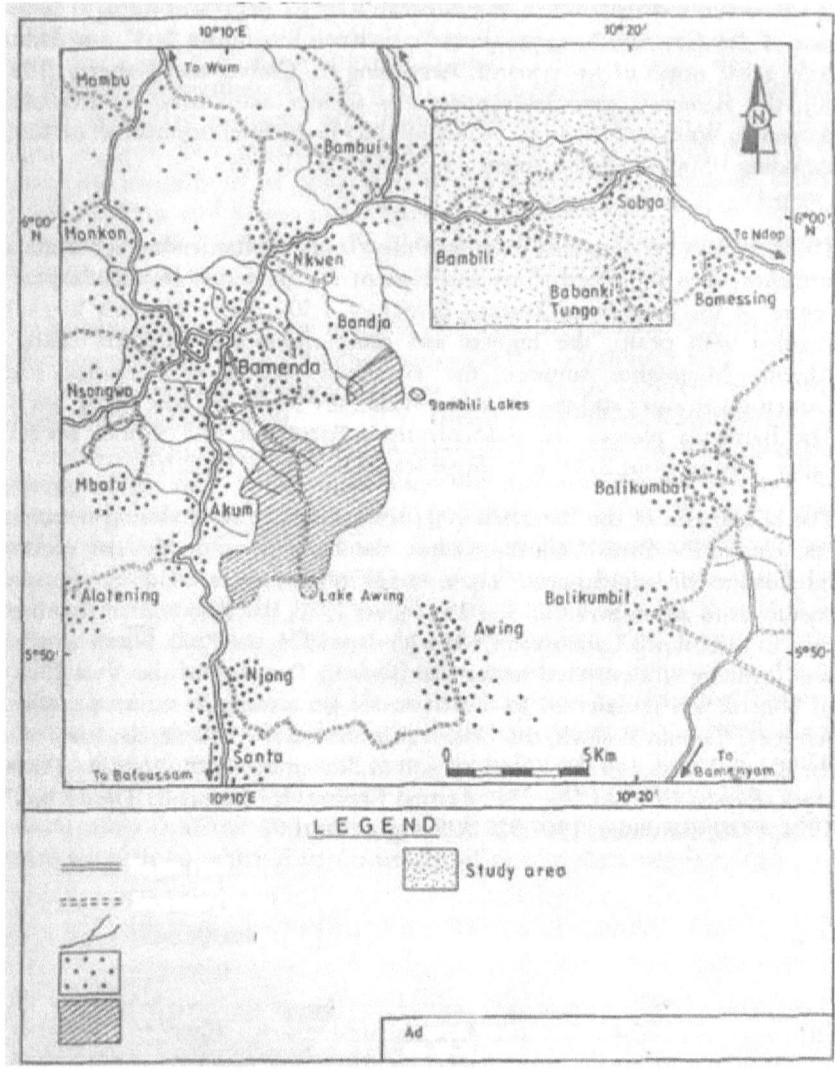

Chapter Three: A History of Bambili/Babanki-Tungoh and the Genesis of the Boundary

The combined forces of climate, bedrock, topography, and living organisms, amongst others have made the soil fertile. The soils of the region are a mixture of forested equatorial and azonal types. A survey carried out in 1953 presented a broad picture of two soil types, viz: reddish, friable porous clays and sandy clays, about 1524.3meters above sea level. The soils are well-drained, strongly leached, and of high humus content. The sandy soil form is derived from the volcanic rocks. These are more fertile than any other predominantly reddish friable porous soils[6]. This therefore means that the region under study is blessed with fertile soils, but Babanki-Tungoh is more fertile because it is situated in a valley, though in terms of area coverage she is not all around as fertile as Bambili which is found on the slopes. The fertility of Bambili is explained by the fact the Bambili people use "mechanized" farming in which they apply cow dung to the earth in order to make it fertile.

The arrival of the Germans in this region in the 1890s signalled the introduction of cash crops like Arabica coffee[7]. Babanki-Tungoh which is blessed with a rich and fertile soil produces more food and limited land for cultivation. Besides, the production of crops like vegetables, groundnuts, yams and maize flourish in this region. The coming of the cattle rearing Fulani was accompanied by another type of farming - Animal Husbandry. This was however, to be more a problem because arable land was to be used now for cattle rearing thereby making it scarce.

In the late -twentieth century, most of the inhabitants diverted their line of occupation to commercial services. For instance, traders trade on a variety of items. Many other fields of occupation were also encouraged through education. Nonetheless, it could be deduced that it is because of the fertility of the land which is suitable for agriculture all year long that the two villages are having persistent boundary disputes. Before the boundary dispute erupted in the 1950's these two neighbouring villages were living in peace.

C) From Fraternal Friends (up to 1950s) to Fraternal Enemies?

The people of Bambili/Babanki have lived at their present sites for more than a century. From the period when they arrived at their present site to the early 1950's, these two villages which shared a common boundary, lived peacefully so to say.

The administration of the R.J. Hook in the 1920's as the Assistant Divisional Officer (A.D.O.) for the Bamenda Province, he made the villages to live in peace. This was facilitated by creating "The Seven Head Chiefs in Council" which constituted all the seven chiefs making up the Bafut Native Area. The head chiefs declared that they were going to work hand in glove with each other. This meant that none of them was going to make or execute any law without the consent of the other chiefs. There was also a consensus of doing everything in union, and this seemed a good reason to accept the assembled chiefs as individuals, and at the same time as a collective unit of the Native authority to the Bafut area. This could be seen as all the villages jointly operated a single court at Bafut which worked "satisfactorily" and was headed by the chiefs of Bafut and Big-Babanki (which later gave birth to Babanki-Tungoh). Apart from this legislative aspect, the two neighbours paid taxes into a common treasury at Bafut.

Furthermore, the inhabitants of the two villages for more than a century have been freely intermarrying. This therefore meant that they must have experienced social inter-course through market interactions, cultural ceremonies and other festivities. Yet, each village seemed to hold herself aloof. While in the field informants maintain that, in the early times no chief would visit another chief not even his own brother, but would send messages. This was applicable only to the chiefs of the area. But in the early period of the 20th century the situation had changed. This manifested itself in that no chief could pass to another village for a visit during the night. He could only do this during the day, and only after he has been granted permission[8].

From the foregoing , it is tempting to conclude that the relationship between Bambili and Babanki Tungoh was very cordial. Bambili and Babanki-Tungoh constitute an "ethnic" group. Fukui and Markaki (1993:4-6) maintains that, "ethnic" groups are not a group because of ethnicity, but because they engaged in common action and share common interests. The usefulness of the ethnic label, both in political rhetoric and popular discourses, is based on the assumption that mere consciousness of shared origins is enough to constitute a group [9]. Adadevoh(2002: 80) states that ethnic groups are not necessarily homogenous entities either linguistically or culturally because it is visibly clear that minor linguistic variations and cultural differences often exist within the group, forming the basis for the delineation of sub-ethnic ethnic systems. Rangers and Hobsbwam (1985) sees the phenomenon of ethnicity as an invention. However, Bambili-Babanki and Tungoh no doubt shared these common characteristics which went closer to those examined by Fukui and Markaki as well as Rangers and Hobsbwam.

Despite the unanimity and harmony with which the chiefs exercised their duties in the Bafut Native Area, they nonetheless, displayed frequent envy of each other, as one was either larger than the other in terms of territory, stronger than the other in times of war, more influential in administrative matters or one village hosted most of the institutions in the region and even in the revenue allocation. This could be illustrated by the fact that other chiefs of the Bafut area petitioned the position and influence of the Bafut Chief in the area over administrative and transitional issues[10]. Each chief was determined to resist the exercise of any authority except his own inside his territory. The two chiefs were also suspicious of neighbouring villages which allegedly nursed aggressive and expansionist tendencies on them.

Above all, it should be emphasised that if peace reigned during the last half of the nineteenth century and the first half of the twentieth century, it was because of the tact and practical commonsense which the colonial administrators used. Both the Germans and, to a small extent, the British used the divide and rule principle, indirect system or forceful policies - in maintaining peace. It was partly because of this reason and several others that "peace" had reined in the region. No doubt by the 1950's the border between Bambili and Babanki-Tungoh became a bone of contention. In examining the *casus belli* of the boundary conflict it will be realised that other variables, not directly related to the boundary, aggravated the boundary conflict.

D) Contending issues: causes of the boundary conflict between Bambili and Babanki-Tungoh

The causes of the boundary dispute between Bambili and Babanki-Tungoh can be examined under political, economic, social and psychological domains. Politically, the two neighbours believed in expansionist, hegemonistic and annexationists' tendencies. At one time or the other, these two villages attempted, although without much success to subjugate their neighbours. For instance, the Bambili had boundary disputes with Nkwen, Bambui and Babanki-Tungoh. Babanki-Tungoh also had boundary conflicts with Bamessing, Balikumbat and Bambili. The Bambili and Babanki-Tungoh, in addition have a problem with their settlement patterns. A case in point is Bambili which is completely hemmed in. This situation is further compounded by the fact that her population is ever expanding and the available land is *ipso facto* getting smaller and smaller.

The scarcity of land to the Bambili people can be attributed to the government policies in the area since 1960s. The Cameroon College of Arts Science and Technology (CCAST) which was opened in 1963 took considerable hectares of arable land from the Bambili. It was not long afterwards that Ecole Normale Superieur Annex (ENS), The Regional School of Agriculture, School of Health Sciences (CUSS) and the Gendarmerie Brigade were opened. All these took up Bambili land and the only way for Bambili to survive was to expand at the expense of their neighbours.

Conversely, Babanki-Tungoh also found herself in an uncomfortable geographical location. Their region of settlement is at the rocky and narrow end of the Ndop plain. At the initial time of settlement, the first hamlet was in the valley and it was enough to sustain the small population which necessitated an outward expansion. In an attempt to expand and annex their neighbours, the Bambili and Babanki-Tungoh clashed on their common border leading to the boundary conflict. Nonetheless, some informants argue that the need for self-defence and not expansionism led to the border conflict[11].

Furthermore, inter-tribal wars have not been a new phenomenon in this region. In the nineteenth century, Bambili and Balikumbat went to war. The causes of this include, amongst others, the expansionist policies of Balikumbat. During this war, Babanki—Tungoh reached an entente with Balikumbat and gave her full military co-operation. The resultant effect was that Bambili was defeated. The agreement that ended this war imposed very harsh terms upon the Bambili. These terms include: Bambili was to be vassalage to Balikumbat until the payment of tribute was completed.[12] Bambili felt humiliated and decided to revenge on Babanki, an ally of Balikumbat. The attempt to revenge against Babanki-Tungoh for having assisted Balikumbat is one of the causes of the on-going Bambili and Babanki-Tungoh boundary conflict.

Another political factor that led to the Bambili and Babanki-Tungoh boundary conflict was the uncontrolled circulation of guns and ammunition around the sub region. Cameroon Criminal Law requires that to possess a gun, one has to be granted a license by the government[13]. The selling and ownership of arms is commonplace in this region. At the time that guns were strictly controlled, killings in the region were minimal. Fighting with guns during conflicts has become common in the last two decades of the 20th Century as against the use of sticks, stones and knives. Dillon (1980:80) reports that in the Bamenda Grassfields a gesture of submission during fighting was enough to inhibit a man from killing his defeated adversary, and running away may keep fatal outcome of fighting to a minimum[14]. As far as the Babanki-Tungoh and Bambili were concerned, the presence and free movement of guns had rendered that assertion an illusion.

With this advancement and lawlessness, the weapons used in tribal warfare have changed. With the new situation, killings have become rampant and destruction is immense. In a confidential note of 1978, it was noted that:"...Information worthy of trust revealed to a service agent that *Kwifon,* the highest secret traditional society in Bambui have privately instructed all men in Bambui to possess dane guns in preparation for a war against Funge people at any moment from now...."[15]

From the foregoing, two points can be deduced. Firstly, that the arms circulation, indirectly affect Bambili and Babanki-Tungoh boundary relations because the geo-political locations of Bambili and Bambui are close with a permeable boundary. The permeability of the boundary show that what affects Bambui affected Bambili indirectly and/or directly. Secondly, it might be true that without the arms, the violence between Bambili and the Babanki-Tungoh communities would still have arisen. It was also true to say that the application of such weapons have accentuated the amount of destruction and causalities.

Another political cause of the boundary conflict was the laxity of the civil administration who attempted demarcating this boundary which led to a thaw in the Bambili and Babanki-Tungoh relations. But between 1965 and 1995 several complaints have been brought before the court. What was more about these complaints was that court injunctions are contravened by both villages. When that happened, effective sanctions were not carried out on the individuals who went against the law or court ruling.

To make the point of the laxity of administration more lucid, it will be realised that the two villages reached an "entente" on July 25, 1973.[16]. Unfortunately, the understanding was violated by the Babanki Tungoh and they were never brought to order neither was the Fon of Babanki-Tungoh called for interrogation. This certainly gave the impression that the agreement was not considered serious even by the government of the area.

In a related vein, the activities of James Samuel Jones (pseudonym) - one of the highest educated elite in Bambili as given rise to a school of thought which holds that he was behind the boundary conflict. In a confidential release, James Samuel Jones closest associate revealed that James Samuel Jones armed the Bambili people with automatic rifles to "crush" the Babanki people "next time"[17].

Economically, the border between these two villages is principally used for economic activities. When the two villages settled in their respective areas, this border was jointly used for hunting. When the fertility of this land was discovered and a corresponding increases in the populations of the two villages, it became a bone of contention. The border in dispute was farmed throughout the year, and informants attested to the fact that eighty percent of the vegetables supplied in the Bamenda metropolitan town and its environs come from this area. This means that this fertile piece of land sustains the livelihood of these villages, socially and economically. To show how the economic factor was very important in the boundary dispute, a confidential release on November 15, 1971, from the Prime Minister's office stated: ". . . It is desirable for the Babanki people to have a market for their potatoes about this area, and so a piece of land should be sliced from the Bambili land on this area and allocated to Babanki-Tungoh for this purpose . . . ."[18]

This communiqué shows that economic imperatives were behind the boundary misunderstanding., Taking away land from Bambili and giving to Babanki-Tungoh for economic purpose was not accepted by the Bambili.

The economic imperatives are compounded by the fact that this area is also used for cattle farming or grazing land. The Fulanis who arrived in this region at the end of the 19th century preferred to graze their cattle in the higher slopes free from disease-bearing insects. In carrying out these activities, the piece of land remains limited in supply. The limitation of land coupled up with an increase in demand for the products, facilitated the two neighbours "stepping on each other's toes". To drive home the point, an official cattle market was opened at Sabga which is purportedly under Babanki-Tungoh by the British colonial administration and the buying of cattle elsewhere in the region other than in the cattle market was strictly prohibited[19]. It could be noted that the grazier farmer conflict which gave a final push to the boundary conflict stemmed, in the main, from the co-existence of two different patterns of land exploitation. In other words, land use and land holding were not often mutually harmonized.

Another cause of this boundary conflict can be found in the psychological domain[20]. The instinct theory is an innate or genetically predetermined disposition to behave in a particular way when confronted with certain stimuli. Those who unleashed the boundary conflict in the 1950's might not be alive today, but the boundary conflict is persecuted by their progenitors. In carrying out the "duty" they are defending their "fatherland." Thus the Latin adage *Dulce et Decorum et pro Patricia Mora*, which meant that it is a nice thing to fight and die for the fatherland. The boundary conflict between Bambili and Babanki-Tungoh flared up in the 1950's, because of a fertile piece of land found between these two villages. Since then, it has been claimed and counter claimed by the two villages. In the 1990's the claims took a different dimension - warfare, causing enormous damages to both villages.

The boundary dispute is because of a piece of land as has already been mentioned. This large tract of land is found on top of Sabga. On the high ground adjacent to Bambili the land is purely grazing land. It then drops suddenly into a valley. This valley was claimed to be very fertile and it was extensively farmed and built over by the Babanki-Tungoh people. Babanki-Tungoh village was over the ridge on the far side of the valley on the edge of the Ndop plain.

The Bambili people did arrive in this area prior to the Babanki people and the highland now in dispute was "no man's land". Both parties were probably using it for hunting. Then the Fulanis arrived in the 19th century with their cattle and settled on it. With the introduction of law and order some Babanki-Tungoh people left the valley that they had originally settled in, being short of farming land. They started to farm in the highland known now as the area under dispute.

From the mid-20th century the two villages have made claims and counter claims over this land. What is more disturbing is who owns the disputed land? If we take into consideration the fact that the Bambili people arrived first, then we could as well accept the fact that the disputed land belongs to Bambili. But there is a difference on who makes a claim over the land and who effectively occupies the land? In as much as the Babanki Tungoh people have built and are farming on the land, one is tempted to conclude that the land belongs to them. However, for a better understanding of the history of the conflict it is imperative to look at land ownership on the eve of colonization.

Land was one of the most important reasons for the formation of states in the Bamenda Grassfields. Even within the states, the ruling authorities struggled to control the resources; land was important for agriculture, hunting, fishing, settlement, crafts and manufacturing, amongst others. Due to these reasons the land tenure system evolved to be fundamentally communal[21]. The colonialists met the land tenure system on a political basis of control. The land was placed under the household, lineage or clan heads by the state. Each family, as a constituent of a lineage, had the right to land; ownership was transferred to the offspring on inscriptive basis. This took place when the male offspring was getting married and needed land. In this case therefore, land constituted the basic form of property, status and prestige in the society[22].

However, the development of monarchical system of government and social stratification transformed the basis of land ownership to include other forms of private ownership. In this case, it existed either individually or collectively. Nonetheless, the communal ownership dominated, and all land was, in principle, under the control of the *Fons* who administered it through their administrative officials like the quarter, ward or village heads; lineage heads; *sub-fons* and developed local laws and customs prohibiting the sale or pledge of land, but made it possible for easy transfer from one noble to another. Under this arrangement, the right to perform sacrifices to a local god or other ancestors was also transferred. On these, nobles could own large tracts of land or be designated to do the transfers.

Similarly, land could be distributed to non-lineage members, but only after having first considered the interest of the immediate lineage and dependants. In the same way, settlement on any land within a polity by an outsider was only permitted by the Fon through his administrative officials[23]. The coming of the British colonial administration in 1916 saw the introduction of the certificate of occupancy. This meant that when the Fon possessed land he could lease it out for a period of ninety-nine years to his subjects or tenants. But it should be noted that this did not confer titles because it was leased to the individual, yet the Fon or chamberlain remained the "lord manor". According to the 1974 land ordinances, the certificate of occupancy was abolished and following Decree N° 76/165/27 of April 1974, new conditions were established for obtaining the new document, land certificate. Article one of the Decree stipulates that "land certificate shall be the only authentic document of real property rights"[24] to land. This meant that without this document it was difficult, if not impossible, to claim land.

With regard to Bambili and Babanki-Tungoh, they have been claiming the piece of land on their border, yet none of them is prepared to show any document to this claim. Instead, the Bambili point to the lake as their ancestral home. They also maintain that libations are poured into this lake once a year to appease the ancestors and to have a good harvest during the farming season. The Babanki-Tungoh also pointed to the lake as theirs and the entire piece of land. What is more is that both villages do not seem to possess a land certificate or the defunct certificate of occupancy. As a matter of fact it is unwise and unthinkable to start to feel that these two African communities should only claim legitimacy by showing a land certificate. What should obviously be the proof into this land should be the resort to the traditional way of boundary making and settlement of African boundaries long before the advent of colonialism in the 1880's. The puzzle here therefore is why the administrators despite the fact that they are all Africans, could not look below their nostrils to handle the boundary in the African traditional way. It appears unfortunate.

What we mean here is that the failure of Bambili and Babanki-Tungoh to produce a land certificate might be attributed to their ignorance. They are ignorant because they had not known such inventions in boundary making like the land certificate. The administration could have taken off time to orientate them but the administrators always rushed to the disputed area for inspection. A case in point was the Divisional Officer, Bamenda Central Sub-Division, Oben Peter Ashu, who on June 26, 1975, inspected the disputed area and issued letter N° ABA.23/681 of 18 September 1975. In that letter he gave directives to Ardo Jacky of Sabga, Babanki-Tungoh and the farmers of Chuku Babanki-Tungoh on what should be done before farming on the areas[25].

What is important is that all what Ashu asked the people to do did not include the land certificate. The land became state land. The fact that it became state land was confirmed by the Honourable S.N. Kindo, educated elite of Bambili, when he said ". . . it is the role of the Government to make the best use of the land they have and not to allow it stand wasted. . . ."[26]. Kindo based his arguments on grounds that neither Babanki-Tungoh nor Bambili had any title to claim the land.

What is disturbing as far as titleship to land is concerned is who should produce the certificate. Is it the individual or the community? If it is the community, could it be possible for the whole community to possess one certificate? Here the role of the Fon becomes very important. He was according to what existed before colonization, the "lord of the manor" and leases out land to his subjects. This is evident in a letter written by the Fon of Babanki-Tungoh, on June 29, 1973, addressed to the Assistant Cattle Control Officer, Bafut Area Council. In that letter, the Fon said:". . . This is to satisfy that I the Fon of Babanki-Tungoh, have given a plot to Mr. Fulum Joseph of Mbuateh-Tengam nearest to Aigh Ale at the lake. He is going to do farming there and to make a fence round the farming plot. So I hereby wish to inform you and your office so as to let you know. . ."[27].

Chapter Three: A History of Bambili/Babanki-Tungoh and the Genesis of the Boundary

With this, it is clear that the Fon owns the land and leases or distributes it to his subjects. In the event of border conflict, it is logical that his subjects will come out to defend the boundary, firstly because the Fon is looked up to as the "hope" of the tribe. However, since the 1950's the boundary conflict between these two villages has manifested itself in various ways.

E) The Manifestation of the Boundary Conflict c. 1950 -1955: The epoch of Law Suits

The boundary conflict was manifested in three principal ways: from c.1950 to 1958 it was mainly in law suits filed by the contestants; from 1958 to 1973, when it led to the signing of the Babanki-Tungoh and Bambili entente. This second period can be called the "thaw" in the boundary manifestation. The last period was from 1973 to 1995. This period was characterised by skirmishes, threats, suspicion and outright warfare. It ended in 1995 with yet another law suit.

The Bambili people brought a suit against the Babanki-Tungoh people in the Bafut native court, Civil Suit N°23/53. As already mentioned, this claim was made over a piece of land bordering the Bambili-Babanki-Tungoh. The court judgment of December 11, 1953, situated the boundary on the hills on the West side of the outlet of the lake and valley. The court granted Bambili part of the land which the Bambili had claimed. This land stretched from the German boundary of Babanki-Tungoh with Medankwe at "Kukets", to the hills west of the lake and valley.

The Bambili were not, however, satisfied with the decision. As a result of this, they appealed and in its judgment of July 15, 1955, the Appeals Court shifted the line to the high grazing land near to the escarpment beyond which is Bambili village. Yet, they were still not satisfied and called for a review by the Colonial District Officer. On September 8, 1956, the Assistant Divisional Officer Ward, rendered his review judgment. According to Ward, the boundary began: "At the very high peak at the boundary with Babulue into the Tuentueng stream. It will follow streams in the same general direction until it reaches the cattle trace near markets ruga. There a cairn will be erected and the boundary will go in a straight line to the raffia bush on the stream that comes across the main road just beyond mile 13"[28].

Ward's review judgment came close to giving Bambili most of their claim. He went on to add:". . . Anybody from either village, who now finds himself on land not owned by his own people, will have the choice of moving to his own village land or staying where he is and paying tax to the next village. If he chooses to do the latter he will be permitted to stay and farm. Persons who choose to move must do so before January 1, 1957. This will give them time to harvest their crops . . . ."[29] What pushed Ward to arrive at this was that he doubted whether the boundary between Bambili and Babanki-Tungoh had ever been defined. He made this clear when he said:

> . . . in my [his] opinion correctly, I do not think that the boundary had ever been defined between the parties. It is my opinion that the decisions of the court of first instance and the appeal court were no more than attempts to arbitrate. They both failed because they chose an unsuitable and artificial line. It is my intention to create a more suitable natural boundary[30].

His judgment appeared one sided as although many Babanki Tungoh people were to be affected, no single Bambili person was required to make the choice. It is practical commonsense that in these days one will not expect a large number of people who have lived on a piece of land for a very long time without interference, to suddenly pack up and to move leaving their stock and land. In any case he was only attempting to provide a solution to the boundary conflict. In an attempt to "create a more suitable natural boundary" Ward aroused the disgruntleness of the Babanki-Tungoh people. It was as a result of this discontent that the indigenes of Babanki-Tungoh asked for a review. On May 15, 1958, A. B. Westmacott, Colonial resident in Bamenda gave his judgment in Review No. 84/56 in File No. 361(569). According to Westmacott Ward's decision was one-sided since he maintained that many Babanki-Tungoh people were affected and no Bambili man was even required to make a choice.

A. B. Westmacott, after having inspected the land for three days, decided In the Review Jurisdiction of the Resident, Bamenda holden at Bafut on 15 May 1958 that:

After carefully inspecting the land I have decided that Babanki-Tungoh should remain in possession of the land which they now occupy but that all the grazing land on the Bambili side which is [was] now unoccupied - with the exception of three Babanki-Tungoh [sic] and several Fulani rugas, - should be confirmed as belonging to Bambili. Starting from Bambili Lake, the boundary will be as decided by the Appeal Court until it approaches the footpath running from Babanki-Tungoh to Bamenda. It will then bear almost due north from this point along the grassy spur until it reaches a rocky outcrop on the steep escarpment defining the valley. It will run along the edge of this escarpment until the cliff like feature ends and the land becomes rolling down land. The boundary will then follow the line as defined by Cairns until it reaches the main Bamenda-Kumbo-Nkambe road (The Ring Road) at the sharp corner just beyond mile post 13. The village head of Bambili to have the right of carrying out sacrifices at the spot in the valley now on Babanki Tungoh land as heretofore".[31]

The manifestation of the boundary problem between the Babanki-Tungoh and Bambili communities, judging from the above evidence indicates that it moved from one court to another. From the Bafut Native Court to the High Court of Appeal; from the Divisional Officer Bamenda through advisory bodies to the Resident, Westmacott.

The Westmacott decision has remained on the map. What was required was that the decision on the map should be utilised for the demarcation of the disputed area. However, when this decision was arrived at on May 15, 1958, the J.J. Mbafor who surveyed the land in accordance with the decision of delimitation,[32] encountered insurmountable problems carrying out his duties.

Bambili people, it was reported, were not satisfied with the decision. In April 1959, the Fon of Bambili petitioned in civil suit No. 23/53 against the decision to the Government of the Southern Cameroons. On July 8, 1959, the Deputy Commissioner of the Southern Cameroons, J.A.A. Tamkoh, replied to the petition in No.361 (569)/T/19 in the following words: "I am directed to refer to your petition of April 1959, and to inform you that it is regretted that Government cannot interfere with the judgment of the Resident. I have the honour, Sir, Your Obedient Servant, Deputy Commissioner of the Cameroons"[33]. The laxity of the colonial administration vis-à-vis the implementation of the West Macott's decision could only be better appreciated within the objective of the colonial enterprise and even the post colonial regime as the post colonial state has not shown much difference with the colonial state except in name. Overall colonialism as a system was a dehumanizing and was pegged on exploitation. To that end it treated the people of the colonized territory as though they were technological objects who were used as a mechanism for accomplishing the colonial enterprise. That could quickly explain why Westmacott was lumping up people as though they were commodities.

One common contemporary denominator which could be deduced from Wesmacott's attempt is that just as the colonial enterprise was a European project and they chose Africans that they wanted to participate in it for the sake of helping them to achieve their goals, as it is today, globalization and technological innovation in the form of mobile phone and internet is by and large a project of developed and semi-developed countries, that allow ordinary people such as in Africa to participate in it. The fact that Wesmacott concentrated in attempted to demarcate people whose history was peripheral to him illustrates the fact dearly held by colonial apologists that colonialism was an enlightenment project which was rooted in evolutionary theory propounded by Charles Darwin. Behind the minds of the chief priest of colonialism was the dear belief that some human beings were/and are at the lower rung of the evolutionary chain and it was the responsibility or burden of the civilized to civilize the brutes

Furthermore the saying that "government cannot interfere with the judgement of the resident" needs further explanation. It shows the contradictions within the organizational structure of the colonial domination. In concrete terms it shows how the Resident was ill-informed about situations on the ground. The government, whatever that means was more informed with the nuances on the ground. In the post colonial state the situation has not changed either. The Divisional officer who is and might be conversant with the ground situation is not often allowed to take and execute decisions according to the dictates of his mind as the central government in Yaounde often over rules most of the decisions taken at provincial level.

That notwithstanding the Babanki-Tungoh people were not satisfied with the Westmacott decision either. However, the Fons of both villages had a meeting in 1965 and signed by J.N.Foncha. The full text of the decision agreed by the Fon's meeting which met on 13 February 1965 read as follows:

F) Decision on Land Dispute Between Babanki-tungoh And Bambili Agreed Upon By The Bafut

Chiefs Meeting In Their Council On 13/2/65

1. That the area in dispute was allocated to Bambili following the Westmarcott Boundary of 1956.

2. That it is desirable for the Babanki Tungoh people to have a market for their potatoes about this area, and so a piece of land should be sliced from the Bambili land on this area and allocated to Babanki-Tungoh for this purpose. This piece of land will start from the present V.H.F. beacon to a point somewhat westwards to a point 10 metres away from the brick building now being constructed by one Babanki man somewhat Southwards into Bambili land. Hereafter to join the Wetmarcott boundary straight ahead. The rest of the boundary to follow the Westmarcott demarcation towards its terminus near Lake Bambili.

3. All compounds built by Babanki Tungoh people on Bambili land to remain Bambili property and their occupants to pay tax to Bambili and be known as Bambili people or to quit into Babanki Tungoh. A statement to this effect to be got from these men who will enable the administration and the Bambili village council to decide whether they should remain or quit.

4. The surveyor to be accompanied by four representatives of Bafut Clan Area drawn from Bafut West and Bafut East constituencies. Stones to be collected by both villages to pile up a various point on the boundary to be visible readily.

5. A copy of the amended Westmarcott Map with the statement was agreed upon by the Bafut Clan Chiefs to be given to the Chief of each of the villages.

Signed: J.N. Foncha
P.M. 15/2/65.
S.D.O.

The above are my draft minutes. You will produce the full minutes please, and give the necessary instructions to the Surveyor etc.

Signed: J.N. Foncha
P.M. 15/2/65.

    The minutes of the meeting with the chiefs which were signed by the J.N.Foncha shows how the post colonial state has succeeded the colonial state without much difference. The chiefs who represented the traditional elites and Foncha who represented the political elites all held tied to the tail coat of Westmacott's decision. The chief's meeting further strengthens Westmacott's decision by dividing the people as though they were ignorant of the traditional methods of land arbitration that existed long before the colonial arrival in the area.

    According to the other village, Bambili, the Westmacott decision was not in their favour. As a result of this, the Bambili paid the sum of 138,400CFA francs in July 1967 as deposit for an appeal against part of the boundary marked by the 1958 decision. Unfortunately, this appeal was never heard for reasons that were never made known. In 1972 another meeting by the traditional council headed by the political elites of both communities-Hon. Mukong and Hon. Kindo for Babanki Tungoh and Bambili, respectively was held. The attempt was to pacify both villages. The minutes and deliberations are reproduced in full below:

Traditional Council Meeting With Hon. Mukong And Hon. Kindo On The 16-1-72 In The Chief's Palace In Babanki-tungo To Find Out A Peaceful Solution To The Babanki-tungo/Bambili Boundary Dispute

At 2.30 p.m. Hon. B. N. Mukong, in the presence of the Chief, Transitional Council members, and a host of other Babanki-Tungoh people, introduced the Hon. S.N. Kindo and the topic of this visit. In his brief introduction, Hon. Mukong told the house that on the 13th January 1972, Hon. Kindo, the district Officer, Mezam, the Surveyor and himself went to the disputed boundary, and saw things for themselves. He then told the Babanki-Tungoh people that as the leaders of the area and also sons of the two villages had deemed it expedient to address the two villages in order to seek ways and means by which they could end the long standing boundary dispute between the two villages. He **then** concluded by saying that, that was the reason why they were in the palace that day. He declared the floor opened for Kindo to speak to the people of Babanki-Tungoh.

Having addressed the **Chief, His Council** and the people, Hon. S.N. Kindo told the house that the boundary dispute between the two villages was one of a long standing. He went on to say that, they the Parliamentarians of the area had come to seek from the people ways by which the matter could be ended. He pointed out that Parliamentarians come and go, and **that** they could leave Parliament tomorrow. Continuing, he said that since they were the children of the two villages, they **were** out to find a suitable solution to the dispute. He added. He added that if they are changed or leave Parliament next day, new persons coming might not all the time be children from Babanki-Tungoh and Barnbili, and as such might not know the problems of the people very well, and consequently might not tender the right cure to their problems.

Kindo Hon., said that in the multi-party days there was a lot of enmity, nepotism and tribalism among people but today under the C.N.U. Government peace and security are the only media of solving disputes. We went to the boundary site, Hon. Kindo went on and saw that one village claims land and puts it into effective use, **but** on the **contrary** the other village claims land **and never** puts into use at all. He said that there he was going to call the spade a spade. Kindo pointed out that it is the role of the government to make the best use of the land they have and not to allow it stand wasted. Hon. Kindo appealed to the house to think constructively and to resolve at a peaceful and lasting solution to the boundary issue. As an eye witness of the boundary from start to the finish, Hon. Kindo observed:

a) That one village is claiming land and using it, while the other is not doing so.

b) That in certain places on the boundary as showed by Westmacott, Babanki-Tungoh had trespassed into Bambili had one vice versa(sic).

c) That when he first came into Parliament he was received first in Buea by Babanki elements and that Mukong and himself were not well loved by all in the two villages, he then revealed that the hatred for them cannot make Mukong give part of Babanki land to Bambili or claim part of Bambili and give to Babanki, likewise himself.

d) That in certain places on the boundary site, he took on himself the powers of the D.O. to suggest to the Surveyor to change the boundary so as to avoid problems from either village.

e) That the deposits given by the two villages calling on the land Tribunal was not to be returned and that it was small, and should be increased so as to meet up with the cost of tones, sand and labour in the construction of a permanent boundary between Babanki-Tungoh and Bambili.

f) That he Kindo was free of blames in Babanki-Tungoh because if he knows of any cause to be blamed he would not have come to be blamed he would not have come to address the Babanki-Tungoh people without fear. He then opened room for questions from the people.

Chapter Three: A History of Bambili/Babanki-Tungoh and the Genesis of the Boundary

Questions

1) The first member of the Council asked:- From the time of the Germans to the time of the British rule we had no boundary disputes between Bambili/Babanki-Tungoh, why are these disputes coming up this time when the aborigine of Cameroon are ruling themselves?

Hon. Kindo gave no answer to this question.

2) The Chairman of the Council asked:- I have always been present at the boundary site from the time of the decisions of the law court to this time. I also travelled with Westmarcott for three days along this boundary, why is the map drawn to show Westmacott's decisions not in accordance with his decision? Hon. Kindo did not answer the question.

3) Westmarcott made a boundary between Babanki and Bambili in 1958 and gave a decision but never drew a map of the area he visited. In his decision he gave out 3 Babanki-Tungoh compounds to Bambili namely: Toh Meshi, Che Veghwo, and Jaff Mukom. The giving out of the compounds did not satisfy the Babanki people, and as such they raised a deposit calling on the land Tribunal to decide the matter.

(a) What has happened that the land Tribunal has not come to the boundary site?

(b) What has become of the deposit given? Hon. Kindo said that the deposit given was small to do the work on the boundary and as such it should be increased to make up the cost of sand, stones and labour force to be given.

4) Another Council member asked: When one makes a summons, he wants that his case be tried. If he is tried and he loses the case, then the courts forfeits his summons, do the Babankis now presume that they have lost the three compounds to Bambili? If they did not lost the case:

(a) What therefore were the decisions of the land Tribunal?

(b) Where is the Deposit of the Babanki Tungoh people? Hon. Mukong in response said that Hon. Kindo in his talk appeal to the Babanki-Tungoh people to forget the past and to explore ways and means to end this boundary issue, because they Politicians did not come as judges to as peace makers to end the dispute.

5) There were four people who visited the boundary site on the 13-1-72. Why was it not possible that all of them come to address this Council today? There was no answer to this question.

6) Between miles Posts 12 and 13, the Babanki-Tungoh have a common boundary with Bambui, why do surveyors and Government Officers who came to make the Bambili/ Babanki-Tungo boundary always begin their boundary trace from mile post 13, on the Ring Road to Nso?

In Hon. Kindo's attempts to answer the questions, said that they were not out to receive blames but rather, the people of Babanki-Tungoh would have praised him, and made suggestions as to what they as their representatives could do to end the situation.

A member of the Council suggested that a conciliation committee could be formed consisting of members from Babanki-Tugoh villages to sit and study the situation at the dispute area and to suggest ways of ending the matter.

The Chief and people of Babanki resolved as follows:

1) That for the purpose of peace, the Westmacott map showing the boundary map showing the boundary should be corrected to work in accordance with his decisions since it was drawn from the said decision.

2) That the law court boundary of 1953 between the two villages be respected to a peace both villages.

3) That something should be done about the deposit if the land Tribunal will not come to the boundary site.

4) That the Council and entire people of Babanki are happy and grateful for the giant step taken by Hon. Kindo and Hon. Mukong in their attempts to end this matter. The Council and Chief wished them every success.

5) That after consultation with the Council and entire people of Babanki— Tungoh, and after a serious study of the situation the Council and people will tender a report later on the Hons. Kindo/Mukong mission to Babanki-Tungoh on the 16th January 1972.

Hon. Mukong thanked the Hon. S.N. Kindo for his endeavour to end the Babanki-Tungoh/Bambili boundary dispute. He called on all Babanki-Tungoh people to do same.

Hon. Kindo thanked the entire population of Babanki-Tungoh for the time and patience sacrificed to come and listen to what he had said. He told the Babanki to wait on the information of the District Officer on when to come to the boundary site for final arrangements. He prayed for a peaceful solution when time came. In conclusion, he said the Governments decisions were final. They rally at 5.30 p.m.

Signed Peter Vewerro
Chairman -B. Tungoh
Traditional Council
Copy: To Hon. D.N. Mukong
-To District Officer - Mezam
-To Hon. S.N. Kindo

Signed: Secretary
B. Tungoh T. Council

The two parliamentarians saw the boundary misunderstanding as a venue for them to propagate the political ideals of the Head of State, Ahmadou Ahidjo. That explains why they started by talking about the disadvantages of the multi party days when there was rancour and hatred and that the one party state was out to maintain peace. Cameroon became independent in 1960/61 and was styled the Federal Republic of Cameroon. Ten years later, the President and his politicians preached the disadvantages of the multi-party era and in 1972 organised a referendum which was claimed that 99.99 percent voted. Cameroon then became a Unites Republic of Cameroon and the sole aim was to forge a national unity. The politicians therefore did not mince their words and took the boundary misunderstanding as platform to remind the people about a unitary state. Yet one could see that they were like using coercion rather than using tact and common sense to settle the boundary problem.

However, a year later, on July 25, 1973 both villages signed an agreement acknowledging and accepting the Westmacott decision as the only authentic document. It was hoped that the decision would put an end to the long standing dispute between the two communities. The "entente" was signed by the Fons of Babanki-Tungoh and Bambili for their communities. This understanding was witnessed by the Cameroon government representative, Ngonge Sone, B. N. Mukong for Babanki-Tungoh, S.N. Kindo for Bambili and several land and surveys officers. The entente stated *inter alia*:

> We the undersigned Fons of Bambili and Babanki-Tungoh do hereby accept the Westmacott decision on our existing land dispute as being the only and authentic administrative decision that can put an end to our long standing dispute. We are fully prepared to collaborate with the team of surveyors that will be sent by the administration to trace and define the boundary between our people. Our people will carry stones and sand for the successful accomplishment of this task. In addition we will accept the technical advice that will be given us by surveyors to demarcate this boundary. He could bring along with him the Native Authorities surveyor who drew the maps which are now in our possessions. Finally, we are going to request our people to refrain from carrying out any activities on the supposed disputed area until the final demarcation is made by the survey team. Any person encroaching on this disputed area will be penalised by the administration. We are fully prepared to maintain and respect each other's interest on this area until the final demarcation[34].

As a result of the entente, peace reigned in the sub-region albeit fears, threats and scepticism persisted. Every possible effort was made by the administration of the Bamenda Division to provide a peaceful solution to the problem. In addition solutions were also sought for the Farmer/Grazier conflicts during this period which came about by the transgression of section 13, par 2, of the Farmer/Grazier law of 1962 by some farmers of the disputed areas.[35] Further farming activities were authorised by the Farmer/Grazier Department and all persons who were authorised to retain their farms in this area to obtain farming permits from the Farmer/Grazier Branch in regularisation of the land they occupied in the area.

Though some degree of peace reigned for more than a decade after the Westmacott Decision and the 1973 accord, the boundary manifestation took a different dimension and magnitude in the early 1990s. This was because the early 1990s witnessed the accumulation of weapons, the rising aspirations of the indigenes and their rulers to expand and annex the piece of land under dispute, the involvement of politicians and the training of local militia men. Above all, the 1990s was one of the most tumultuous years in the political history of Africa South of the Sahara and Cameroon was not exempt.

Important, to emphasise here that the year 1990 witnessed the end of the cold war and the re-introduction of multiparty politics in Africa. Politicians who wanted to remain in office developed various strategies to remain in power. The fear of the immigrant population in most cities of Cameroon by the politicians of the day, that they will support opposition and turn the scales of election led to citizenship crises as the politicians decided to call some citizens sons and daughters of the soil and the others as strangers. These factors increased the amount of threats, tensions and fears amongst the indigenes of both villages which culminated in open armed clashes in 1991, 1993 and 1995.

G) The War Period

It is interesting to bear in mind that before the 1991 outbreak of war, the 1973 peace accord had been violated. On August 1, 1981, the Fon of Bambili reported to the Civil Administration that the Babanki-Tungoh people were still continuing their activities in the disputed area. In response to this, on April 17, 1986, the District officer of Tubah reported to the Divisional Officer for Mezam. He called it a "provocative trespass" into Bambili land by the Babanki-Tungoh people. In his reply, the Divisional Officer for Mezam stated that he had convoked the "ring leaders" of the aggressive groups to his office for interrogation and cautioning. The provocation nonetheless continued uninterrupted.

On May 24, 1991, the Bambili people, men and women, went to the disputed area and started farming. On May 25, 1991, Babanki Tungoh people through their regent reported to the Civil Administration of Tubah that the Bambili people had illegally started activities on the disputed area. From this account it is obvious that the violation of the agreement between the two communities facilitated the escalation of the armed conflict. The terms of the agreement explained that any person encroaching on the disputed area would "be penalised by the administration." This was not done. The only thing that was done to the trespassers was that the "ring leaders" were called and cautioned by the District Officer.

During the Bambili and Babanki-Tungoh confrontation, property and lives were destroyed and several families were rendered homeless. Bambili people blocked the main road leading to Babanki, they stopped and searched vehicles for Babanki people and tortured them. Some students who were writing their General Certificate Examinations, especially Babanki students, in Cameroon College of Arts Science and Technology (CCAST) were not spared, as they were harassed. Some "vandals" from Bambili stormed the examination halls, instilled fear and distress in them and momentarily disrupted their examination[36].

When the dust finally settled, the Administration of Tubah under the District Officer, Martin Jum, and the Mezam Divisional Administration under the Senior Divisional Officer, Bell Luc Rene, set up an administrative commission to investigate and resolve the problem. A Prefectoral Order No.194/712/s.1 of 27 March 1991 created a commission with the principal objective which was to trace and demarcate the boundary according to Westmacott decision of 1958. The commission was in accordance of the provisions of Decree No. 78/322 of 3/8/78 instituting a commission for the settlement of boundary disputes concerning administrative areas under Traditional Authority, an Inter-Village Boundary Commission was thereby appointed to delve into the Boundary Dispute between Bambili and Babanki Tungoh in Tubah Sub Division. In the nascent stage the two communities appeared not to be cooperating with the Administration. Consequently, they were compelled to corporate following the Letter Ref. No.E.29 01.2/165/235 from the Divisional Officer for Tubah, Tangwa Joseph Fover to the Senior Divisional Officer, Mezam, Bamenda. Written on 16 April 1993 the letter stated amongst other things:

> I have the honour to forward to you copies of the last minutes of the meeting the Commission held on this issue which after pleading for long the parties do not seem to agree. I will then strongly recommend that the parties should be invited by the Prefect and cautioned of the consequences of their intransigencies. They should be warned to collaborate with the Commission and furnish the needed materials for the work. However, the Bambili have promised to supply their share of the materials. Lastly, they should be warned that no farming should be carried out in the disputed area until the final solution is taken and parties officially informed. The Commission has decided to interpret the Westmacot decision putting the two parties aside and needs strongly the advisory and moral support of the Hierarchy. The 1991 Commission began by attempting to retrace the boundary to satisfy both parties with the following being the members of that commission:

- Mr. Jum Martin Ndiyeng, Divisional Officer, Tubah was chairman
- Mr. Nfonbe Hosea Thadeus, chief of Service Lands Mezam was secretary
- Mr. Alain Bome, Representing the chief of service Surveys, Mezam was member
- Mr. Nyamboli John, Municipal Administrator Tubah, Member
- Mr. Che Hosea Ambe, Sub-Section President of CPDM Tubah, Member
- The Divisional Delegate of Agriculture Mezam, Member

-Fon Awemo11, The fon of Bambili Village Member
-Mr. Aban Anthony, Delegate of Bambili Member
-Mr. Asang Shuigelai, Delegate of Bambili Member
-Mr. John Amuntum, Delegate of Bambili Member
-Mr. Aseh Cornelius, Regent of Babanki Tungoh Member
-Mr. Mukong B.N. Delegate of Babanki-Tungoh Member
-Mr. Tohnayor Emmanuel, Delegate of Babanki Tungoh Member
Mr. Vitung William, Delegate of Babanki Tungoh Member
Mr. Gwalle Jacob Menang, Delegate of Babanki-Tugoh Member

On the 2 April 1991 all the members settled at the Divisional Officer's office, Tubah except the Divisional Delegate of Agriculture, Mezam, Mr. Aban Anthony and Mr. Asanga Tchwimei Delegates of Bambili and Mr. Aseh Cornilius, the Regent, Mr. Tohnayor Emmanuel, Mr. Gwalle Jacob Delegates from Bambili. According to the minutes of that meeting, the Commission members assembled at the Divisional Office, Tubah, and proceeded to the site at 12:15 p.m. The Members arrived Chuku-Babanki and the Divisional Officer made reference to P.O. No.194/P.O./712/s.1 of 27/03/91. He expressed disappointment at this absenteeism and lateness of the fon of Bambili and went ahead to say that the exercise cannot be suspended notwithstanding. He called upon them to make provision for the necessary logistics to facilitate effective work, in the implementation of the Westmacott decision. That is provision like Transport, Feeding, and Materials for cairns and labour force to transport materials. Six people were selected from each of the communities including a mason.

The chairman called upon other members to say something where upon the Municipal Administrator of Tubah re-iterated the team spirit to characterize the exercise to complete action on a sound decision of previous administration. The Sub-Section CPDM President taking a turn, appealed to the participants to take a peaceful approach to the realization of this exercise, since peace is the pre-requisite of any successful action or achievement. The Divisional Chief of Service for Lands, Mezam explained further on the technical aspects of the job and ran down the estimates of the material drawn up by the Representative of the Divisional Chief of Service of Surveys for Mezam as follows:

-5 bags cement-12 cairns (60 bags cement)
-14 head pans sand-12 cairns (168 head pans sand)
-14 head pans gravel-12 cairns (168 head pans gravel)
-1.5 rod 10mm-12 cairns (12x 1.5)
- Spades, head pans, pig axes, trowels, water cans, hammers, cutlasses and six concrete boxes.

The chairman opened up for suggestions and after several suggestions it was agreed that there should be a reconnaissance survey on 11/04/91 before the practical exercise of planting the pillars and surveying.

The chairman thanked all the members for their contribution in the planning of the exercise which is meant for the establishment of this artificial boundary. He also advised them to know that such a boundary had nothing to add to or subtract from the peaceful and social atmosphere existing between the two communities hitherto".

On 11 April 1991 the Commission assembled at 9:00a.m., at the agreed site at Kifiemle and after a roll call it was noted that all the members were present except the Divisional Delegate of Agriculture. Also absent from the delegations of both parties were:

-Mr. Aban Anthony from Bambili

-All the five persons from Babanki except Mr. Ndifor Michael who had been co-opted in the previous meeting to replace one other Babanki Tungo delegate appeared alone accompanied by four persons to add to the labour force. He declined assisting in the exercise and explained that as a co-opted delegate he could not go out alone to represent the interest of his people without the mandate of the Regent and the other four delegates officially appointed by Prefectoral Order No.194/PO/712/S.1 of 27/03/91. He asked the Commission to wait for them to come as he believed they were on their way coming, where upon the Commission gladly consented and waited in the open chilly field for two hours. It

was at this juncture again that Ndifor Michael called for an adjournment to a later date. The members joined the Chairman in expressing their disappointment at the whimsical attitude of the delegates of Kedjom Ketinguh who have so far proved to be ungrateful to the seriousness of the members in helping the two communities to live in peace. On the other hand the commission also noted with satisfaction the seriousness of the Bambili delegates who were all present and had provided:
-Six persons to augment the labour force
-Gravel for concrete mixture
-Three concrete boxes for the cairns

After a brief discussion it was unanimously agreed that the chairman should make contact with Kedjom Ketinguh delegates in the presence of Bambili delegates before fixing the next date for meeting. The chairman also instructed Ndifor Michael to keep his absent colleagues properly informed of the day's deliberations and to note that this was going to be the last adjournment.

On 7/5/1991 the Commission members assembled at 10 a.m. Before the commission proceeded to the demarcating site the Divisional Officer of Tubah called for peace and read out a statement from Westmacott decision which went thus: "Anybody from either village, who now finds himself on the land not owned by his own people will have the choice of moving to his own village land or staying where he is and paying tax to the new village". The roll call showed that only the Divisional Delegate of Agriculture was not present. Mr. Asang Taniform, a Bambili delegate was not also present and Mr. Mukong from Babanki was not present too and was replaced by Mr. Anguh Loh.

The commission first started by proceeding to the highest peak being led by the two quarter heads from both villages, i.e. Mr. Ndifor Michael from Kedjom Ketinguh and Mr. Yufanwi Chwimia from Bambili. On that highest peak the Divisional Officer who was at the same time the chairman repeatedly called for peace and also warned for any disturbance from each party before the Reconnaissance Survey. He also called for effective implementation of Westmacott decision.

When most of the informants were contacted in the field from both villages, they maintained that the decision was read out by the chairman and that it was not easy to start. The Regent from Babanki Tungoh referred the commission to the phrase on the last paragraph of Westmacott decision which stated "starting from Bambili Lake". The Regent and his people now insisted that the starting will only be taken from the outlet of Lake Bambili. The commission refused and also the chairman said that the Commission will not give chances to what is not in the decision. Mr. Bogne Allain the surveyor, called for both parties to listen. He said that according to survey rules, he cannot go down into the lake. That he can only take the starting from the highest peak near the lake. After a serious argument, the people of Kedjom Ketinguh accepted the going ahead.

A point was marked on the top of that high peak for a cairn to be planted. This first cairn was given to the people of Bambili and the next cairn was supposed to be given to the people of Kedjom Ketinguh. Just about 70 meters from the top of the high peak, the Kedjom Ketinguh insisted again that they will only take from the outlet of Lake Bambili. The chairman rolled out the point. Mr. Malley Asong , one of the Delegates from Kedjom Ketinguh said that his people will not continue if the commission does not take from what they want. The Regent of Ketinguh asked for permission from the chairman to enable them (the both parties) have a meeting of reconciliation and it yielded no fruit. Later on the Regent of Kedjom Ketinguh called for a suspension which will enable him to meet his notables for consultations. The Fon of Bambili was very annoyed and insisted that this matter should not be suspended. After a serious argument between the two parties the chairman made mention of the financial problem, which the transport fare of his commission members will soon get finished. He called the Regent of Kedjom Ketinguh and the fon of Bambili to meet in his office on a later date. The Injunction Order was reinforced.

From the above discussion it will be noted that almost all the efforts to arrive a peaceful solution was rendered futile and also that in spite of all the "painstaking efforts" to resolve the dispute, the inhabitants of Babanki and Bambili violated one of the agreed terms of the commission, which was that there was to be no farming around the disputed area. The villagers of both villages farmed on the disputed area. Crops and eucalyptus trees were planted and fences were built around the farms. The inhabitants from both villages attempted to expand their farms and by so doing they transgressed beyond the boundary line. There were also reports that the Babanki people had struggled to "dry up" the Bambili Lake so as to use the water on their farms. The Babanki people were also accused on grounds that they sounded war trumpets, chanted war songs and threatened Bambili women on their farms around the disputed areas. The Bambili people on their part were blamed for having trained fighters and destroyed crops in the farms owned by Babanki people and blocked the Bamenda-Ndop-Kumbo road as well as the Bambili-Mbingo Highway. These convulsions eventually led to another war.

On January 23, 1993, there were fresh provocations. The Babanki people asserted that the Bambili indigenes came up to their side of the boundary and embarked on crop destruction, chopped down a young eucalyptus forest and set a Babanki man's compound on fire. This act was immediately reported to the administration by the Babanki elites who claimed that there was no evidence to show that it was the Bambili people who had caused the destruction.[37]

According to the Cameroon administration, the Bambili people should have been arrested when they were in the process of causing the destruction. On January 26, 1993, Bambili people blocked the road leading from Bamenda to Ndop and from Bamenda through Bandja to Babanki and attacked the Babanki people[38]. This strategy, according to the Babanki people, was because most of them had gone to Big Babanki for the annual traditional festival, *Kebenkendong*. The Babanki rushed back and confronted the Bambili. Before the Bambili could launch an assault the Babanki people had burnt down some houses and several people were wounded.

The Senior Divisional Officer for Mezam, Samuel Sufo, went to the battle front on January 27, 1993, and attempted to appease the two communities. The warring factions retreated but fighting resumed the next day and continued for more than a week before the Administration brought in the gendarmes. Six "ring leaders" were arrested from Babanki and detained in the Gendarmerie Brigade, Tubah, for having instigated the fighting[39]. It is important to note that the war broke out when the 1991 commission set up by the Administration was still at work in its attempt to find solutions to the dispute.

When the battle was over, it was gathered from informants that the Divisional Officer for Tubah inspected the area and found out that the boundary had been violated by both sides[40]. To further demarcate the boundary he planted pillars and pegs in the absence of the two parties involved, holding that they could protest after he must have finished the job. He ignored the 1958 Westmacott Decision and as a result evoked the annoyance and disappointment of the both parties[41]. The first bullet of protest was fired from the people of Babanki Tungoh. The trigger of the protest was pulled on 30 January 1993 by the chairman of the village traditional council to the Divisional Officer, Tubah in a protest letter which was copied to the Prime Minister; Minister of Territorial Administration; Governor of the Northwest Province; Senior Divisional Officer, Mezam; Divisional Officer, Tubah and State Council. The letter was captioned,

A Letter of Protest Against the Unjust Treatment of the Ketinguh People

The traditional Council of Kedjom Keinguh once more writes to you in connection with the recent outbreak of hostilities between Bambili and Kedjom Ketinguh and point out how unfair the Tubah Administration has been to the Kedjom Ketinguh people and which unfairness has resulted to the loss of lives and great material damage. Having carefully analysed the situation of things as they are, we would like to point out the following to the Administration

1) As early as August 1992, the Bambili people started provoking the Kedjom Ketinguh people by climbing up to the so called disputed area (which in fact is Kedjom Ketinguh land) where they fired guns, played drums and sang

provocative songs of war. Reports of these activities were made to the Administration both verbally and written. These demonstrations were later on intensified by the looting of food belonging to the Kedjom people. The destruction of property including farms, fences and houses then followed. All this was reported to the Administration step by step. The reports yielded no fruits as the Administration went right to the scene, saw the destruction even as fresh as it was, but would not believe it, arguing that the Bambili people should have been arrested when they were carrying out the destruction.

We would like to point out here that our people exercised exemplary patience and restraint and should be congratulated for that.

2) As soon as the hostilities broke out, the Bambili people were very quick to block the Ring Road (which is a national road) since they had planned to cut off any links that the Kedjom people have with any administrative unit in Mezam. This gave them satisfaction as a few weeks earlier; they the Bambili people had blocked the road through Banjah to Kedjom Ketinguh. These road blocks had two devilish intents. First of all, the Bambili people wanted to suffocate the Kedjom people economically (and have actually succeeded in doing so) and secondly to be able to check vehicles, extort money and most wickedly to pull out Kedjom people (both Kedjom Keku and Kedjom Ketinguh) and kill. Five Kedjom people were actually pulled out of cars (4 from Kedjom Keku and 1 from Kedjom Ketinguh). Of this number, one was wounded and three were rescued. Though we cannot account for the one missing person from Kedjom Ketinguh, we thank God for sparing the lives of the four innocent people who may have been murdered in cool blood. As soon as it was discovered that the Administration was not willing to clear the blocks, the Kedjom people also set-up their own blocks so as to save the lives of their people who may have innocently walked into the death trap in Bambili. As soon as the Administration learned of this, forces were sent they tore

through barriers in Bambili to go and arrest Kedjom people for making road blocks. Instead of catching people at the barrier, they went into a person's compound and in their usual brutal manner collected innocent people who were conversing under the guise that they were planning war. The questions to ask here are many:

a) Was the Administration incapable of clearing the road blocks in Bambili or it was with complicity that they were left there?

b) How can a Divisional Officer pretend to say that he was chased back from the road when he has forces at his disposal?

c) How many houses or compounds in Bambili were raided as the ones in Kedjom which were raided under false pretences?

d) What justification is there that people caught for being accused of mounting road blocks are driven through road blocks mounted by other people who are not caught?

e) When finally out of some two or three Bambili people were taken to Bamenda for the same offence, why were they released almost immediately while our people continue to be held behind the bars for no actual crime committed?

f) As the Bambili people confessed, they blocked the road so as to stop weapons from getting to the Kedjom people, who gave them the authority? Has a national road become the property of one village? Many more questions could be posed on the very obscure role of the Tubah Administration in this conflict, but suffice it to say that we are very sceptical about the intensions of the Administration.

3) At the meeting at the S.D.O., Office on Tuesday January in the evening, it was decided that the S.D.O. Mezam, the D.O. Tubah, the forces of Law and Order and the Chairman of the Traditional Council of the two villages in dispute would visit the areas where fighting was going on the following day, Wednesday 27th January 1993 at 7:00a.m. This actually took place. The Chairman of the Kedjom Ketinguh Traditional Council was taken to the scene by the S.D.O. for Mezam while that of the Bambili Traditional council was taken to the scene by the D.O. Tubah. While the S.D.O. for Mezam was pleading peace, the Chairman of the Bambili Traditional Council was busy with his people planning out war strategies. That is why he was not present to talk to his people. The Kedjom Ketinguh people respected the terms of the peace agreement and went home to celebrate the peace agreement, little knowing that the so called peace mission was a trap for them.

Early on the morning of Thursday 28th January, they were awakened by heavy gun fire of Bambili people who had invaded their land, burnt down compounds and killed Kedjom people. It then dawned on them that the peace talks were a farce to the Bambili people who meant serious people. What could have stopped the Kedjom people from taking up arms again under such conditions? Even angels would not have done otherwise.

The question here is why was Mr. Awemu, the Chairman of the Bambili Traditional Council absent from the peace talks whereas he had been taken up to the disputed area by the D.O. Tubah? Does his absence which was not questioned by the Administration not indicate some bit of complicity? Who would have been preaching peace to the Bambili people as was done by the Chairman of the Kedjom Ketinguh Traditional Council? What was Mr. Awemu's role in the journey up to the hills?

4) After the meeting on Saturday January 30th with the Divisional Officer, the forces of Law and Order, the Municipal Administrator of the Tubah Rural Council, Dr. Yembe of E.N.S. Bambili and a team of technicians in the company of

delegations from the two villages headed by their chiefs, the D.O. Tubah convened a private meeting in his office of the two chairmen of the Traditional Councils of the two villages. In this private meeting, the chairman of the Bambili Traditional Councils was again conspicuously absent. Surprisingly, not a single remark was made about this absence, even in passing. Whatever is going on is yet to be understood.

5) To crown all these events, the D.O. in Tubah in a communiqué read at the meeting and broadcast over Radio Bamenda, the so-called disputed area has been declared a "no man's land" and has been placed under military control with firm instructions that nobody should even pass near the area in dispute, under pain of death. This is an administrative death blow on the face of Kedjom Ketinguh people. First of all does the Administration know the limits of the so-called disputed area? The Kedjom Ketinguh people have been living on this land for Centuries. What does the Administration intend to do with these people; send them away as refugees?

6) The Administration knows just too well that in a dispute situation, there is always a victor and a vanquished or loser. We see no reason why whenever we are attacked and we push back the attackers, the Administration then steps in to suppress us. The Administration which arbitrates in such matters should be fair enough to allow each side maintain what has been captured. After all that is what war means?

Even if the Administration must take sides, it should not be as clearly shown as it has been in this case. It is very provocative for the Fon of Bambili and Mr. Aban Anthony to have followed our people who were unjustly arrested right from the place of arrest to Bamenda where they were detained. It would appear that it was the Bambili people who had to work out the modalities of the detention of these innocent Kedjom Ketinguh people. After all, it should be made clear that while Administration changes hands, the so-called disputed area and the two villages remain.

In passing, we are alarmed at the type of weaponry that the Bambili people are using against the Kedjom Ketinguh people. We are also alarmed that a village in Cameroon has such sophisticated weapons to use on another village

In any sense of the word the letter showed the bias nature which the peaceful decision was sorted by the administration especially through the Divisional Officer. It also showed in a way that the people knew their rights and what belonged to them. The letter achieved its desired effects. As on 16 April 1993, the Divisional Officer; Joseph Tangwa, in an attempt to "pour palm oil on troubled waters" invited both Bambili and Babanki-Tungoh for a reconciliatory meeting. In the invitation letter he cautioned that no farming should take place in the disputed area. He went ahead to maintain that the demarcation of the boundary will be done according to the decision of Westmacott. In the letter which has been scanned and presented below he said:

> A sub-technical commission was formed in 1994 charged with special functions of settling the boundary dispute in a way acceptable to all the factions. The sub-technical commission, as a matter of fact, made futile efforts to settle the boundary feud. Yet, activities still went on unabated in the disputed areas against the terms of the Commission. The historicity of commissions in Cameroon in recent years has been a sad one, to say the least. The administration in an attempt to circumvent its responsibilities always tries to set up commissions. These commissions found difficulties in succeeding because the members were never completely empowered to carry out their duties. The 1994 commission was just one of such commissions and no doubt, the end-result was the war of 1995.

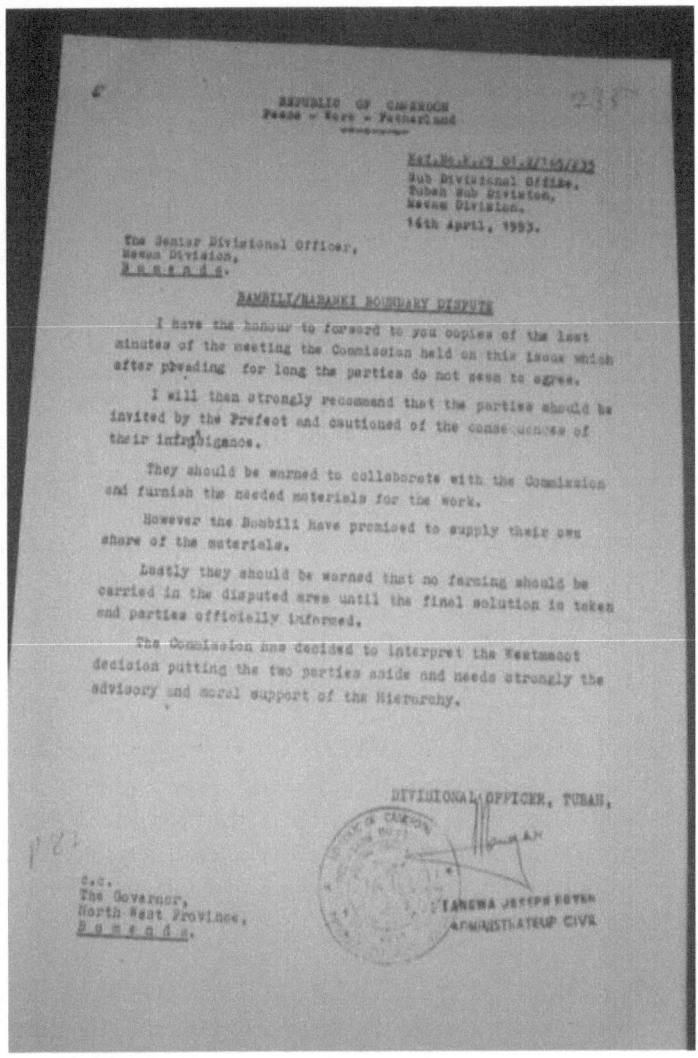

H) The 1995 War

Farming continued in the disputed area, in defiance of the terms of the 1994 Commission. There was every evidence to show that conflicts caused by petty quarrels, threats and disagreements could arise in the nearest future in the form of war[42]. As a result on 13

March 1995, the Fon of Bambili reprimanded the Senior Divisional Officer for Mezam in a letter which he addressed to: The Sub Divisional Officer, Tubah; The Municipal Administrator, Tubah; The Brigade Commander, Tubah and The Commissioner Special Branch, Tubah. He said:

POLICE SECURITY FOR BAMBILI WOMEN AS THEY PLANT THEIR FARMS IN PARTS OF BAMBILI OUTSIDE THE DISPUTE AREA PRESENTLY OCCUPIED BY BABANKI TUNGO INVADERS. "Following the recent invasion of Bambili and the destruction of the properties of Bambili people by the Babanki Tungo invaders, we would wish here to request the Administration to provide and guarantee adequate security to displaced Bambili people to return to their compounds and to carry out planting activities as the rains have already come and planting is taking place all over the country. The recent Babanki Tungo invasion has rendered many Bambili families homeless even in areas outside of the dispute area. Added to their homelessness, these destitute families cannot safely return to their compounds to carry out planting on their farms they had farmed before the Babanki Tungo invasion. The administration should therefore dislodge the Babanki Tungo invaders from these parts of Bambili land outside of the dispute zone between the two villages to enable the Bambili people carry out their farming activities on their legitimate lands...."

Another remote cause could be traced to the destruction of boundary beacons by the Babanki Tungoh people. This is evidenced in a letter which was written by the Fon of Bambili, Awemo 11 to the Senior Divisional Officer who doubled up as the Chairman, Bambili/Babanki Boundary Commission on 21 April 1995. The letter was copied to His Excellency, The Prime Minister and Head of Government; The Governor, Northwest Province; The Divisional Officer, Tubah; The second Assistant Divisional Officer, Mezam; Brigade Commander Gendarmerie, Tubah; The Commissioner Special Branch, Tubah and the Technicians concerned. The letter stated inter alia: "Sir, I wish to bring to your notice the destruction of the first beacon (pillar) which was planted on the 19/04/95 by the Technical Commission which you supervised. This destruction is carried out by the people of Babanki Tungoh". He went ahead to sound a warning to the administration in the following words:

> If the administration does not take this serious, there are possibilities that the rest of the beacons may be destroyed. I am appealing very strongly that the security forces should be placed on alert to check this wanton destruction. As I have always mentioned in my letters to the administration, the Babanki Tungoh people are not interested to end this dispute. This is evident in the fact that they have refused to supply labour and material for this job. My people have been supplying material and labour only for them to come and destroy. The administration should not let the job of the technicians to end in vain.

It will appear that the plea of Fon Awemo fell on deaf ears as the administration never took his words seriously. As a result he wrote another letter, this time in a harder style. In the letter Ref:002/FPBAM/BV/95, written on 25 April 1995 addressed to the Senior Divisional Officer for Mezam and copied to The Prime Minister, Head of Government; The Governor of the Northwest Province; The Sub Divisional Officer, Tubah; The Brigade Commander, Tubah; The Commissioner, Special Branch, Tubah; The Municipal Administrator, Tubah and the Technicians concerned, he put his letter in seven points.

Sir,
I refer to my letter of 21st April, 1995, reporting the destruction of the first boundary pillar at the peak of Lake Bambili by the Babanki Tungoh people.
I wish once more to report that they have again destroyed the rest of the pillars so far planted.
It should be noted that the Babanki Tungo people have refused to participate in the following:

a) To contribute for the purchase of materials for the construction of the pillars
b) To supply labour for the transportation of the materials to the site
c) To provide food for the workers

I am calling the Chairman's attention to the following points:

1) That the present Babanki-Tungo market at mile 13 was burnt down under the supervision of Police Commissioner Mr. Ntoni on the orders of the Senior Divisional Officer for Mezam, Mr. Nchami Vincent, to evict the Babanki's from their illegal occupation of Bambili land. They immediately reconstructed the market on the same site and government took no action.

2) The Babanki Tungo people uprooted the provisional materials which D.O. Tangwa of Tubah Sub Divisional office used to demarcate the boundary, and this received no government action.

3) Various administrative injunction orders issued from 1958 have been violated with impunity by the Babanki's with no penalty from the administration.

4) The kidnapping of Yufanwi (a Bambili man) during one of their furious invasions has never received adequate treatment despite the fact that the administration was furnished with the National Identity Cards lost on the scene by the kidnappers.

5) That I protest against the comprises like the application of the West Macott Decision that is being carefully manipulated by the administration to favour and appease the Babanki Tungoh people, who are still arrogantly destroying all the efforts of Government to bring about the peace.

6) That I have lost human beings, property, and a lot of money which have helped in retarding the development of my village.

7) That the lawless attitude of the Babanki Tungo people with no corresponding sanctions from the Government seems to reveal the weakness of the latter.
In view of the above, I pray the Government to use the machinery at her disposal to put an end to this vexing problem or accept the version of the assailants that the administration is not serious". This appeared not as serious to the administration as the wordings of the letter appeared. For that reason war clouds gradually gathered momentum in the skies of the two communities and the end result was the war of 1995

The immediate cause of the third Bambili and Babanki war of April 1995 was the exchange of gun-firing by two hunters from the rival villages who found themselves around the boundary line while on a hunting expedition. In the process the Babanki hunter was killed. The Babanki immediately declared war on Bambili. The War was fought with renewed ferocity by both belligerents for three days, until the forces of law and order intervened and stopped it. The prompt intervention of the forces of law and order never gave breathing room for any "terms" to be deliberated upon. And when Samuel Sufo attempted another demarcation, the Babanki-Tungoh "dragged" him to the Bamenda High Court on July 3, 1995.

The hearing of the judgment was in the High Court of Mezam Division Holden at Bamenda before his Lordship Justice Moma Macaulay Che on "Monday 3rd Day of July 1995 suit No.HCB/28/95 BETWEEN Vivansi Ezekiel Anguh Suing on behalf of the People and village of Kedjom Ketinguh other wise known as Babanki Tungoh
AND
SENIOR DIVISIONAL OFFICER MEZAM DIVISION......Defendant
Plaintiff present
Defendant present
Mr. Nyo Wakai and Mr. Monie for the plaintiff

Defendant unrepresented. The intensity of our work renders us to revisit the entire judgment here in order to better appreciate the role of the law in the conflict business.

"REPUBLIC OF CAMEROON"
IN THE NAME OF THE PEOPLE OF CAMEROON
JUDGEMENT

Pursuant to leave being granted to the bailiff in HCB/42H/95 to represent the chief and people of Kedjom Ketinguh otherwise referred to as Babanki-Tungoh, the plaintiff herein has by this originating summons, through his counsel brought this action praying this court to place a construction of the Review Judgment No.84/56 of May 15 by N.A.B. West Macott, resident in Bamenda Province by determining

1) Whether or not the Review Judgment No. 84/56 of May 15 1958 did not determine definitely the boundaries between villages of Kedjom-Ketinguh otherwise known as Babanki-Tungoh and Bambili

2) Whether any person or authority has any right or power to go outside that decision which had never been reversed by a higher jurisdiction. The Court is further invited by the plaintiff to prevent the S.D.O. Mezam from carrying out the planting of pillars as a means of demarcating the boundaries between Kedjom Ketinguh village and that of Bambili. But if at all, he further prays the Court, pillars have to be planted; the S.D.O. should do so in consonance with the Review decision of West Macott in Review No.84/56 of May 15, 1958.

There is an affidavit of 43 paragraphs deposed to by the plaintiff in support of his prayers. Also attached to the affidavit are two annextures, the one sketch map of the area that was drawn by the Bafut Native Court and the other the West Macott Review decision No. 84/56 of the May 1958.

In reply to this summons the defendant wrote a memorandum to the president of the Court raising the following questions:

1) That this Court is competent to hear and determine the issues in The plaintiffs summons because the Review decision though being an administrative Officer he acted as both Judge and an administrative Officers. He then concluded by saying that this action should have been taken to the administrative Court of the Supreme Court.

Furthermore he stated in his memorandum that it would be eerie after 37 years for the plaintiff to bring this suit demanding an interpretation of a decision that had been taken. He then asked the question "Where is then is the principle of prescription. Finally he urged the Court to dismiss plaintiff's action".

Plaintiff's counsel at the hearing adopted and relied on the summons, affidavit and annextures. Counsel argued that the crime before the Court is for the Court to determine whether or not the West Macott Review decision was a final decision concerning the boundaries between Bambili and Babanki without more. Defendant also relied intoto on his written submission.

Here I have to remark that the facts as stated in the 43 paragraph affidavit are true since the defendant made no effort to rebut them. Even if he had to raise a preliminary objection as he has done to his submission he would have contradicted the facts contained in the plaintiff's affidavit. His submission though I am taking it into consideration is off the target to the procedural laws known and practiced on this side of the country.

The saga of the boundary problem between Babanki and Bambili depicts that it moved from one court to the other-to wit, from the Native Bafut Court, to the Native Court of Appeal, the Divisional Officer Bamenda and then to the President West Macott. In tense these was the hierarchy of Native Courts in those days. And in those days the Customary Courts had jurisdiction over land.

Consequently when the matter went to the President West Macott for Review he acted as a Judge in a Court and any decision that he took was binding on the parties as a Court decision and not an administrative one. Therefore the only construction that I can place determining on the West Macott decision is that it was a final decision-determining the boundaries between the two villages. The defendant recognises this for when cross-examined by the Court as to the essence of the West Macott decision the reply was: "We believe in the judgment of the President".

The answer to the question asked in the summons is in the affirmative being in the affirmative it would be strange enough for any authority to essay to veer a decision that was passed since 37 years ago and both parties were satisfied with the said decision as there was no appeal.

To me this is a quite temet application made to prevent any authority from interfering with the West Macott decision as the plaintiff raises fears of this in his paragraph 40 of the affidavit which states: "That an inquiry from the supposed experts what the next step would be, the parties were informed by the experts that they had instructions from Yaounde to come and merely implement a document that had been given them in Yaounde". This paragraph of affidavit in support of the motion has not been challenged by the defendant. For purposes of repetition, the West Macott decision was one that determined and definitely too the boundaries between Kedjom-Ketinguh and Bambili.

WHEREFORE, the President of the Republic of Cameroon commands and enjoins all bailiffs and process-servers to enforce this Judgment, the Procureur General and State Counsel to lend them support and all Commanders and Officers of the Armed Forces and the Police Force to lend them assistance when so required by law: IN WITNESS whereof the present judgment has been signed by the Judge and the Registrar-in-chief.

One thing comes out very clearly in the above judgment- that the Court Judgment in Suit No.HCB/28/95 of Monday 3rd July 1995 ruled and confirmed the Westmacott decision of 1958 and also confirmed the entente that was signed between these two villages on 25 July 1973. The judgement in itself appeared biased and lopsided. The preponderant importance constantly attached to the Westmacott decision over the years makes us lend a commentary to it at this juncture. But before we turned to attempt an appraisal of the Westmacott decision it is incumbent to examine the situation just preceding the Bamenda High Court of Appeal.

It would be interesting to note that despite that judgement one would have expected that the conflict was resolved but the Babanki Tungoh resisted the judgement and even refused the said land to called disputed land. On 9th October 1995 a letter was written from the Fon of Babanki Tango's office to the Divisional Officer, Tubah and copied the S.D.O. Mezam; The Brigade Commander Gendarmerie Tubah and the Commissioner of Special Branch, Tubah. While reacting to a letter written by the divisional officer, Tubah the letter read as follows:

Sir,
UNAUTHORISED ACTIVITIES AT THE DISPUTED AREA BETWEEN BAMBILI/KEDJOM KETINGUH
With reference to your letter No. E.29 01.2/165/299 of 28/09/95, I wish to inform you that there is no nothing like disputed area between Bambili and Kedjom Ketinguh.
Once more, be informed that this dispute was settled by West Macott Vide his decision dated 15/5/58 and in the Contrary it was the Kedjom Ketinguh people who were not satisfied and later paid in the Sum of 138,400 Francs on the 26/7/67 as deposit for appeal against part of the boundary but unfortunately this appeal was never heard.
Furthermore, on the 18/09/75, Mr. Oben Peter Ashu, the present Governor of the South West Province, who was then the Divisional Officer Bamenda Central Sub Division, after inspecting the place on the 26/6/76 did issued letter No. ABA 23/681 of 18th September 1975, giving directives to Ardo Jacky of Sabga Babanki Tungoh and the Farmers of Chuku Babanki Tungoh, how and what to do before farming in that area.
The Bambili people accepted the West-Macott Decision and have all along respected that decision till about 1991 when

they started their Criminal activities perhaps being supported by some administrative authorities, to be naming some area in Kedjom Ketinguh as "Disputed Land".

'I wish to state further that, this matter was disposed of by the High Court of Bamenda holding on 3rd day of July, Ref. Suit No.HCB/28/95.

If the Bambili people or the administration is not satisfied with the decisions taken so far, they may take further action to the proper authorities than going through Criminal ways of which we are not afraid.

I sincerely appeal to you to ask the Bambili people in the name of peace to immediately stop any trespass into Kedjom Ketinguh Land.

What is very intriguing at this juncture is the fact that so much attention has been attached to the Resident's judgement of 1958- A.B.Westmacott. The next section attempts to examine the place of Westmacott as the only way which the two belligerents feel that should be used to arbitrate the boundary conflict.

H) The Wesmacott's myth: a commentary

Mr. A.B. Westmacott was the highest British colonial administrator known in colonial jargon as the resident in the Bamenda Division in 1958. As at 1958, the Bambili and Babanki Tungoh boundary palaver was common currency. It had hopped from court to court to court and since the resident at the same time could judge cases it reached his court. His ruling overruled that of his predecessors but the boundary was never demarcated. It all remained a decision on paper. Interestingly enough, the two communities have kept on pontificating on that decision and at times when the administration wants to implement that decision either one of the communities or the other will step in to disturb the procedure. So far the translation of the Westmacott decision into reality has remained an illusion.

In an address to His Excellency, The Minister of Territorial Administration titled,

A POSITION PAPER PRESENTED BY THE FON OF BABANKI TUNGO (KEDJOM KETINGUH) TO HIS EXCELLENCY THE MINISTER OF TERRITORIAL

ADMINISTRATION, CHAIRMAN OF THE NATIONAL COMMISSION FOR BAMBILI/ KEDJOM KETINGUH BOUNDARY DISPUTE ON WEDNESDAY 23RD FEBRUARY, 2000, the Fon, His Royal Highness, Fon Viyouh Nelson Shiteh, said: " Your Excellency, we have in possession a decision which both parties have pledged to accept as the only document which if well interpreted will bring lasting peace between the two villages. This decision popularly known as the Westmacott Decision was taken on the 15th May 1958 by the then Resident, A.B. Westmacott (Ref. Review No. 84/56 File 361(569)..." To further show how the Westmacott boundary was so dear to the parties he went ahead to say amongst other things: "Your Excellency, it is unfortunate that though the boundary as defined by Westmacott stresses on the use of an Appeal Court Boundary, NONE, of the many maps presented as showing the Westmacott boundary has in its key the Appeal Court Boundary. We have gone at length to research on this Boundary Dispute because we discovered to our utter dismay that our neighbours, the Bambili people have been doing everything to blur our findings on the series of interventions that have taken place in this protracted dispute. Our problem your Excellency has been to reconcile the prescriptions given by Westmacott in his boundary quoted above with what appears in the map, Plan No.BD. 235. We are happy to inform you that the Good Lord has revealed the truth to us at last. This map (Plan No. BD. 235) was drawn way back on the 27 July 1957 by one Mr. J.M. Mbafor, a Native Authority Surveyor. The Appeal Court Boundary in this map has been re-titled "THE BABANKI TUNGO CLAIM". So far, we have discovered four versions of this infamous map, Plan No. BD. 235....

After the creation of the Christian Justice and Peace Commission by the Bambui Parish priest to handle the boundary situation, its findings pointed yet to the Westmacott decision. That Commission reaffirmed the Westmacott decision in the following words:

From all our findings given above and working with impartiality, honesty and objectivity expected of such a justice and peace commission we have come out with Bambili/ Babanki Tungo boundary as follows: From the boundary moves straight towards the direction of the foot path up to a point 100m away from the source of the first tributary of the outlet (to the right facing the footpath). This is the point that initiates an angle from where the boundary shoots straight taking an average of the high knolls to the right flank of the new road on the foot of that hill. From here it follows the new road for 100 meters and moves right from some 50m and shoots straight along the grassy spur till a heavy rocky outcrop with a fig tree is reached. This is as described by Westmacott, shown by surveyors and confirmed by the members of the commission.

After the rocky outcrop the boundary moves along the cliff top edge over looking Babanki Tungoh built up area to the right in the valley. Westmacott had set aside S.D.O. Ward's Decision because it puts too many Babanki Tungoh people on Bambili side needing displacement and this boundary was at Tuengtueng stream down the valley. Westmacott also saw all the grazing land on the Bambili side which is now occupied with the exception of the three Babanki Tungo houses and several Fulani rugers should be confirmed as belonging to Bambili.

At the end of the escarpment the boundary follows a line below the knoll to the end. (This point is in a valley and there is a small footpath moving up there). This area is the rolling down lands. From here the boundary shoots straight to the foot of the highest conical hill recently excavated for laterite and over looking the road of Babanki village and below which there are some small streams.

From the base of this hill a straight line moves towards mile post 13. Over the Babanki Tungo market on the right side of the road going to the Babanki Tungo village there is a tree which marks another point. From that tree the boundary shoots straight splitting the Babanki Tungo market into two and ending at the sharp bend beyond mile post 13. All these spots were identified to be showed the two villages in the field. Remember the description is from the Bambili lake through the famous footpath to mile post 13 area. We understand there are many similar geographical features in the area. Sequence of their occurrence has helped us a lot. The fact that no original boundary claim was ever been accepted and that no decision ever used the lake outlet as boundary; we stand by this decision....

We the members of the commission understand it is a long time (40 years) since the boundary was made. Much development has taken place in the disputed area; sometimes with the thinking that such effective occupation would yield the area in the long run to the developer. The commission frowns at this. Yet such a development is bound to attract sympathies now. We recognise the fact that these sympathies would come up on both sides but advise that it is left to you the Bambili and Babanki Tungoh brothers and sisters to willingly put your heads and hearts together and talk to one another on these areas of sympathies. That will be left to you people. We may only be of assistance if requested. Our reference was the Westmacott boundary of 1958 between Babanki Tungo and Bambili and that is just what we have done and is the end of the commission's work.

To further lend credibility to the "darling Westmacott" on 19 April 1995 the Babanki Tungoh people through their chairman, Loh Mufe Emmanuel, wrote to the Senior Divisional Officer for Mezam and copied amongst others the Honourable Prime Minister; Vice Prime Minister of Territorial Administration and the Governor of the N.W. Province. The letter read as follows:

Sir,
PETITION AGAINST THE SO-CALLED DEMARCATION OF THE BOUNDARY BETWEEN BAMBILI AND BABANKI TUNGO ACCORDING TO THE WESTMACOT DECISION BY THE SO-CALLED EXPERTS FROM YAOUNDE.
We, the people of Kedjom Ketinguh (Babanki-Tungo) would

like to express our objection to the work that was started yesterday, 18th April 1995 by the so-called experts from Yaounde and to point out to the S.D.O. that what they are doing does not in the least come close to the dictates of the Westmacot decision of 1958 which the public media advertised that the S.D.O. had decided was going to be used to retrace and demarcate the boundary between Bambili and Kedjom Ketinguh.

Sir, we would like to register that all efforts made by our delegation in your office on 17 April, 1995 to have the commission made up of five delegates each from Bambili and Kedjom Ketinguh, prior to going to the field ensure that the experts were going to interpret the Westmacot decision and not to impose a boundary fabricated in Yaounde were shouted down. We were told that the interpretation will be done on the field, but when we requested on 18th April 1995 on the field that the commission talk with the experts before retracing took off, the S.D.O. refused and to our utter dismay, the expert pulled out from his bag a map displaying an ink demarcation line and told us he had his directives from Yaounde. (One would have expected the said expert to know his bearings, but he was not ashamed to ask where the lake was).

Our first reaction was not to be party to the masquerade that was not in the least going to solve the unfortunate conflict that has cost our two villages too much in human life and property, but we decided to give the said experts a chance and follow them to the lake where the Westmacot decision of 1958, page two, paragraph five, line six clearly states where the boundary starts from, but the experts and the S.D.O.'s, party went parallel to and far beyond the lake to take their bearing and from there descended, rather embarrassingly, into the Kedjom Ketinguh village where people live long before the Westmacot decision of 1958....To implement the Westmacot decision, the Appeal Court sketch map, a copy of which we obtained from the Native court archives in Tubah, must be used to retrace the boundary from the lake up to the footpath as mentioned in the Westmacot decision.

The above examples illustrate how dear to the communities the Westmacott decision has been. It remains a puzzle that the two communities are still clinging to this decision long after it was decided upon. Perhaps, this appears like the tip of an iceberg given the fact that Africa South of the Sahara today tend to believe so much on European decisions that were taken in their territories. The two communities have traditional councils and one wonders the functions of a traditional council if the boundary question could not be resolved by them. One is tempted to call the Westmacott syndrome, a myth. The mystification stems from the fact that it has taken fifty years or so and the communities as well as the administration still feel that they should attached importance to the decision, surprisingly when the top level administrator like the Senior Divisional Officer attempts even to strike a balance he also refers to Westmacott.

Conclusion

The chapter has focused on the origins, migratory and geo-political setting of the Bambili and Babanki-Tungoh. It has further examined the period in their history when they were fraternal friends. In addition, the causes of the boundary feud have been examined. These causes are centred on a fertile piece of land. This chapter has ended with a discussion of the various ways the boundary conflict has manifested itself since the 1950s. Between 1995 and 2005 there existed a period of "silence". That means that no major war or outbreak of the nature before 1995 occurres. The next chapter sets out to examine these "cool years" and its impact on the boundary misunderstandings.

Notes

1. The Bantu languages are spoken in Africa South of the Sahara in a line running roughly from the Bight of Biafra to the Indian Ocean near the Kenya-Somali border. The group includes more than four hundred languages, all as closely related to each other as are Germanic languages. The Bantu-Speakers occupy a huge area not only in Africa but in Cameroon. For more on Bantu and Semi-Bantu see Philip Curtin et al., *African History*, 26-30; Joseph C. Anene & Godrey Brown, *Africa*

in the Nineteenth and Twentieth Centuries (Ibadan, Nigeria: Ibadan University Press 1966) 283; George Murdock, *Africa: Its Peoples and their Culture History* (New York: McGraw Hill, 1959), 46-50.

2. E.G. Hawkesworth, "Assessment Report on Bafut Tribal Area of Bamenda Division," 1926, NAB; Interview with Shomboin David, Bambili, North West Province, 28 December 1997.

3. Ibid.

4. Interview with Buteh Joseph, Bambili 8 August 1997. This view was further confirmed by Akuli Innocent a retired, police officer who is an indigene of Babanki-Tungoh, 10 November 1997. When I visited the field again in October 2008 I met this informant who repeated the information cited here without mincing words.

5. Hawkesworth, "Assessment Report on Bafut Tribal Area of Bamenda Division," 1926 R. J. Hook, An Intelligence Report on the Associated Village groups occupying the Bafut Native Authority Area of the Bamenda Division of Cameroon Province" 1934 (N.A.B.).

6. M.G. Bawden and I. Lagdale-Brown (eds.) *An Aerial photographic Reconnaissance of the Present and Possible Land Use in the Bamenda Area, Southern Cameroons* (Department of Technical Cooperation, directorate of Overseas Surveys, Forestry land use, 1962), 1- 2 Cited in Mbutruh, "The Economy and Society of Southern Cameroons under British Colonial Domination C. 1916 - 1961," 42 -43.

7. For reasons why the Germans penetrated the hinterlands see Harry R. Rudin, *Germans in the Cameroons 1884 - 1914: A Case Study in Modern Imperialism* (New York: Yale University Press, 1938), 76 - 78; Ngoh, *History of Cameroon Since 1800,* 77.

8. Files No. A B 3 (b) B 30665 (N.A.B.), Ab 3 B 3065, Interview with Joseph Buteh, Nkwen, Bamenda 22 December 1997. This view was also confirmed by James Kohfor, Quarter Head Membi, Bambili, interviewed 24 December 1999.

9. For more on ethnicity see, Katsuyoshi Fukui and John Markakis (eds.) *Ethnicity and Conflict in the Horn of Africa* (Athens: Ohio University Press, 1993), 4-6. Some Bambili informants failed to admit the fact that they have never had anything in common with the Babanki-Tungoh. A case in point was traditional elite, James Kohfor, interviewed, 28 December 1997. But historical evidence has shown that the two ethnic

Chapter Three: A History of Bambili/Babanki-Tungoh and the Genesis of the Boundary

groups have interacted in their histories of origin, settlement and socio-cultural and political organisations.

10. File No. Ab 3, The Bamenda Grassfields peoples (b) A 3065, (NAB)
11. According to Pa Robert, (an informant who asked that his real name should not be used Babanki-Tungoh neighbours are jealous of their fertile land and the extent of their development in terms of education, a point further affirmed by Shomboin David. On the other hand Pa Akuli Innocent holds the view that Babanki-Tungoh neighbours want to salvage them (Bambili) because they are very industrious and equally having fertile land. Besides, the neighbours are jealous because they appear the smallest group in the region Joseph Buteh supported this view.
12. Interview with Commissioner Chumboin Pius, Dibombari, Douala, 31 November 1997, Inspector Julius Ngong, Buea emigration, 10 October 1997. All of them confirmed this view.
13. Interview with Shomboin David, Bambili, Tubah Sub Division, 20 August 1997.
14. The presence of guns in the sub region could be attributed to the iron industrial complex that had existed in the area since the 18th Century. Blacksmiths were able to manufacture their own guns and in addition most guns were also imported into the area from the long distance trade which existed between the Bamenda grassfields and the Bight of Biafra.
15. Confidential Note, Ref. No.0212/CLL/B/29/744 Receipt, 102/9.21 of 3rd August 1978.
16. Some of the terms of the Accord included amongst others, that anybody who will encroach on the disputed area will be punished by the administration. But when the Babanki-Tungoh violated this clause the leaders were called and cautioned by the district Officer.
17. Interview with Beatrice Ajouh Ngam, Bambili, 8 September 1997. She is teaching in the Kindergarten. She is not an inhabitant of Bambili neither does she hails from Babanki-Tungoh. She holds the view that Samuel Jones (pseudonym) strongly has hand in the boundary conflict. This view was further confirmed by a senior Professor of the Department of Sociology and Anthropology, University of Buea, interviewed 10 July 1997. He is a very close friend of Samuel Jones (pseudonym), interview with Shomboin David, Bambili palace and

held the opinion that Samuel Jones has been playing a mediatory role. He further maintained that Johnny kept a football trophy in August 1997 to reconcile the two factions. A point much disputed by Akuli. Evidence seems to show that the real aim of the cup was perhaps to "smoke the screen" by the accused. Although the case is much disputed it is very difficult to discard the point held by this school of thought. What makes the Samuel Jones factor more convincing is the fact that he owns a cattle ranch around the area under dispute and there are indications that if this area falls under Bambili he will be the greatest beneficiary.

18. Confidential Note Ref. No. PM 398/17117 of 15th November 1971, 2. This was re-emphasising a previous communiqué issued by the Bafut Chiefs Meeting in their council on 13/2/65 and signed by J.N. Foncha as Vice President of the Republic on tour in Bamenda on 27 July 1965.

19. Annual Reports for Bamenda Division for the years 1946, 1947, and 1948 (NAB).

20. Psychology is the branch of biological sciences which studies the phenomena of conscious life in their origin, development and manifestation. It deals with the mind and its relation to the course of conflicts between human societies could be very complex but the simple fact is that the psyche of people has much to do with the relations with their neighbours. For more on psychology see, James Denver, *A Dictionary of Psychology* (London: Penguin Books, 1952), 227, Andrew Crinder *et. al.*, *Psychology* London: (London: Penguin Books, 1964), 173-177.

21. Mbutruh, "The Economy and Society of Southern Cameroons under British Colonial Domination c. 1916 - 1961", 94.

22. Ibid.

23. Ibid, 96.

24. [K. Wilson] *Land Tenure and State Land* (Yaounde: National Printing Press, 1981), p. 98, Interview with Lucas Atanga, Provincial Delegation of Land and Surveys, Bamenda, 24 August 1997, this was further confirmed by Edward Ndi Timngum, Provincial Chief of Lands and Surveys, Buea, 5 January 1998.I visited him in January 2008 but this time he was Edward was the Delegate for the Provincial land and Surveys Department in Bamenda capital of, Northwest Region of Cameroon.

25. Letter from the Office of the Fon, Babanki-Tungoh (Kedjom Ketinguh) to the Divisional Officer, Tubah Sub-Division, 9 October 1995.

26. Minutes of the traditional Council Meeting with Hon. Mukong and Hon. Kindo on 16 January 1972 in the Chiefs palace in Babanki-Tungoh to find out a peaceful solution to the Babanki-Tungoh/Bambili Boundary Dispute, 2.

27. Fon of Babanki-Tungoh to the Assistant Cattle Control Officer, Bafut Area Council, 29 June 1973.

28. The Native Courts Ordinance Cap. 142, Laws of Nigeria Cited in the Review Jurisdiction of the Resident, Bamenda holden at Bafut, Review No. 84/56, File No. 361 (569) 15 May 1958. (See Appendix I).

29. Ibid.

30. Ibid, (emphasis added).

31. Ibid, (emphasis added).

32. Minutes of a Traditional Council Meeting with Hon. Mukong and Hon. Kindo at the Fon's Palace in Babanki-Tungoh, signed by the chairman of Babanki-Tungoh Traditional Council, 16 January 1972.

33. J.A.A. Tamkoh to the Fon of Bambili, Letter No. 362-569/T/19 of 9 July 1959.

34. A copy of the Bambili/Babanki-Tungoh entente terms reached between the respective Fons on 25 July 1973, in the presence of a Cameroon administrative witness, Ngonge Sone. S.N. Kindo and B.N. Mukong, witnesses for Bambili/Babanki-Tungoh respectively.

35. For more on the Grazier/farmer problem see, *Report on the Cameroon Under United Kingdom Trusteeship for the Year 1949* (London: H.M.S.O. 1950), 87, *Report on the Cameroons Under United Kingdom Trusteeship for the Year 1948* (London: H.M.S.O., 1949), 280.

36. Report by Mr. Jum, District Officer, for Tubah on the Babanki-Tungoh War of 1991, 10 August 1991.

37. Report by the Bambili Cultural and Development Association on October 7, 1993, on the Bambili boundary dispute. This point was further affirmed by Loh Emmanuel interviewed 24 August 1997, Bamenda.

38. Ibid.
39. Interview with Chomboin Pius, Dibombari Douala, 25 August 1997.
40. Ibid.
41. Ibid, The view was further confirmed by Joseph Buteh, interviewed 24 December 1997.
42. Ibid.

Chapter Four

The "Cold" Years, 1995-2005

Introduction

This section focuses on the cold period when there was no overt outbreak of hostilities amongst the two communities but which at the same time was characterised by correspondences, tensions, and rumours and disobeying of the Injunction Orders by the two communities. The period also witnessed the introduction of new players into the field of the boundary conflict.

A) The Complaints Period

On 8 July, 1998, His Royal Highness, the Fon of Bambili, addressed a letter to the Divisional Officer of Tubah complaining about the Babanki Tunguh people who had trespassed into the Bambili land and started farming. He said amongst other things that the Babanki people "have again started extensive farming on Bambili land and are harvesting eucalyptus trees which are on Bambili land". That information in the letter appeared to have been unfounded and thus was rumour. To show that it was rumour the Divisional Officer, Tubah Sub Division, Kamga, in the letter Ref. No.E29-01.2/165/329 wrote to the Fon of Bambili and copied The Governor, North West Province; The Senior Divisional Officer, Mezam; The Legion Commander, Bamenda; The Brigade Commander, Tubah and The Commissioner of Special Branch, Tubah. In that letter he said:

> Following the latter(sic) which you wrote to me complaining that the Babanki-Tungoh people have entered the disputed land and were harvesting eucalyptus trees, I proceeded to the field on the 15 July 1998 in company of: the Chairman of Bambili Traditional Council, The President of MBECUDA, two notables of Bambili, the Brigade commander, Gendarmerie Brigade, Tubah, the Commissioner Special Branch, Tubah; with the aim of witnessing the provocative acts reported and taking appropriate measures thereafter to preserve the peace. While on the spot, I was shocked to notice

that your report to me were very far from the truth, as the activities being carried out by few Babanki people are taking place on the disputed land and not inside Bambili. From what we saw the Babanki people are to be blamed for farming on the disputed area in violation of the injunction order, but not of intrusion inside Bambili land. The Administration has the duty to bring the defaulters to order, and will not fail to do so. On your part, you should keep on sensitizing your population so as to make sure that no Bambili citizen follows the bad example of Babanki people, i.e. violates the administrative injunction order. Furthermore while appreciating your constant endeavour to inform the Administration on all facts and happenings likely to compromise the peace between your community and your neighbours, I want to stress on the vital need to always ascertain the facts before sending any report to the Administration, as false reports may bring the Administration to take inappropriate decisions and thereby compromise the peace as well. I am therefore appealing to you, to take all necessary measures henceforth, in order to make sure that your future reports contain nothing but accurate information. I count so much on your usual understanding.

Apparently not satisfied with the letter and anxious to exercise his duties, the Divisional Officer wrote another letter Ref. No.E29-01.2/165/330, to His Royal Highness, Fon of Kedjom on the same date, 31 July 1998. He said:

On the 15/7/98, I undertook an inspection on the land in dispute between your community and Bambili people, and I was very sad to notice that despite the administrative injunction order restraining both Bambili and Babanki Tungo peoples from carrying out any activity on the disputed area, despite my several warnings to Babanki people, some of your subjects were working, new farms on the said area in addition to those they worked at the beginning of the current farming season. As you very well know, the aim of the administrative injunction decision, dated 21/7/92, and copy of which I personally sent to you for implementation, was to prevent further bloody confrontations between your village and Bambili. Furthermore, I don't need to remind you that, the Traditional Ruler you are, being an arm of the Administration, (emphasis in the original) is charge, amongst others, with the maintenance of law and order, the implementation and administrative decisions in his area of jurisdiction. Therefore, your constant failure to implement this administrative injunction or at least to inform the Administration of the violation of said decision by some of your subjects is questionable. Should I understand that the Fon of Kedjom Ketinguh careless about our struggle to bring peace between Bambili and his village and wishes the conflict to last and fighting to continue? Whatever the case, the Administration shall not allow this state of affairs to continue, as it is going against the line of the Government policy of peace and development. I am therefore anxious to appreciate the action you'll take immediately to stop your subjects from violating the administrative injunction decision.

The Fon of Babanki Tungoh was blamed in the letter for allowing his subjects to violate the injunction orders which were placed in the disputed area for the two communities to refrain from any activity. Since to a larger extent the Divisional Officer believed that the Fon of Babanki and his people were responsible and also contravening the government policy it became imperative for him to reprimand the Fon who was the "be-all and the end- all" of his people. It is even more interesting that the Divisional Officer was talking about peace and development being a government policy. Since the 1990s the government of Cameroon had taken as a policy of engendering divide and rule and inventing more citizens by denizising others through the stranger/son of the soil virus. These had created tension between people and to have been saying what the Divisional Officer was saying is more unfortunate. The situation remained far from being a peaceful one as tension continued to mount. The introduction of the Christian, Justice and Peace Commission although starting off in a good footing did not do much to help matters.

Responding to such a haphazard situation the Divisional Officer of Tubah wrote another letter Ref. No.E29-03165/336 on 15 September 1999. Amongst other things he said:

> Despite several attempts made by the Administration and, of recent, by the Clergy of Tubah Subdivision, the old boundary dispute between Bambili and Kedjom Ketinguh villages is yet to be settled. We all placed our hopes on the venture of the Christian, Justice and Peace Commission, but it couldn't succeed to bring the two parties to a compromise. All the same, a great step has been made forward, towards the final solution of the dispute. The findings and resolutions of the Commission are certainly going to be of great help to the National Commission, which is now handling the matter. Let's hope that its decision will not delay any longer. But in the meantime we should not relent our efforts in maintaining the peace between the two belligerent communities. The relative peace prevailing since 1996 has to be preserved, and this will require our joint efforts. Presently, the situation is not encouraging, as the administrative injunction order prohibiting farming activities on the disputed area is being grossly violated and most especially by some farmers of Kedjom Ketinguh origin. It should be understood that such attitude of the farmers constitutes a serious threat to peace, and therefore can no longer be tolerated. (Emphasis is in the original). The Administration is determined to ensure the strict respect of the injunction order by all, but this cannot be possible without the full cooperation of the Traditional Authorities and the Clergy. It is my appeal to the Clergy to continue, through the Christian, Justice and Peace Commission, to educate the both communities as they did during the past three years. As concerns the two Traditional Authorities, they should, each in his own capacity, take all necessary measures to see to it that the illegal occupants withdraw from the disputed area immediately. They must start from now to warn these defaulters, and should report all cases of resistance to the administration for exemplary punitive measures to be taken against recalcitrant one. I count very much on your usual

cooperation, for peace to reign between Bambili and Kedjom Ketinguh pending the final decision on the boundary dispute opposing the two villages.

Although there had been no outbreak of violent clashes between the two communities tension and suspicion was becoming a common occurrence to the administration. From the letter we realise the introduction of a new player, Christian and Justice and Peace Commission, Tubah. It was formed in June 1996 as a joint venture by the major Christian churches and communities in Tubah Subdivision with the main objective of seeking a Christian solution to the numerous wars and conflicts plaguing the area. The commission was made up of the clergy and lay people. As at this date it had 12 commission meetings, 4 visits to the disputed area, acquired and studied relevant court judgement, pacts, agreements, maps, interviews, sketch-maps and other investigations.

According to the letter written by the Parish Priest of Bambui, Henry Mesue on 18 June, 1998, through the Divisional Officer Tubah Sub Division, to the Senior Divisional Officer, Mezam "…. Both villages accepted the commission's project to end the dispute. They promised to assist the commission for the final solution and wished the commission to end the work with government administration together with both villages putting in place a final boundary…."

Although the two communities had accepted the work of the Commission two outstanding issues stood in the way of the commission to accomplish their job. In that regards the Parish Priest continued in the following words: "Sir, the final issue now is to determine two points for clarification. These are:

1) the point linking the foot path to the lake as endorse by Westmacott

2) the point from the rolling down land to the sharp corner just beyond Mile Post 13 on the Bamenda Banso part of the ring road. So, only a surveyor can help us here. The commission should be grateful if the Senior Divisional Officer would help us help these people".

Interestingly enough, it was just wishful thinking that the "two communities had accepted the verdict of the Commission. On the 26th May 1999, the fon of Bambili, His Royal Highness, Awemo 11 wrote to the Divisional Officer, Tubah and copied all the paraphernalia of the Cameroon administration, at both divisional and provincial level accusing the Babanki people for intruding into the disputed land which the Commission had already ruled as belonging to the Bambili people. He wrote in the following words:

Dear Sir, Bambili/ Babanki-Tungoh Boundary Dispute

I regret that I have to write to you on the above subject once more. But I do not have any choice in the matter particularly as I do not like to see any blood-shed between my subjects and the Babanki Tungoh people. But it seems to me that some of the Babanki Tungoh people are taking advantage of this policy of mine and are carrying on extensive farming on areas which by the final findings and resolutions of the Christian, Justice and Peace Commission have confirmed the Westmacott decision as Bambili land. Mr. Divisional Officer, as you are aware in February this year, Hon. Dr. Abety, Minister of Special Duties at the Presidency of the Republic, as part of his services to the people of his subdivision, made a motorable road from around mile 12 to Ngohbege and in the process passing through parts of the disputed land, now confirmed by the final findings of the Christian, Justice and Peace Commission to be Bambili land. It was thanks only to the praiseworthy efforts of HRH the Fon of Babanki-Tungoh that the road was completed. It was indeed a great surprise to me and indeed to any reasonable person who became aware of the situation, that some Babanki people resisted vehemently the construction of a road which was being constructed entirely on Bambili land but which will be useful to both the Bambili and the Babanki-Tungoh people. As soon as the road was completed, these same Babanki-Tungoh people turned round and pointed to it as the new and acceptable boundary between them and Bambili and then went ahead to partition the side bordering their village among themselves and cultivated it. More recently, some Babanki-Tungoh people have crossed into my village and have caused extensive damages to my village forest reserve at Akonui: they fell a lot of trees, saw them into wood and carted them to Bamenda and elsewhere for sale, in the process using the road whose construction was they had opposed in February of this year. I want to appeal to you once more, Mr. Divisional Officer, to use your good offices to stop these provocative actions of the Babanki-Tungoh people and so avert the possible bloodshed which some of them are anxious to see. In particular, Mr. Divisional Officer, kindly get government surveyors to plant the necessary boundary pillars in accordance with the Westmacott decision now confirmed by the final findings and conclusions of the CJPC (Christian Justice and Peace Commission)

As to whether the land was ever given to Bambili by the Christian Justice and Peace Commission remains a subject of speculation. That is so because the commission was set up most recently and it would have been quite premature for the commission to have already handed over the piece of disputed land that has been a bone of contention after a very long time to Bambili. That notwithstanding, on 17 July 1999 the Fon of Bambili wrote another letter to the Divisional Officer and this time further copied His Grace, Archbishop of the Bamenda Archdiocese and The Chairman, The Christian Justice and Peace Commission, Bambui Parish.

In that letter he was pointing out to the further aggression of the Babanki Tungoh people who had entered the farms of the Bambili people and were destroying crops before the eyes of the farmers from Bambili. He further maintained in that letter that his people did not retaliate because he had cautioned them never to do so. Furthermore, he was still holding very strongly to the fact that the commission had handed over to Bambili the disputed land. The Fon took off time to warn the administration to step in and avert an imminent danger or else relations between the two communities would escalate into total war. He concluded his letter in the following words:

....Mr. Divisional Officer, I think that the time has now come for the administration to step into this matter and stop Babanki Tungoh people from farming on Bambili land and especially to plant the boundary marks. I see this as the only way of averting an imminent confrontation and further worsening of the relationship between the two villages. I restate here our commitment to peaceful co-existence and we stand ready to cooperate with the administration at all times to see that this long standing and vexing matter is settled once and for all....

To further strengthen the point of the Land which was handed over to the Bambili, on the 8 June, 2000, the fon of Bambili wrote another letter which was quite contradictory. He maintained that the Babanki people were still provoking the Bambili by farming on the disputed land despite an injunction order. He said "....I have the honour to report to you once more about the provocative acts of the Babanki Tungoh people by farming extensively in the disputed area between our two villages on which there is an administrative injunction...." It is common and practical commonsense that if the land had been handed over to the Bambili people there would have been no place for an injunction order which the Bambili people themselves were claiming and which the Babanki Tungoh were trespassing.

B) The Koungo Edima Commission

The Bambili-Babanki Tungoh "tug of war", so to say, over their common boundary which was causing considerable headache not only to the two communities but to the Cameroon Government as well called for the prompt intervention. The Cameroon Government decided to set up a commission under the Minister of Territorial Administration manned by His Excellency Koungo Edima to read the political barometer and diagnose the treatment of the boundary disease once and for all. In a country which was virtually obsessed by decrees, or arêtes the commission was to operate under *Arete No.00210/A/MINAT/DOT/SDOA/SCA Portant approbation du process-verbal du 9 mai 2000 de la Commission Nationale pour le reglement du litige de limites Territoriales entre les Commnautes BAMBILI et BABANKI-TUNGOH.(Departement de la MEZAM)* For a full text of the arête see appendix.

On the 25 June, 2000, the National Commission charged with the settlement of Inter-village Disputes, and accompanied by the full "Etat Major" of Mezam Division visited the disputed area. After briefing by the technicians the National Commission determined the boundary between Bambili and Babanki Tungoh and Ministerial Arete No.00210/AMINAT/DOT/SDOA/SCA date 16 August, 2000, was issued. Instead of the boundary headache being cured it instead caused more convulsions and complications in solving the boundary conflict.

The implementation of that arête was opposed by the Babanki Tungo with impunity despite the fact that the Senior Divisional Officer for Mezam had set up a Technical Committee headed by the Divisional Officer for Tubah charged specifically to implement the Ministerial arête. That committee however visited the area on the 2nd and 4th of July 2001 and the positions of boundary pillars were identified in the presence of full delegation of the two villages, including the two Fons.

On 6th July 2001, the Divisional Officer and the full technical team and Bambili delegation assembled to start work but the Babanki delegation boycotted thereby making the work practically impossible. Despite the boycott the technical team continued work on 9th July 2001. They were now assaulted and held hostage by a large mob of Babanki people and the materials brought for the erection of the pillars seized, spades iron rods, buckets and boxes.

The chain effect of the Ministerial arête continued. Following the incidence above the Senior Divisional Officer for Mezam in his letter No.390/L/E/29/PS OF 1ST August 2001 again invited the two villages and the technical committee to his office on 7th August 2001, and severely warned the Babanki Tungo people about the consequences of their actions in holding the technical team hostage, threatening their lives and destroying the boundary pillars built with state funds. He told them that by boycotting a meeting called by the administration amounts to contempt of authority and is punishable. He reiterated that their attitude in the matter could no longer be tolerated and that the administration could have taken very drastic action to impose state authority. He emphasised that he was giving them the last chance because he believed that dialogue and concertation was very important to end the boundary conflict.

He also reminded them that the National Commission charged with settlement of inter-village disputes whose decision he was executing is the supreme authority and its decision is final given the fact that all land is state land.

The talk of the Senior Divisional Officer was like "throwing water on a duck's back" especially as the Babanki Tungoh whom he spoke to them most, remained very stubborn. Such actions carried out either by Babanki or Bambili only helped to delay the peace process. On 12 September 2001, the Fon of Bambili, Awemo 11 addressed a letter to the Senior Divisional Officer, Mezam, through the Divisional Officer, Tubah Sub Division to that effect and copied The Minister of Territorial Administration; the Governor of the NW Province (NWP); the Procureur General NWP; The Legion Commander NWP; The Provincial chief of National Security NWP; the Brigade Commander, Gendarmerie Tubah and the commissioner of Special Branch Tubah. He said amongst other things:

> Dear Sir,
> PETITION AGAINST THE MANNER OF HANDLING THE ERECTION OF DEMARCATION CAIRNS BETWEEN BAMBILI AND BABANKI TUNGOH
>
> 1) Further to our letter dated 10th September 2001, we wish to report to you once more the resolved determination of the Babanki Tungoh people to frustrate the erection of the demarcation pillars between us and them which is the only way to bring to a stop to the periodical conflict between the two villages.
>
> 2) We are totally at a loss as to what the Babanki Tungoh people want. The R.C. Ward decision was the decision which was acceptable to us even though we lost some land to the Babanki Tungoh people. Then came the Westmacott decision which virtually deprived us of our land including the temple of our gods, although Westmacott accepted in his judgement that we should continue to use this temple to offer sacrifices to our gods.

3) In April last year, the Minister of Territorial Administration and the National Commission for the settlement of Inter-Village Disputes determined the present boundary which largely followed the Westmacott decision. It will be recalled that in 1973 the two Fons signed an agreement which was witnessed by the Administration accepting to abide by Westmacott decision.

4) Following the decision of the National Commission for the settlement of Inter-Village disputes and backed by Ministerial Arretes No.00210/A/MINAT/DOT/SDOA/SCA dated 16 August 2000 relating to the "Process Verbal" of the National Commission for the Disputed Boundary between Bambili and Babanki Tungoh of 9th May 2000, the present boundary was determined. After several disrupted attempts by Babanki Tungoh, the Divisional Officer for Tubah Sub Division and Chairman of the Technical Committee convened a meeting at his office on the 3rd of September 2001 in which it was agreed to continued work on the 10th September 2001. On this day a large population of Babanki people came out and declared that the work was not to continue unless a 1913 map which they produced was used. At earlier meetings convened by the Senior Divisional Officer, and the Divisional Officer Tubah, no objection was raised by them nor was any map produced. In any case we do not think that any person could petition against the decision of the National Commission for the settlement of Inter-Village Disputes since this is the highest competent authority in this matter. Following the incident of the 10th September 2001, the Chairman of the Technical Committee and the D.O. of Tubah Sub Division, detained the Fon of Babanki and his delegation but we have learned that they were released almost immediately and the material meant for building the pillars (namely pillars, sand, gravel, cement, iron rods etc) have been brought back and dumped somewhere. We are extremely disturbed by these happenings and are beginning to wonder whether in a matter of this nature it should be one of the parties to dictate to the government of a sovereign state.

5) It is to be noted that the Babanki Tungoh people have challenged the authority of the state in the following ways:

   i. The Babanki Tungohs have violated with impunity all administrative injunction orders placed over the disputed area.

   ii. Earlier cairns built by the administration were destroyed by the Babanki Tungoh people. Although some of their ring leaders were arrested and detained they were later released and no further action was taken against them.

   iii. Most administrative meetings convened by both SDO Mezam and DO Tubah were boycotted by the Babanki Tungoh people.

   iv. Cairns erected on the 9th July 2001 by the Technical Committee were again destroyed by the Babanki Tugoh people and we are not aware of any punitive action taken against them.

   v. On the 10th September 2001, when the Technical Committee went to the field to continue its work the Babanki Tungoh perturbed the work by introducing a map which they claimed was drawn in 1913 and insisted that the work could not continue unless this map is followed, thereby instructing the administration what to do.

6) In the light of the above the sovereignty of the state is being seriously challenged by a village (Babanki-Tungoh). We draw attention to the provision of article 4 of the Ministerial Arrete No.00210/A/MINAT/DOT/SDOA/SCA of 16th August 2000 which calls for sanctions against any person contravening the terms of the arête in accordance with the laws in force.

7) Despite of this we remain firmly committed to the cause of peace in this matter and pledge our cooperation at all times with the administration.

The manner in which the Babanki Tungoh people handled the boundary palaver with Bambili did not go on *sine die*. On 11 March, 2003, they decided to back paddle their position. By so doing they, through their fon addressed a letter to the Divisional Officer Tubah in the following words:

> Sir, PROPOSALS TOWARDS A PEACEFUL SOLUTION OF THE PROTRACTED (CHRONIC) LAND DISPUTE BETWEEN MY VILLAGE (KEDJOM KETINGUH) AND OUR BROTHERLY VILLAGE OF BAMBILI
> I write first of all to thank you from the bottom of my heart and on behalf of my peace-loving objects for the very wise decision you took to invite suggestions from both villages once more on how a peaceful solution could be sought to the long standing land dispute.
> It is my greatest wish that a solution be sought to this aching problem so that the brotherly people of these two villages that are condemned by history and geography to be neighbours live as peacefully as they did up to 1988.
> Sir, I would like to start by stating categorically that the Kedjom Ketingoh people are, and have always been law-abiding and always would want to stand by their word. This explains why our position on the subject is that the Westmacott decision still remains the only authentic document whose accurate and unbiased interpretation and implementation will achieve the desired goal. Our position is backed by the following facts and documents:
>
> 1) The peace pact signed by both villages on 25th July 1973;
>
> 2) The Bamenda High Court Judgement of 3rd July 1995;
>
> 3) Our position paper presented to the Honourable Minister of Territorial Administration on the 23rd of February 2002 in which we tried to prove that there

exist more than one version of falsified maps on this boundary issue produced by the Bambili people in an attempt to distort facts;

4) The Westmacott decision is actually being respected by the two villages and I can assure you that my people respect it 100 percent. If there are any problems, these arise from fabricated stories and intoxication. Each time we have had to fight it has been purely in self defence. We have never been and will never be at the origin of the skirmishes between our two villages.

In accepting the Westmacott decision, I am very aware of the sacrifices my people have made and are still making, especially with the discovery of the first map of the grassfield area drawn by the Germans in 1913 and which shows the original boundary between Babanki-Tungoh (now Kedjom Ketinguh) and Bambili. Since we the Kedjom Ketinguh people had committed ourselves in the Peace Pact of 1973, we are condemned to respect it to the letter and do everything possible to help in the actualization of this decision.

I plead that you give my village a chance to prove that Westmacott boundary is being respected in its entirety by my village and in part (certain parts) by the Bambili people. We are prepared to be called up at any time to throw more light on our stand.

We sincerely pray that peace exists between our two villages. Accept my highest regards",

    Viyouh Nelson Sheteh (Fon of Babanki-Tungoh)

From the above one could say that the Bambili people presented themselves as "good guys". They claimed to be peace loving people who want to live with their neighbours and "brothers" in peace and prosperity. It is simply interesting that from the facts on the ground it does not leave any person in doubt that the Babanki people are the ones that could be singled out as those who posed the greatest problems on the way to resolving the boundary conflict. Suddenly, they arose from their slumber and suggest ways of bringing the protracted boundary conflict to an end is like a child's play or an April fool's joke. A child's play more because one could see how confusing their suggestions appear on paper. At one time they attached preference to the 1913 German map; at another they hung very strongly to the tail coat of Westmacott decision. Above all their suggestions only went a long way to show how dishonest they could be. The facts which they presented as suggestions were arguable. This was borne out by the fact that barely two years later (2005) they started constructing a church in the disputed area.

The District Officer for Tubah issued injunction Order No.18 of 4 July 2005 stopping any work on the site. The Babanki Tungoh people fired back on 26th August 2005 refusing as usual to abide by the injunction order (see appendix). This led to the intervention of the Senior Divisional Officer for Mezam, Jacob Musima, who reacted as if he had been stung by an angry wasp by immediately issuing Letter Ref.E29.03/165/494 on 8 November 2005 by which he concretised the injunction order already placed by his junior colleague. He wrote:

Subject:

INJUNCTION ORDER ON CHURCH CONSTRUCTION SITE IN KEDJOM KETINGUH

I have the honour to refer to your letter no.472/L/E.29/2306 of 13th October 2005 on the subject matter supra and wish to sate as follows:

a) That the said site where the purported church construction was to take place is a disputed piece of land between the Bambili and the Kedjom Ketinguh villages.

b) That this inter-village boundary dispute saw the intervention of the Hon. Minister of State in charge of Territorial Administration and Decentralisation some years ago, who came in with a national commission to determine the boundary.

c) That the actualization of the boundary by the commission on the ground through putting of cairns was hampered by the Kedjom Ketinguh community who destroyed the first two cairns and attacked the technicians, thereby stopping the actualization work.

d) That all attempts by the administration to let the actualization of the boundary continue to the end has not been successful as the people of Kedjom Ketinguh have not paid their share, of fees or contribution for the commission to continue work, and are making no efforts to pay same.

e) That it is only when the actualization exercise of the boundary between Bambili and Kedjom Ketinguh shall have been through and done that it would be clear as to whether the church site is on Kedjom Ketinguh land or Bambili land.

f) That the Fon of Bambili is very much against the construction of the said church house until it is determined on whose land the church is situated, even though the church is a public utility. From the foregoing, it is but expedient that the actualization of the boundary be concluded to determine on whose land the church site is situated, and for this to take place, the people of Kedjom Ketinguh should be made to pay their own share of the fee for the realization of the job which stands at 1,000,000 FRS. Bambili paid 650,000 FRS and have their balance ready as of now. The sooner the actualization of the boundary is done or realised, the better for the two communities of Bambili and Kedjom Ketinguh, whose impending and crucial boundary dispute shall have been resolved once and for all.

Conclusion

As per 2005, the so called Ministerial arête had not been implemented and although there was no overt escalation of warfare the final decision to resolve the boundary conflict was still a far cry to the peace loving people. The protracted boundary conflict had serious repercussions on communities and beyond. The next section focuses on the ramifications of the boundary conflict in all its facets and even proffer solutions which perhaps if implemented will bring the two communities and the Cameroon government out of the long protracted boundary misunderstanding.

Chapter Five
Consequences of the Bambili and Babanki-Tungoh Boundary Conflict and Some Suggested Solutions

Introduction
The boundary conflict between the two neighbouring villages of Bambili and Babanki-Tungoh had lasting ramifications which have adversely affected the socio-economic, cultural and political lives of the people of both villages. This chapter focuses on the consequences on the two communities and their neighbours. It will further examine the efforts carried out towards the resolution of the boundary conflict by various administrative bodies and why these attempts have failed. The chapter will end with suggested solutions and a conclusion. For a better appreciation of the consequences I have decided to treat them under the social, economic and political rubrics.

A) Social Consequences
Socially, both villages suffered considerable number of deaths during the wars. Much property like houses, cattle and other fixed assets were damaged. Men, women and children have been rendered homeless and some without families; others have been maimed and rendered inactive for the rest of their lives. For instance, in the early hours of Saturday May 25, 1991, a group of Babanki-Tungoh people attacked Yafamwi Chimia, the "claimed" quarter head of the disputed area by the Bambili[1]. His cows and money were taken away and his property was damaged. Those who were involved reportedly carried guns, cutlasses and spears. With these weapons considerable damage was caused to the victim, his three fences and crops (plantains, maize and bananas) were either destroyed or looted[2]. As the Bambili people rushed to the scene to rescue the children, some of them were shot and others sustained injuries[3] (see Table I for the number of victims and the magnitude of the injury, which they sustained.)

Furthermore, when the boundary conflict crystallised into warfare in the early 1990s, Babanki-Tungoh students studying in Bambili were prevented from writing their end-of-year examinations. According to letters Nos. E. 2901.2/165/109 and E/2901.2/C.2/10/4/11 respectively, captioned "Insecurity of Students in Institutions in Bambili..." from the Fon's palace, Bambili, and accepted by the Director of ENS and principal of CCAST, Bambili, to the Divisional Officer, Tubah Sub Division, the Fon wrote in the following words:

> In so far as concerns your earlier correspondence, I wish to dare say that it was due to specific circumstances which generated this state of insecurity, namely, the invasion of my village by the neighbouring Babanki-tungoh and the consequent repercussions of destruction of property around this semi-urban agglomeration over a boundary dispute which has remained unresolved since the colonial days... (It) was not felt within the CCAST complex only, it shrouded my entire village and students of Babanki-Tungoh went without exams.... [4]

The Fon was reacting to the Babanki-Tungoh version that their students were completely sifted out from examination by the Bambili people sent by the Fon. The Fon of Bambili maintained that the act was carried out by "vandals" from Bambili who were not sent by him. Whatever the case, Babanki-Tungoh students were momentarily prevented from writing their examinations in CCAST Bambili[5].

The Divisional Officer for Tubah, Martin Ndiyeng, in Letter Ref., No.E2901.2/165/109 wrote on 31st May 1991 to His Royal Highness, The Fon of Bambili. The subject of the letter was insecurity of students in Institutions in Bambili. Amongst other things he said:

> Information continues to reach me that your subjects have continued to threaten the lives of students who are not of Bambili origin studying in the Government or Private Institutions situated in your village.

This attitude has caused many students to abandon classes or are writing their final exams in total fear whose after effects will be regrettable both to the students and their parents.

Considering that your village accommodates all the highest educational institutions in the province, it is obligatory that you use your traditional powers to put your subjects under control and protect the Government institutions implanted in your village.

You are to be reminded that the administration has viewed and is viewing these acts of vandalism with concern and will be obliged to take sterner measures should they persist.

I will like to know what action you have taken within the shortest possible time. Accept my best wishes as I wait for your usual cooperation.

The Babanki Tungoh people took the relay baton from the hand of the S.D.O and handed it over to the Minister of National Education in very strong terms. In response to that situation, the Babanki Tungoh people on 20th August 1992 wrote a letter directed to the Minister of National Education and copied the Presidency of the Republic; Prime Minister of the Republic; S.D.O. Mezam; Provincial Delegate for Education Bamenda; D.O. Tubah Sub Division; Municipal Administrator, Tubah; Councillors Tubah and other people.

Sir,
WE WANT OUR OWN CCAST
For many years our village has been having many problems about land matters with the people of Bambili village. Last year there was a great fight and some of our people were killed on their farms and our people who worked in Bambili: E.N.S., CCAST, Agriculture School, IRZ and IRA were beaten and their houses burnt and some of our children were also beaten and their books and other things were burnt. Because of that situation we asked our children who were admitted in CCAST not to go there.

Since the government has gone into the case, we thought that our children will be able to go and attend CCAST this school year, but one Dr. Abety Peter who works in the Prime Minister's office came recently and held a meeting with his Bambili people and told them that he will work hard so that our people whose things were damaged by Bambili people are not paid compensation and that he will make a Bambili man, Mr. Ndofor to be the principal of CCAST so as to show our people pepper. Because of this we shall not allow any of our children to go to CCAST Bambili again. We used to think that CCAST Bambili was a school for all children from this part of our country but since the Bambili people say it is only for them and they want their village man to be principal in order to destroy our children, we want the Honourable Minister to create our own CCAST High School in our own village too.

Apart from students, the entire Babanki-Tungoh community appeared unsafe. This was shown in a communiqué which they wrote to the Governor of the North West Province, Bell Luc Rene. According to the Babanki-Tungoh:

....every bit of thing in Bambili that had any relation to a Kedjom-Ketinguh (Babanki-Tungoh) element, including our houses, cars, domestic [sic] animals and household property... (were destroyed). We now find it absolutely impossible for us to live and work in Bambili as we are completely unsafe in the place... We are therefore appealing very strongly to the Governor to come to our aid now that most of us are refugees in our own province since we cannot pass through Bambili to our relation in the village....[6]

This meant that the Babanki-Tungoh community in Bambili lived in perpetual fear and insecurity as a result of the boundary conflict. There were about 181 Babanki-Tungoh living in Bambili and they exerted a considerable influence in the daily activities in the region[7]. Unfortunately, Babanki-Tungoh threatened their existence in Bambili. The issue of Babanki-Tungoh people, writing to the Minister of National Education in need of their own CCAST needs further attention here. That appeared the climax of the paradox of the sons and daughters of the soil. As they rightly put it in their letter, CCAST was meant for all the Cameroonian children whose intellectual aptitude qualified them to further their education. For Bambili people to claim that they could appropriate the institution at the detriment of the children of Babanki people because of a war that was not even perpetuated by these children was a bizarre situation.

Furthermore the war of 1991 caused considerable damage to both material things and human lives. It would appear that this weighed more on the Bambili people. The table below shows the number of people who were wounded during the 1991 clashes alone.

Table 1: The List of Victims Wounded During the Bambili/ Babanki-Tungoh Clash Of 25 May 1991 and Gunshot Victims Operated and Bullets Removed at the Bambili Health Centre

No.	Name	Sex	Quarter	Village	No. of Bullets
1	John Tafa	M	Manka	Bambili	1
2	Shombong David	M	Menteng	Bambili	2
3	Ndumo Paul	M	Agham	Bambili	1
4	Richard Bajong	M	Bujung	Bambili	1
5	Zachaues Asanga	M	Achi	Bambili	1
6	Benedict Ashangmbeng	M	Ntembang	Bambili	1
7	Ndumu Joseph	M	Ntembang	Bambili	1
8	Joseph Takang	M	Mbeyo	Bambili	1
9	Christopher Chenui	M	Achi	Bambili	1
10	Christopher	M	Mbecha	Bambili	5 and referred to hospital.
11	Taminang Chigsi Joe	M	Nibie	Bambili	Referred to the hospital
12	Joseph Tamukom	M	Mempi	Bambili	Referred to hospital
13	Mabo Augustine	M	Ntembang	Bambili	Referred to hospital
14	Ashano John	M	Mempi	Bambili	Referred to hospital
15	Martina Sandoh	M	Achi	Bambili	Referred to hospital
16	Richard Achinui	M	Caps	Bambili	In a state of comma
17	Afegenui Isaac	M	Achi	Bambili	Referred to hospital

18	Mushongong George	M	Ntembang	Bambili	Treated and sent home
19	David Tih Achu	M	Ntigi	Bambili	Treated and sent home
20	Christina Formbong	F	Achi	Bambili	Treated and sent home
21	Rahel Lem	F	Mbecha	Bambili	Treated and sent home
22	Awantang Valintine	M	Achi	Bambili	Treated and sent home
23	Nicodemus Ikongne	M	Menteng	Bambili	Treated and sent home
24	David Akongnui	M	Nibie	Bambili	Treated and sent home
25	Peter Forbigi	M	Mendam	Bambili	Treated and sent home
26	Max Ajeh	M	Mempi	Bambili	Treated and sent home
27	Gregory Anuafor	M	Achi	Bambili	Treated and sent home
28	Christopher Chenui	M	Achi	Bambili	Treated and sent home
29	Gregory Takui	M	Ntembang	Bambili	Treated and sent home
30	Anthony Asongwe	M	Achi	Bambili	Treated and sent to home
31	Martin Awemo	M	Menteng	Bambili	Treated and sent to home
32	Peter Nforkeh	M	Mbenshi	Bambili	Treated and sent to home
33	Nkeh Denis	M	-Nchoken	Bambili	Treated and sent to home
34	Forlum Tenislo	M	Nibie	Bambili	Treated and sent to home
35	Gregory Che	M	Ntembang	Bambili	Treated and sent home
36	Tangie Fungsa	M	Achi	Bambili	Treated and sent home
37	Ashongwe Peter	M	Achi	Bambili	Treated and sent home
38	Zuh Francis	M	Babanki-Tungoh	Babanki-Tungoh	Victimised at his shoe mending shop at 3 corners, Bambili and referred to the Bamenda Provincial Hospital.

Source: Bambili Developed Teaching Health Centre Archives

From the above table, it could be read that in all, 10 patients were operated on and had their bullets removed at the Health Centre. Seven patients were referred to the hospital for x-ray of soft tissue damage to identify situation of bullets for removal amongst, One critical and in comma due to head injury. Twenty-one patients had their bullets and/or wounds treated and sent home to report everyday for wound dressings unless complications set in thenceforth. One patient was from Babanki-Tungoh and was victimized at the

Bambili three corners and was referred to the Bamenda Provincial hospital. A total of thirty one victims were received. Two are said to have died at the battle front and the administration ordered for the burial. A total of 15 bullets were parcelled and they accompanied this report. (From MINPUBLIC HEALTH/MESIRES,BAMBILI DEVELOPED TEACHING HEALTH CENTRE, REF.No.150/ BDTHC/TSD/A4 to THE SUBDIVISIONAL OFFICER, TUBAH).

Following the Report of hostilities between the People of Bambili and Babanki Tungoh written by the Divisional Officer Tubah, Jum Martin Ndiyeng on 25 May 1991, three people died as a result of the hostilities. They were: Awemo Martin of Bambili; Martin Asongwe of Bambili and Zhuh Ngononge Emmanuel of Babanki Tungoh. The report also went ahead to provide a list of refugees who were of Babanki origin and who had been displaced by the war and were in Bamenda looking for safety. The table below shows the total number of the refugees produced as a result of the war.

Table 2: List of Refugees Rendered by the Bambili/Babanki Tungoh War

Name	Number of wives/husbands	Number of children
1) Tifah Elias Tinsuh	2 wives	5 children
2) Anuh Martin	3 wives	12 children
3) Abuh David	1 wife	14 children
4) Nkwoh Jonson	3 wives	8 children
5) Akongwe James	1 wife	3 children
6) Makwando Z. Nse	1 wife	7 children
7) Nse Peter Abong	No wife	No children
8) Kendong Benita N.	1 husband	4 children
9) Joseph Nkwih	1 husband	No children
10) Nyingchuo Mathias	1 wife	5 children
11) Kenyu Joseph	1 wife	4 children
12) Chumbom Moses	No wife	No children
13) Mukengu Isaac	No wife	No children
14) Zhuh Francis	1 wife	5 children
15) Augustine Tum	1 wife	5 children

16) Chuyum David	1 wife	7 children
17) Kubam Emmanuel	1 wife	3 children
18) Mufui Esther	No husband	8 children
19) Anguh Peter Kenyim	1 wife	5 children
20) Akuli Joseph	3 wives	19 children
21) Alfred Nkwain	1 wife	5 children
22) Ategfon Silvester	1 wife	4 children
23) Ngong Benjamin	2 wives	10 children

In sum about 183 people including children were displaced from Babanki- Tungoh alone during the 1991 assault. Most of the above persons were civil servants attached to T.S.A.; MINEPIA; R.C.A.; CCAST; E.N.S.; Health centre ONAREP and also business men.

The gravity and intensity of the social relations emanating from the Babanki Tungoh/ Bambili fracas was most felt by the people in Table 2 who wrote about their predicaments on the 28th May 1991 to His Excellency, The Governor of North West Province. They wrote in the following words:

Your Excellency,

SUBJECT: INSECURITY OF KEDJOM CIVIL SERVANTS, BUSINESS MEN AND THEIR FAMILIES IN BAMBILI VILLAGE

We write to bring to the notice of the Governor the horrible experiences we of the Kedjom Ketingoh origin residing and working in Bambili have gone through since Saturday 25th of May 1991 till now that we are writing this report.

It was on this fateful day that hostilities broke out between the two neighbouring villages of Kedjom Ketinguh and Bambili. The Bambili people waged a full scale war against the Kedjom Ketinguh people living and working in Bambili. They chased all of us out as each person ran for his life. A few of us were caught and severely beaten and could only be saved by the forces of law and order to whom we are very thankful.

They destroyed every bit of thing in Bambili that had any relation to a Kedjom Ketinguh element, including our houses, cars, domestic animals and household property. Thank God none of us was killed.

We now find it absolutely impossible for us to live and work in Bambili as we are now completely unsafe in the place and worse still, no houses or household equipment such as beds, utensils etc to use.

We are therefore appealing very strongly to the Governor to come to our aid now that most of us are refugees in our own very Province since we cannot pass through Bambili to see our relation in the village. There is total insecurity as there is continued harassment of the Kedjom Ketinguh people even in private and public cars, as well as our children who are now writing the G.C.E. in CCAST BAMBILI. Our children in Primary Schools can no longer go to school since they are out with us.

We may not be pointing an accusing finger at any body but would like to point out that we were shocked at the way in which the Tubah Administration exposed those of us to whom they offered protection after a threat by the Bambili people to burn the District and Brigade officers. We are however thankful that some of us were protected in the Council hall for one night.

Your Excellency, one last thing which looks really absurd to us is that not as much as a single Bambili man has been detained since the problem started. Is it a share coincidence or it is a planned act? Sir, we rely on you for a detailed and thorough investigation into this matter so as to render justice where necessary.

We are anxiously waiting for your action.

In a related issue, some of the Babanki-Tungoh who were working in Bambili preferred to be transferred as a result of the antagonistic sentiments shown towards them by the Bambili. A report written by the chief of Bambili Developed Teaching Health Centre, Shey Ngafi Francis, stated that one of his workers "... Mrs. Kendong Bertha holds the view that with the present insecurity she will prefer against her wish, a transfer from Bambili to another health unit where her security could at least be guaranteed for now.. .."[8] Bertha was a nurse working at the Bambili Health Centre when the conflagration erupted in the month of May. Her only misfortune was that she came from Babanki Tungoh. While the war was raging on she was busy with her profession attending to the war victims. That was not recognised by the people of Bambili as they attacked the health centre putting Bertha on the run. She was rescued by her boss Shey Ngafi Francis alongside with her husband and the kids. In a personal communication with Bertha on 14 April,, 2004, she confirmed that she was seriously brutalized by the Bambili people and if not for her strength and courage she would have been raped.

Shey Ngafi Francis made the point of Mrs Kendong Bertha more lucid and detail in the letter Ref.No.152/bdthc/TSDA4 of 27th May 1991, which he wrote to the Divisional Chief of Service Public Health, Mezam Division Bamenda in the following words:

Subject: Staff Member Victim of Aggression: Mrs Kendong Bertha

> Mrs Kendong Bertha, Nursing Aid serving in this Health centre is of Babanki Tungo origin, the village in land dispute conflict with neighbouring Bambili. On 25th May 1991, these two villages engaged in an aggressive fighting which resulted in two Bambili people killed and 37 wounded and transported to this centre for care. This situation alienated the Bambili population. They then organised a systematic man hunt and destruction of houses and property belonging to the Babanki Tungo people irrespective of whether they were at war front or not.
>
> Mrs Kendong Bertha, who at this material moment was engaged in the reception and treatment of the wounded

Bambili people at the health centre, was a victim. All her property was burnt to ashes and her children allegedly kidnapped away. She equally received threats from the angry population who came to see their patients being treated by her who held that they were to deal with her come what may. In spite of all these threats she worked with me calmly and conscientiously.

At about 5;00 pm, I organised and uplifted her to the Gendarmerie Brigade Tubah for security. Came back looked for the children and uplifted them to the mother and father at same place. I received minor threats for doing so. Mrs Kendong Bertha left Bambili with one skirt, one blouse, one pant, one breast ware and a pair of slippers, same for husband and children. She is presently under the care of the administration as a refugee and cannot be expected to come to work, since Bambili seems very unsafe for her and the family. It is necessary to note that Mrs Kendong Bertha has worked proficiently, sympathetically, devotedly, conscientiously, respecting constituted health, traditional and administrative authorities, maintaining good human relations with both staff and the entire population of Bambili up to the last moment when her people were at war with the Bambili people not mining whether her own victims at home were cared for or not. Mrs Kendong Bertha holds the view that with the present insecurity she will prefer against her wish a transfer from Bambili to another health unit where her security could at least be guaranteed for now.

In view of the foregoing, I propose that Mrs Kendong Bertha be moved to a health unit of her preference even temporarily. Her opinion could be sought for this.

In another development, the two midwives I have in this centre are of Bambili origin. I usually engage them in the supervision of the two Primary Health Care Posts situated at Babanki Tungo village. The presence of a midwife for this exercise is indispensable. This present agitation makes it totally and temporarily suspended their journeys to the two health posts at Babanki villages to discuss the matter with you closely.

The health centre personnel and students are functioning normally without any threat from anybody since the only Babanki staff has left.
Submitted for your appreciation.

The letter of Shey showed that the Bambili/Babanki-Tungoh boundary war had even surpassed the International Conventions guarding and regulating war situations. As a matter of fact following the Geneva Convention in war situation, medical personnel or Red Cross workers remained untouched. The case of Kendong Bertha was an example of the violation of such conventions.

Another socio-economic impact of the boundary conflict were the contributions made both in kind and cash, by the inhabitants of the two villages living in the "diaspora." Both the people of Bambili and Babanki-Tungoh in the "diaspora" provided monthly contributions to sustain the war efforts of their respective villages"[9].

Furthermore, Bambili erected road blockades against their enemies, Babanki. The consequences of the road blockades were grave especially on the Babanki-Tungoh community. Almost all the Civil and Health services are located in Bambili. The blockades therefore, cut off the Babanki-Tungoh people from these social amenities. During the conflict the blockades made it difficult, if not impossible, for the victims of the war to be evacuated to government medical health centres at Bambili and/or Bamenda, as well as mission hospitals at Bafut and Mbingo. Apart from the evacuation of war victims, the inhabitants of Babanki-Tungoh were barred from passing through Bambili.

The Babanki-Tungoh people could not retaliate because the Bambili people had nothing to gain in Babanki-Tungoh. In order to "balance the equation", the Big-Babanki Tungoh people who claimed cultural affiliation with Babanki-Tungoh, erected road blockades against Bambili people. The Big-Babanki people however, had an additional reason for raising road blockades. One of their pronounced princes and heir apparent to the throne was killed during a confrontation with the people of Bambili[10].

In reaction to the road blockade the Kedjom Ketinguh Traditional Council wrote to the Divisional Officer, Tubah Sub Division in the following words:

Chapter Five: Consequences of the Bambili and Babanki-Tungoh Boundary Conflict

Sir,

BLOCK-ADE BY THE BAMBILI PEOPLE

On the 7th of January 1991 the Bambili people blocked the Banjah/Kedjom Ketinguh road and seized the Kedjom Ketinguh citizens from vehicles, brutalized them and took them to the Fon, palace Bambili from where they were handed over to the Administration at Tubah. Since the 7th of March 1995 when the Bambili people shot and killed Tseubom Fele in his farm, the Bamenda/Banjah/Kedjom Ketinguh road has remained blocked to the Kedjom Ketinguh citizen who dared to follow his master's cows from the cattle market through the road was almost beaten to death but for the intervention of some good Samaritans. Since then all cow boys taking cows to the cattle market are censored by the Bambili people to make sure that no cow goes to the cattle market from a Kedjom man. Cow boys whose cattle record from the last Veterinary Post shows a difference are forces (sic) to pay for the extra cows.

-Considering that every citizen has the right to live and move freely;
-Considering that the Administration has allowed the Bambili people to impose a toll on the Kedjom Ketinguh cows going to the cattle market;
-Considering that the citizens pay taxes in return for protection of their rights by the Administration;
-Considering that the Administration has not done anything to check the economic blockade imposed on Kedjom Ketinguh cattle owners and farmers by the Bambili people;
-We therefore appeal to you to use your good office to remove the blockade so that the Kedjom Ketinguh citizens can pass to the cattle market and the farmers to evacuate their crops in order to sell their cattle and crops and be able to pay their taxes.

The letter showed a wide variety of issues that were affected by the road blockade and most of the Babanki people had to bear the brunt.

B) Economic Consequences

Economically, whenever, the boundary conflict flared, it was difficult for fresh vegetable and other farm produce from the fertile boundary area to be transported to the Bamenda metropolitan market and even beyond. The consequences of this were two-fold: firstly, there was scarcity of vegetables and its resulting price hikes; and secondly, the farmer's experienced extreme hardship because, the sole source of their income was from selling vegetables. The trade and interaction that had been going on between the two villages effectively became difficult to be implemented. With the advent of the boundary conflict in the 1950s the cordial interaction between the two villages ceased, which caused more difficulties on the inhabitants.

Besides, the constant road blockades led to the opening of the Babanki-Tungoh-Bandja highway. This acted as a safety valve for the Babanki-Tungoh who were most affected as a result of the road blockades. The opening of this highway gave the region a better road network. Socio-economically, the road blockades pushed the people of Babanki-Tungoh to cement their ties with the Balikumbat and Bamessing to look upon them as their "saviour". In like manner, their century - old enemy-brother, Big Babanki, normalised relations with them. It can be argued that the Bambili-Babanki-Tungoh boundary conflict produced something positive. In addition, it led to a normalisation of relations, between the Babanki-Tungoh on the one hand and the Balikumbat, Bamessing and Big Babanki on the other hand.

Another economic consequence was that the touristic industry in the Tubah Sub-Division was negatively affected. The geographical location of Lake Bambili attracted tourists from around and beyond the North West Province. This was because the lake is found in the disputed area. Besides, the killing and looting of cows did not only affect the owners adversely but also affected the government. The only source for the Fulani people was the proceed from the sale of cattle and livelihood was jeopardized when they were unable to sell

sell their cattle. In as much as the government was concerned, the inability of the Fulanis to sell their cattle meant a reduction in the jangili tax, hence national income.[11]

C) Political Consequences

Politically, the boundary conflict exposed the weaknesses or the inability of the administration to solve the boundary conflict. The Fon of Babanki-Tungoh who signed the 1973 accord not call on his people to stop their activities on the disputed area was agreed to by both parties. Yet, neither him nor the people involved were penalised. This certainly gave the impression that the accord was not considered serious by the government. The weaknesses of the civil administration were further shown by the fact that the administration did not understand the historicity of the boundary conflict. Following an interview in the *Cameroon Tribune*, Bell Luc Rene said:

> I have said it over and over that the solution to this problem is not exclusively that of the administration. It concerns all of us. All of the disputes are old. For example, the Bambili/Babanki-Tungoh case was resolved in 1958 by the colonial master. The real problem lies in the implementation of the decision taken at that time. The people are not helping the administration to solve this problem. I am only there to help. I am not a native of the North West Province and do not know the boundaries. I cannot sway from decisions taken before or be expected to work on empty files[12].

Certain points could be deduced from the above quotation. Firstly, that 1958 was pronounced as being the year which gave a final solution to the Bambili and Babanki-Tungoh boundary conflict seems to portray the ignorance of the administration. This was because before the 1958 decision was taken by the colonial administrators had been pre-occupied since 1953. In that year, Ward, the Colonial resident in Bamenda attempted a solution. Five years later, in 1958, his successor A. B. Westmacott modified Ward's attempted solution. Owing to the fact that British Southern Cameroons gained independence in October 1961 through reunification, the British colonial administrators were obliged to quit the territory. Since the attempted solution of the boundary misunderstanding appeared a continuum since 1953, one expected the Cameroon administration manned by Cameroonians to better handle this issue.

What was more surprising and interesting is that Bell Luc Rene knew and recognised the fact that the 1958 decision solved the problem in "name and not in fact only" because "[T]he real problem lies with implementation". The crux of the problem now is who should implement the 1958 decision? In as much as the civil administration fails to accomplish this decision, it is tempting to say that, she remains at best weak. As if that was not enough, the second pertinent point is the refusal of the Governor willy-nilly, that he is not a native of Bamenda and therefore should not know boundaries. As the highest ranking civil administrator in the region, his statement was unfortunate.

Closely related to the weakness of the civil administration was the corrupt nature of some civil and/or legal administrators. According to letter, Ref. No. ABA/102/50 of March 1, 1970, the two villages were anxious to know what became of the deposits of 138,400 francs paid by each side in the case. It is further confirmed in the letter that the Bambili community paid the above sum of Receipts No. 81/242331 of 11 April 1963 and 41/242959 of 13 July 1963.[13] The letter however expresses worries about the accountability of this money. It is not easy to establish the fact that this money was embezzled. However, the letter issued by the Senior Divisional Officer of Mezam, H.P. Sone, of April 20, 1971 dismissed any phrases aimed at discrediting the administration. Amongst other things, the letter read "... These statements are meant only to discredit the Administration and also to indicate your unwillingness to abide by the decision of Dr. J.N. Foncha then Prime Minister of West Cameroon"....[18]

The Babanki-Tungoh people are portrayed as more aggressive than their Bambili enemies. In order to support this fact it is worth examining three letters which were written to the Senior Divisional Officer in Bamenda by the Bambili elites. In the letter, Ref. No. E290/102/S.9/74 of October 13, 1980, the Bambili elites wrote:

....I [We] have received a complaint from the Fon of Bambili that Saidu Anguh and 400 other in your village have trespassed into the Bambili land (doing farming and fencing the area) despite the Westmacott's Decision which agreement you signed with the Fon of Bambili on 25th day of July 1973 with the effect that both villages were restrained from carrying out any activities on the disputed area which was finally demarcated showing the boundary of your villages i.e. Bambili/Babanki-Tungoh....[5]

Another letter from the Fon's Palace, Bambili captioned "Trespass into Bambili land by the people of Babanki-Tungoh" states: "Your attention is being drawn to the fact that the people of Babanki-Tungoh have continued to cause provocative activities on Bambili land by building fences with barb wires, huts and farming...."[16] The message which is carried by these letters points to the fact that Babanki-Tungoh people were more aggressive than the Bambili. Although it cannot be denied that Bambili, were aggressive, Babanki-Tungoh were more responsible for the outbreak of the boundary conflict.

In the same vein, Babanki-Tungoh has shown their unwillingness to arrive at a consensus with the Bambili people. It should be recalled that the two villages "buried their hatchet" in 1973, but as events later showed, the Babanki-Tungoh became less interested in peaceful solutions[17]. According to letter, Ref. No. ABA 102/2.9/56 of March 8, 1972, "the chief of Babanki-Tungoh and his councillors failed to turn up, although they actually received "my [his] invitation... the chief of Bambili and his councillors agreed that the area surveyor should carry on the erection of the pillars...."[18]

Another communiqué which illustrates the Babanki-Tungoh "foot-dragging" attitude towards the resolution of the boundary differences was lucidly written by the Area Surveyor and Lands Officer, B.K. Simo, to the Senior Divisional Officer for Mezam in the following words: "...I wish to inform you that the job has to be stopped, nay suspended, because the Babanki-Tungoh people have refused to cooperate. When the job started last week, only the Bambili people turned up and continued to work with my team for a couple of days...."[19].All these communiqué could illustrate that

Babanki-Tungoh people were not willing to come to an agreement with their Bambili neighbours. It could also be that they knew their boundary quite well and were not prepared to give up.

Another political ramification of the boundary conflict was that state building had been adversely affected. Since 1950s when the boundary conflict erupted the two villages have exercised aggressive proclivities towards each other[20]. Despite the July 1973 accord, sporadic trespass into each other's zone was noted with much acerbity from the Babanki-Tungoh. Had it been there was a peaceful co-existence, between the two villages it is probable and even possible that the fertile piece of land which is the bone of contention would be effectively utilised to the advantage of both parties. The various contributions made by the inhabitants of the two villages living in "diaspora" would have gone a long way to accentuate the socio-economic development of the two villages.

As a result of this boundary conflict the zone has been turned almost into a "war zone". The Bambili were fighting with the Nkwen and Bambui, and Babanki-Tungoh clashes with the Balikumbat and Bamessing. Furthermore, other neighbouring villages in the Bamenda Grassfields tend to copy the example of the Bambili and Babanki-Tungoh boundary conflict.

In the treatment of the consequences it was realised that they affected areas beyond the two villages. The boundary conflict has not been going on without any attempts at solving it. Several solutions have been attempted by the colonial masters, the Christian denominations civil and legal administrators and the two villages to resolve the conflict.

D) Efforts at Resolving the Boundary Conflict

The previous chapters reveal that the boundary conflict between Babanki-Tungoh and Bambili has been caused by a piece of fertile land which lies between the two villages. They (the two villages) make different claims as to where the boundary is/or should be. Thus, the main difficulty is to establish a boundary acceptable to both villages. In order to better understand the endeavour made towards the demarcation of the boundary, it is necessary to examine the claims of each community on the disputed land with the main aim of resolving the problem.

Chapter Five: Consequences of the Bambili and Babanki-Tungoh Boundary Conflict

Map 3, in the next page, shows the disputed area and this presents the claims of the two communities and the various boundaries that have been drawn in an unsuccessful attempt to resolve the problem. Section "B - W" represents the claims as made by the Babanki-Tungoh, the Bambili claim the section "B - A". None of the communities have been willing to recognise the claim of the other party.

The demarcation of the boundary between these communities by the Bafut Native Court Judgement of December 11, 1953 is indicated by Section "C-T".

This boundary was established in the presence of Fon Awemo of Bambili and Fon Asik of Babanki-Tungoh and it was registered in the Bafut Native Court Civil Suit No. 23/53. Yet it did not satisfy the two communities. After many other attempts, Ward, the British resident in Bamenda province, suggested another boundary which was later rejected by the two communities because it did not coincide with their respective claims. Another boundary, the Westmacott boundary represented by section "M - W", was later established by Westmacott on May 15, 1958 at Bafut.

Beside, several meetings were also convened by the traditional and educated elite of the two neighbouring villages in an attempt to resolve the boundary impasse. On February 13, 1965, a meeting of the Bafut Chiefs took place in the Bafut Council[21]. According to the minutes of that meeting signed by J.N. Foncha on February 15, 1965, the members arrived at a five-point decision[22]. Amongst other things in the five-point decision, the meeting attached great importance to the Westmacott decision and the final demarcation of the disputed area. From the above it is clear that it was difficult to implement the decision. This is because it was not easy for somebody who had been living in a place for a long time to give up his "assets", especially compounds and farms and secondly transfer his "citizenship". What is more, a communiqué of the Senior Divisional Officer to Prime Minister J.N. Foncha on July 27, 1965 rendered the implementation of point III impossible. In the communiqué, the S.D.O. said:

> We have discussed over the demarcation of the boundary between Bambili-Babanki-Tungoh following the decision of the Bafut Clan council of 13/2/65 and I wish to point out

that the word Eastward was wrong as can be seen from the beginning of the 2nd paragraph. The intention is [was] to give more land to Babanki-Tungoh for a market. The direction eastward will curtail the land instead. Therefore the direction westwards should [be] substituted....[23]

Map 3: The Bambili And Babanki Land And Boundary Confilct

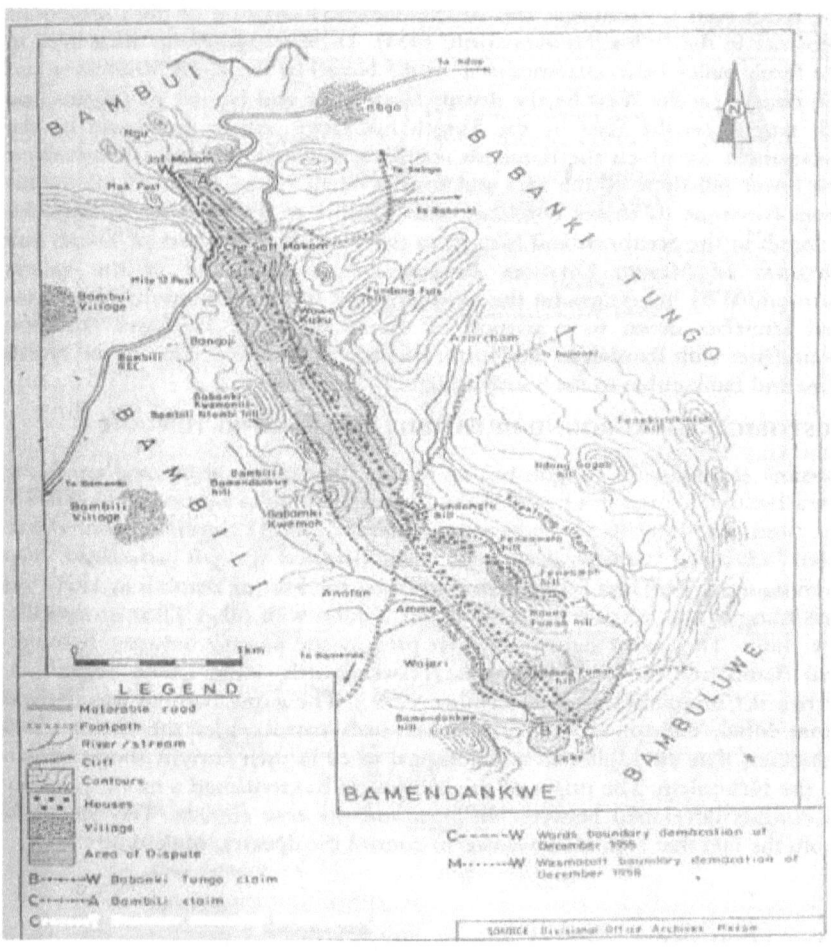

The Bambili people did not accept this interpretation and that led to the failure of the February 15, 1965 decision.

Furthermore, civil administrators from the division and the traditional elite from the warring villages took off time and inspected the disputed area, and also attempted some suggested solutions. This was a result of the 1965 peace initiative which had failed. On June 22, 1971, this delegation inspected the border area and agreed amongst other things, that:

> The new boundary would start from the present J.H.F. beacon (in actual fact, this is an I.G.N. i.e. Institute Geographique Nationale Control point a, near the 13th milestone on the Bamenda-Banso road. From there, it would run to a point 10 metres from a certain Babanki-Banso road. From there, it would run to a point 10 metre from a certain Babanki-Tungoh man's brick building under construction and from there to join the Westmacourt [sic] Boundary straight ahead. The rest of the boundary (from here) [there] would follow the Westmacourt [sic] Boundary Demarcation towards its terminus near lake Bambili)[24].

On June 22, 1971, J.N. Foncha emphasized that the boundary between the two villages, as was agreed upon by Bafut Chiefs Meeting and subsequently accepted by him and his executive council early in 1965, needed modification. He emphasised that this modification was to amend the Westmacott Decision of 1956 in order to give the Babanki-Tungoh people a piece of land on which they could carry out their local potato market[25].

It was confirmed during fieldwork that while following this boundary description, the Area Surveyor and Lands Officer for Mezam, B.K. Simo, tried to get the S.D.O. and Foncha to relate what was described to the Map Plan No. BD 235 that was obtained from the former ministry of Local Government. On the advice and explanation of the Area surveyor, the Senior Divisional Officer for Mezam "informed all those present that the boundary just described and inspected by the team would be properly surveyed and demarcated by the Area Surveyor, Mezam, during the next dry season [November 1971]".[26] He further re-iterated that while the

S.D.O. would provide security,[27] the two villages (Bambili/Babanki-Tungoh) would supply labour for clearing the boundary line as well as collecting and carrying sand, stones and grave for the erection of the pillars.

Unfortunately, the November 1971, attempted demarcation failed because the Babanki-Tungoh people refused to co-operate. This was lucidly expressed by the Area Surveyor to the S.D.O. in the following words: "I wished to inform you [S.D.O.] that the job has had to be stopped, nay suspended, because the Babanki-Tungoh people have refused to cooperate. When the job started last week, only the Bambili people turned up and continued to work with my team for a couple of days...."[28]. Despite the failure, the Area Surveyor did not relent his efforts as on January 15, 1972, he "advised the Administration and the members of Parliament from this area to educate their people properly on this issue"[29].

This information was taken seriously by B.N. Mukong and S.N. Kindo who constituted the cream of the educated elite in Babanki-Tungoh and Bambili with their respective indigenes and the main pre-occupation of these meetings was peace. On January 16, 1972, Mukong and Kindo met the traditional councillors of Babanki-Tungoh in the Fon's palace[30]. In the meeting, the two parliamentarians emphasised that there was no need fighting over a piece of land and that peace was desperately needed for the socio-economic development of the region. According to the minutes of the meeting: "A member of the council suggested that a conciliation committee could be formed consisting of members from Bambili and Babanki-Tungoh villages to sit and study the situation at the disputed area and to suggest ways of ending the matter[31]."

At the end of the meeting the Fon and the people of Babanki-Tungoh, with the aid of their educated elite, resolved as follows: "firstly, that for the purpose of peace, the Westmacott map showing the boundary should be corrected to work in accordance with his decisions since it was drawn from the said decision, secondly, they maintained that the boundary as decided by the Law Court of 1953 between the two villages could be respected to appease the two villages[32]".

A similar meeting took place in the Bambili palace with the Bambili traditional council, two months later. That one was a briefing and a continuation of the peace initiatives of January 16, 1971.

Chapter Five: Consequences of the Bambili and Babanki-Tungoh Boundary Conflict

According to the meeting, the two traditional councils were to participate fully in the demarcation exercise that was to follow. Unfortunately, when the representatives of the two villages and the surveyor arrived on the field for Demarcation exercise, differences developed between Mukong and Kindo. These differences were highlighted in a report by B.N. Mukong, to the Prefect, Mezam Division. According to Mukong:

> Hon. Kindo made a statement that embarrassed me and kept me wondering as to the role we were playing. I have given you Mukong, here [I] and expect you to give Kindo when we get ahead I [he] maintained and still maintain our roles, should be to bring peace and unity so as to enable government carry on her work and as far as possible try to divorce ourselves from our village loyalties. He, Hon. Kindo, also intimated that he was told by his Fon that the boundary passed through my farm and that as I was his Fon's son, he would allow that my farm [to] be kept out....[33]

This shows that differences occurred amongst these elite although they attempted resolving the boundary differences between their villages.

Although these differences erupted between the two elite, their education and orientation yielded fruit on July 25, 1973, when the Fons of the two villages signed a "non-aggression pact." The pact called on the inhabitants of the warring villages to refrain from any action that could provoke war and the two villages were to co-exist as 'brothers." This attempt bore fruit as "peace" reigned in the sub region for a short while[34].

With the advent of the Farmer/Grazier conflict in the disputed zone on September 18, 1975, the Divisional Officer for Mezam, Oben Peter Ashu, inspected the disputed area. According to letter No. ABA 23/681 of 18 September 1975, Oben Peter Ashu said, amongst other things, that:

> During the inspection, it became clear that the land on which these conflicts are [were] brooding had for long been grazing land until 1973 when some farmers, principally, Francis

Asehetech, encroached into it and undertook farming. [It was] because of the encroachment [that] the Farmer/Grazier Branch took action against Francis Aseheteh in Tubah Bafut Criminal Suit No. 5/73-74....[35]

After a thorough inspection of the grazing land and the farms[36] and fences, Oben Peter Ashu, provided a would-be solution to seven farms and instructed that the farmers should obtain farming permits.[37]

Besides, in the 1990s the boundary conflict cropped up again with a vengeance. This was accompanied by the overhauling of the peace initiative machinery. On January 23, 1993, the Divisional Officer for Tubah, Joseph Tangwa Fover, visited the disputed site and realised that a small fence on the Babanki side had been destroyed. His departure from the disputed area was closely followed by the January 26, 1993, crisis between the two villages. Tangwa wrote the report in the following words:

> The Chairman of Bambili Traditional Council ran to my [his] office in the morning [of 21/1/93] to alarm me [him] of the disturbances between the two villages. I [he] immediately moved to the place to seek confirmation at about 11.30 a.m. I [he] did alarm the SDO who immediately went to the spot on Wednesday the 27 January 1993, and appeased the belligerent, pleaded for peace; the people accepted but did not adhere to their promise... Again I [he] contacted the SDO who took steps and enough forces were put at my disposal to move and stop the fighting. We talked to a hostile crowd of about 2.000 on each side through their leaders[38].

To further concretise the attempt towards peace, Tangwa created a Commission on February 5, 1993 with two principal objectives - to trace and demarcate the boundary, and to arrange for the release of the Babanki-Tungoh people who were "trapped" blocking the road when the January 23, 1993, crisis was raging on. This Commission was to start work on February 15, 1993.

One of the set-backs which the February 15, 1993 Commission faced was that the original map of the disputed area could not be seen; to resolve this, another meeting was held on July, 13, 1993.

During the meeting, the representatives of the two villages traditional councils contacted the Director on the National Geographic Centre in Yaounde and a new map was drawn following the A.B. Westmacott Decision of 1958, the map was presented to the different delegations in the meeting.

During the meeting, the SDO for Mezam, Samuel Sufo, read a letter containing two fundamental issues to the representatives: the SDO should assist in the demarcation exercise should the need arise; and secondly, the interpretation of the map should be done on the field with the assistance of topographic experts. Unfortunately, the Babanki-Tungoh delegation opposed the new map, terming it fictitious and insisted that the original map should be presented for the demarcation exercise.

The Bambili delegation, on the other hand, agreed to accept the final decision to be arrived at by the Administration. The Babanki delegation, according to a confidential note, was stubborn, sulky and arrogant[39]. The Bambili delegation suggested that a boundary should be imposed but their suggestion was rejected by the SDO.[40] Before the meeting ended, the SDO advised that any farming activity in the disputed area should stop with immediate effect; and the SDO said that the Westmacott Decision was partially in conformity with the Appeal Court Decision of July 15, 1955. He instructed the chairman of the traditional councils of the two villages to obtain the said decision from the Tubah Customary Court within a week.

Meanwhile, on August 23, 1993, the SDO for Mezam convened another meeting in the Governor's Conference Hall. This meeting was a follow up of the July 23, 1993, meeting which was held a month earlier. It was attended by the representatives of both villages and some prominent administrators of the division.[41] At the meeting, the SDO presented a map drawn up by the National Geographic Centre in Yaounde based on the final decision taken by A.B. Westmacott in 1958. The Babanki-Tungoh delegation, once more, rejected the map and branded it as faulty. It was nonetheless, resolved by the SDO that the Appeal Court Decision relating to the dispute should be obtained from the Tubah Customary Court. It was also agreed that the Appeal Court Decision, the Westmacott Decision, and the newly drawn map should serve as a working instrument during the demarcation exercise.

The August 23, 1993, meeting was a continuous process in an attempt to resolve the boundary conflict. The intransigency of the Babanki-Tungoh people, coupled with the inherent weaknesses showed by the February 15, 1993 commission led to the formation of another commission on March 28, 1994. This commission was baptised the Mezam Sub-Technical Commission. This commission was aimed at overcoming the weaknesses of the 1993 commission and to demarcate the boundary on the field once and for all. After having met in three sessions under heated debates, the members of the Sub-Technical Committee on April 27, 1994, proceeded to the field. They were accompanied by the Divisional Officers, Tubah[42].

In an attempt to interpret the Westmacott Decision on the field, the two parties disagreed. The Bambili delegation disagreed on the grassy spur immediately after the footpath running from Babanki to Bamenda while the Babanki delegation disagreed on the rocky out-crop on the steep escarpment defining the valley and finally on the cliff-like feature. The Babanki-Tungoh blamed the SDO for supporting the Bambili. Despite the fact that the two parties held divergent views as explained above, the commission did not relent its efforts to attempt the demarcation of the boundary as per Westmacott's description?

According to the attempted demarcation, the following bearings were identified: the lake, the footpath running from Babanki-Tungoh to Bamenda, the grassy spur, the rocky outcrop or the steep escarpment defining the valley, the cliff-like feature, the rolling downland cairn, and the sharp corner just beyond mile post 13[43]. However, this genuine attempt to resolve the boundary conflict ended in a failure due to the uncompromising attitude of the two warring villages and several other reasons.

Meanwhile in Confidential letter Ref. No.0045/ PS.179/134 captioned ANOTHER GENUINE STEP IN A BIT TO SOLVE THE LONG STANDING BAMBILI/BABANKI TUNGOH BLOODY LAND DISPUTE IN TUBAH SUB DIVISION, it said:

> On the 23/8/93, the Senior Divisional Officer for Mezam, Mr. Sufo Samuel presided over a meeting in the North West Governor's Conference hall, in the presence of the representatives of Bambili and Babanki Tungoh villages, aimed

Chapter Five: Consequences of the Bambili and Babanki-Tungoh Boundary Conflict

at demarcating the long standing boundary dispute between the two villages. He presented a newly drawn map by the National Geographic Centre in Yaounde following the final decision taken by A.B. Westmacott in 1958. The Babanki Tungoh delegation vehemently opposed the said map and it was finally resolved by the S.D.O. that the Appeal Court Decision relating to the said dispute, be obtained within a week's time from the Customary Court, which has to serve together with the Westmacott Decision, and newly drawn map, as a working instrument during the demarcation exercise.

In a bit to solve the long standing bloody boundary dispute between Bambili and Babanki Tungoh villages in Tubah Subdivision, the Senior Divisional Officer for Mezam, Mr. Sufo Samuel on the 23rd of August 1993, convened and presided for the fourth time in the North West Governor's Conference Hall, a meeting aimed at demarcating a final boundary; prominent in attendance were:

-Mr. Tamadjo Jeanneaux: D.O. Tubah
-Mr. Nyamboli John Ntombe: Municipal Administrator Tubah Council
-Mr. Loh Mufi Emmanuel: Chairman Babanki Tungoh Traditional Council
-The two traditional rulers of the Belligerent villages
-Notables from the two villages
-Technical Team in charge of the surveys exercise amongst others

The S.D.O. for Mezam started the meeting at about 10:40 and revealed that it was his fourth time to convene the same people for the same purpose, and revealed that as it was earlier arranged, on 13 July 1993, together with the two chairmen of the village traditional councils of the belligerent villages, they contacted the Director of the National Geographic Centre in Yaounde. Since the original map of the disputed area could not be traced, a new one had to be drawn following the A.B.Westmacott Decision of 1958. This was effectively done and after two weeks, the director of the National Geographic centre telephoned for its collection. The said map was collected in three copies and in the presence of the Chairman of the Bambili Traditional Council.

In this light, the S.D.O had a letter read out to the audience. The said letter addressed to him in French by the director of National Geographic Centre informed him of the intensions of his service to assist in demarcation exercise should the need arise, and secondly that the interpretation of the map should be done in the field with the assistance of topographic experts. It was translated into English for the comprehension of all. After this the map was spread for the two parties to cross check. The boundary as defined by the Westmacott Decision was traced with ink. But the Babanki Tungoh delegation vehemently opposed the new map, terming it fictitious and asking that the original map must be presented for the demarcation exercise.

While the Bambili Delegation was more sober and more comprehensive and opting to take to the final decision to be arrived at by the administration, the Babanki Tungoh delegation were looking stubborn, sully and arrogant and one Vizhosha of prisons Bamenda who apparently lacked the least respect for the Senior Divisional Officer for Mezam was most stubborn. While developing this advertent behaviour, the S.D.O regretted that the said land dispute arrived at his level because the Divisional Officer for Tubah was being suspected of taking sides and that if such suspicious should continue, he will be forced to push it at the level of Governor or even further.

In other developments, having realised that A.B.Westmacott in his Decision, was partially in conformity with the Appeal Court Decision of 15TH July 1955 relating to some areas of the boundary, the S.D.O instructed the two chairmen of the Traditional Councils of the two belligerent villages to obtain the said decision from the Tubah Customary Court within the framework of the demarcation exercise. When the said document was being obtained, then the commission will proceed to the disputed area for the demarcation exercise in the company of the two experts to be invited from the National Geographic Centre Yaounde. A suggestion from Bambili delegation to impose a boundary was rejected by the S.D.O. The meeting ended about 11: 48 with no incident. When the S.D.O once more warned that any farming activity in the said area should stop with immediate effect....

The foregoing discussion reveals that various attempts were carried out towards the resolution of the Bambili and Babanki-Tungoh boundary conflict. These attempts included meetings convened by the civil administration, traditional and educational elite, the formation of commissions, and attempted demarcations.

Although the endeavour to demarcate the boundary in 1970, 1971 and 1972,[44] failed, it should be noted that they were genuine attempts at bringing about a peaceful resolution of the conflict. Despite the above attempts, the desire to bring a peaceful solution to the boundary conflict had remained an illusion and figment of the imagination of the people. Several factors accounted for the failure of the various attempts. The following section examines some of the factors responsible for the failure.

E) Why the attempted solutions failed

The reasons for the failure of the attempted solutions are many and varied. First of all the belligerents refused to cooperate in the search for peace. On November 16, 1971, an attempt to demarcate the boundary failed principally because of the intransigence of the Babanki-Tungoh. This attitude was lucidly made by the Area Surveyor and Lands Officer, Kay Simo, on November 16, 1971. In letter Ref. No.x.1.1/vol.11/541 to the Senior Divisional Officer titled

THE BAMBILI Vs BABANKI TUNGOH BOUNDARY DISPUTE: SURVEY AND DEMARCATION OF

"Please refer to my letter No.x.1.1/vol.11/535 of 3rd November, 1971, as well as your letter No.DBA/3000/190 of 4th November, 1971 addressed to the Fons of Bambili and Babanki Tungoh.

2) I wish to inform you that the job has had to be stopped nay suspended, because the Babanki Tungoh people have refused to co-operate. When the job started last week only the Bambili people turned up and continued to work with my team for a couple of days: this was reported to the Administration, and last Thursday, the Bamenda Central Sub - Divisional Officer, Officers of Law and Order, and myself met the Fon of Babanki Tungo at his palace, and he promised to send his men on Monday the 15th of November, 1971.

3) Yesterday, when we met in the field, the Babanki Tungoh people objected to the Westmacott Boundary Decision as shown on Map/Plan No.B.D. 235: they claim that the map is/was not drawn in accordance with the Westmacott Decision.

4) I am, by a copy of this letter, informing the Director of Lands and Surveys and the Secretariat of State for the Interior, of the above position please.

Signed: B.K.Simo

AREA SURVEYOR AND LANDS OFFICER (NORTH) BAMENDA.

Simo's report revealed that the demarcation attempt failed because of the attitude of the Babanki-Tungoh people. The Area surveyor and Land Officer and the other administrators used their initiatives to meet the Fon of Babanki-Tungoh to cooperate in the search for a solution. He accepted and sent his own working team, but when the team arrived, it rejected the new map.

The "foot-dragging" attitude adopted by the Babanki delayed the peace process. Their attitude stemmed from the fact that "... they had paid the usual Land Tribunal deposit and had expected that the Tribunal should go into the matter-that they rejected the Westmacott Administrative boundary which is now being imposed on them...."[45]

It was also held that the Babanki-Tungoh people failed to honour an invitation of the Divisional Officer of Bamenda Central Sub-Division, D.N.N. Pufong. On March 8, 1972, Pufong regretted the situation and in his letter to the Area surveyor and Lands Officer said:

> Unfortunately the chief of Babanki-Tungoh and his councillors failed to turn up, although they actually received my invitation. After a short discussion the two parliamentarians (Hon B.N. Mukong and S.N. Kindo), the Fon of Bambili and his councillors agreed that the Area Surveyor should carry on the erection of the pillars according to the Westmacott decision and if the Babanki-Tungoh community felt dissatisfied they were free to petition to the Govenrment....[46]

It is difficult to just agree that the Babanki people did not want peace. They were rather vigilant over what they considered as justice and what they considered to be their own. No doubt their apathetic, attitude did not go on *ad nauseam*. On the 11th March 2003 a letter was written to the Divisional Officer, Tubah which showed that the Babanki Tungoh were not always trouble shooters as claimed. The letter was titled **Proposals towards a peaceful solution of the protracted (chronic) land dispute between my village (Kedjom Ketinguh) and our brotherly village of Bambili.** In that letter the Babanki people said amongst other things that:

> Sir I would like to start by stating categorically that the Kedjom Ketinguh people are, and have been law-abiding and always would want to stand by their word. This explains why our position on the subject is that the Westmacott decision still remains the only authentic document whose accurate and unbiased interpretation and implementation will achieve the desired goal.

It is quite interesting to see how a people wanted peace and were proposing steps to achieve peace. Even at the time of writing, they were rejecting the commission that had been set up by the

Minister of Territorial Administration in Yaounde. They preferred that a commission should be formed within the two communities that had problems in their common border. Their proposals therefore were lopsided as it can be said as evidenced from the above. As already been said elsewhere in this book, the Babanki people knew their right and stood by it. It can be concluded at this juncture that the failure of the Babanki-Tungoh people to cooperate made the efforts towards peaceful solution ineffective only to an extent. As earlier said they appeared as people who wanted justice and peace in the real sense not coloured peace.

Closely related to the above fact, injunction Order No. 2901.2/C.18.162 of 7 January 1991 was, on the other hand, also violated by the Bambili people. This violation took place on May 7, 1991, when the Bambili started farming in the disputed area. [47] With this action, it became difficult to arrive at a peaceful solution to the boundary conflict between the villages - Bambili and Babanki-Tungoh.

Another reason that could explain the failure of the attempted solutions was the inherent determination of these neighbouring villages to seek revenge. In a letter, Ref. No. E2901.72/165/302, from the sub Divisional Officer, Tubah, Kamga, to the Divisional Officer Mezam on November 16, 1995, Kamga remarked:

> It is clear that peace is a far away cry between the two communities [Bambili/Babanki-Tungoh]. The two are full of reciprocal hatreds at all. The solution doesn't lie in confrontation. They don't take into consideration the serious consequences of preceding conflicts. One even wonders if it is for this strip of land at the summit of the hill that they are fighting so much for, it seems to me that the real problem should be the rivalry between the two neighbours and as long as this sentiment of hatred persists, the risk of confrontation shall remain a permanent phenomenon[48].

If we take the letter of the Divisional Officer with "a grain of salt" then this meant that the two neighbouring villages were not prepared to "bury the hatchet." To further labour the point it supports what we have just commented that the Bababnki Tungoh people could not be completely blamed for the slow peaceful process.

Chapter Five: Consequences of the Bambili and Babanki-Tungoh Boundary Conflict

Furthermore, there have been many groups and individuals involved in the attempts to resolve the conflict. For instance, the colonial administration, civil administration, the Bafut Chiefs, Traditional councils, and educated elite, were involved in the attempts to resolve the conflict. What is more, is that these groups failed to refer to the past or what had already been done in order to better understand the problem. Thus, the independent approaches and varying resolutions which were not coordinated, confused the parties concerned, and negatively affected the peace efforts.

The authentic interpretation and implementation for the Westmacott decision was not successful. The two villages initially did not believe the decision but saw it was the only objective map to hang on. But when a map was drawn, it was opposed by the Babanki. This map was reported to be different from that which was approved by Westmacott. For this and several other reasons the Babanki refused to cooperate.

What is even more is the surveyors charged with the responsibility of demarcation were not the "local" surveyors agreed upon in the 1973 agreement. These surveyors displayed ignorance on the field with regard to identifying the bearings on the grounds as they were on the map. In a petition against the demarcation by the Babanki-Tungoh to the Senior Divisional Officer, the ignorance of the "Yaounde experts" was put in the following words:

> ...we decided to give the said experts a chance and follow them to the lake where the Westmacott decision of 1958, page two, paragraph five, line six clearly stated where the boundary starts from but the experts and the S.D.O.'s party went parallel to and far beyond the lake to take their bearing and from there decided, rather embarrassingly, into Kedjom Tinguh (Babanki-tungoh) where people lived long before the Westmacott decision of 1958[49].

The above-citation portrayed that the surveyors from Yaounde knew little or nothing about the disputed site. To drive home the point, the surveyor, B.N. Mukong, educated elite of Babanki-Tungoh, in a report to the Divisional officer for Mezam, dated January 27, 1972, explained that: "We were at a loss where to go next from the lake. I observed here that the outlet of the lake and its course did not show the true position on the land. As to the next hill, we gave diverse directions. The scale of the map itself is misleading. After several proposals we decided to go to the nearest Fulani huts...."[50] The ignorance displayed by the "experts" made any attempt towards a peaceful resolution far-fetched. The two quotations above show that the technocrats from Yaounde were not conversant with the topography.

The suspicion and scepticism of both parties concerning the objectivity of the civil administration also led to the failure of the efforts towards resolving the boundary conflict. Reports from both parties showed that they doubted the honesty of the sub-Divisional Officer for Mezam, Samuel Sufo, who convened several peace meetings in the governor's Hall. He was, at one time, accused of favouring the Bambili and at another time he was accused of favouring the Babanki-Tungoh. It was also because of similar suspicion that the Babanki withdrew their cooperation during the last demarcation attempt in 1995. When matters came to a head, the S.D.O. for Mezam was taken to court to answer whether he had any powers to change or alter the Westmacott decision which was agreed upon by the two communities.

Another reason why attempts at reaching a negotiated settlement failed was because the two villages continuously made claims and counter claims on the disputed area. This was because the disputed land was very fertile and the two villages depended on this piece of land for their livelihood.

Besides, the two communities have failed to recognise the time-lag between the Westmacott decision and current attempts at demarcation. This means that within this long period, new developments have taken place in this area, and because of this any attempt to hinge at the Westmacott decision, without taking into effect the changes ended up in futility. The area Surveyor and Land Officer called the attention of the Director of Lands and surveys Department, Buea on February 15, 1972, and lucidly made the point in the following words: "It must not be forgotten that [the] survey and demarcation of the Bambili/Babanki Tungoh Boundary today is based largely on the Westmacott [sic] Decision taken in 1958, and it is not surprising that several changes and developments have taken place (on the ground) over this long period of 14 to 15 years."[51]

From the foregoing, it can be said that several attempts were carried out to solve the boundary conflict but they failed for several reasons already mentioned. It is within reason at this juncture to suggest some possible solutions for a permanent resolution of the conflict.

F) Suggested Solutions

Boundary conflicts are as old as human beings and there have always been ways and means adopted towards the resolution of boundary conflicts. At times solutions geared towards the resolution of boundary conflicts have failed. It is because attempted solutions to the Bambili and Babanki-Tungoh boundary conflict have failed that the following section provides some suggestions aimed at solving the boundary conflict.

In the foregoing discussions, it was realised that two commissions were formed with the aim of resolving the boundary conflict.[52] These commissions failed for various reasons. However, from the point of view of concrete institution-building, there is perhaps no better evidence than the creation of a boundary commission. This commission should have a legal backing and a good text of application, preferably an act of parliament or a presidential decree. The commission should comprise the representatives of the state: Minister of Defence, Territorial Administration, Justice as well as the Delegate General in charge of Internal Security, one member nominated by the president, and representatives from the village's concerned.[53] Furthermore, the commission will be charged with the sole responsibility of resolving border conflicts and conflict prevention in the country. It should operate through two technical committees under the Ministry of Territorial Administration.

Besides, it has been evident that attempts have failed because of new developments in topography that have taken place since the Westmacott Decision of 1958. One suggestion to this effect is what Boggs refers to as "simplification of the boundary function." The Bambili and Babanki-Tunogh boundary should be retained but its functions should be reduced to allow it to assume more welcome functions as lines of positive and productive contact. The solution to the Bambili and Babanki-Tungoh boundary conflict might rest in the "simplification of the boundary function"[54].

Besides, contact *per se* is a double-edged sword. Although contact is necessary for boundary conflict, it can also be highly conducive for the reduction of boundary conflict; the solution to boundary conflict could lie in increased contact. It is important to note that boundary conflict is further reduced when there is contact between equal status members of Bambili and Babanki-Tungoh. This is possible because the Bambili and Babanki-Tungoh villages are not separated by any natural features like rivers, mountains and valleys. Thus, their permeability gives room for contact and therefore if it is better handled, it will reduce boundary conflict.[55] More so, the borderlanders ought to understand that interaction with the other side is frequently a matter of necessity and even survival. This is especially true with the two neighbouring villages because there is a pronounced level of economic inter-dependence.

Another suggestion that can bring peace between the two warring villages is to determine who owns the disputed land. It is very difficult to know who owns the piece of land because none of the villages is ready to show convincing evidence - land certificate, Decree No. 76-165 of 27 April 1976 established the conditions for obtaining land certificates. Provision 1 Article 1 of the Decree states "The land certificate shall be official certificates of real property.[56] These two villages do not seem to possess the required land certificate. Therefore, the state has the right to claim the disputed piece of land as state land or National Land. According to part II of Ordinance No. 77-1 of 10 January 1977, "National lands shall of right comprise lands which at the date on which the present Ordinance enters into force, are not classed into the public or private property of the state and other public others."[57]

Based on the above, the government can transform it into a national forest. The government can accelerate agricultural activities in the area by opening up an experimentation farm which will be an affiliate to the Regional School of Agriculture in Bambili or I.R.Z., Bambui, situated some four Kilometres from the area of dispute. By doing this, the two villages will retreat from carrying out acts of aggression in the disputed area. The government can build a school or hospital on the disputed piece of land for the people of both villages.

The government can also encourage "Provincialism." This means that the inhabitants should have a sense of belonging to a province and therefore defend the pride of the province. If the Cameroon nation is a combination of provinces which are made up of clan-lineages, it can safely be said that a problem cannot be solved at a macro-level when the micro-level is ignored. In this case, the inhabitants of the province are compelled to know and carve out certain objectives geared towards the socio-economic development of their province. For instance, the North West Elite Association and the Chiefs Conference should be overhauled in terms of objectives and structure. Above all, a regional organisation charged with the development of the Babanki-Tungoh and Bambili could be created. The organisation, if formed, could be Baptised the Bambili-Babanki Tungoh Development Association. (B.B.A.T.U.D.A.)

Another suggestion is that the media should be used to educate and orientate the two contestants. Most of the time the written and audio-visual press have been instruments of revenge and attacks thereby creating a permanent state of instability. Most privately owned newspapers in Cameroon are more interested in headlines that provoke conflicts than those that resolve them. It is generally believed that conflict starts in the mind before it gets on to the battle field; such newspapers whip up war hysteria.[58]

To those who do not understand the English language, vernacular programmes could be overhauled in Radio Bamenda and other regional radios and broadcasting should be carried out every week.[59] The two villages should have seasoned journalists who will always sensitise the villagers. With such a network, the media will become more responsible to human development and more contributive towards nation-building.

Furthermore, a pastoral approach[60] could be used to resolve the boundary conflict. This could be done if the differences that exist among the denominations are reconciled - the Presbyterian, Baptists and Catholics. If an effort is made to use this method, the various denominations should take two fundamental points into consideration: firstly, they should attempt to go beyond conflict resolution and compromise beliefs and values that stand as obstacles to non-violent peace-making, and secondly, they should keep in mind that their objective is not only to avoid harm or injury but also to organise each community to seek the good of the other by making the adversary a friend.

Conclusion

The Chapter has focused on the consequences of the boundary conflict between the belligerents. It has further examined some of the solutions carried out by various bodies in their attempt to solve the Bambili-/Babanki-Tungoh boundary conflict. The chapter has also advanced some reason why the attempts failed. It has ended up by providing some suggested solutions which if implemented might provide a lasting solution to the boundary conflict in question.

Notes

1. Interview with James Kohfor, Bambili, 24 December 1997. He was born in 1943 in Bambili and lived through the saga of the boundary conflict with Babanki. He bitterly laments that the piece of land on the border which Bambili and Babanki Tungoh are fighting over belongs to Bambili.
2. Ibid.
3. Interview with Shomboin David, Bambili 20 August 1997. He is a Babanki Tungoh elite who confirms that he participated in one of the wars. At the same time he regrets that war is a very bad thing.
4. Fon of Bambili, Awemo II, to the Divisional officer, Tubah Sub-Division, 14 June 1998, 1999 and 2000. Emphasis are mine.
5. Interview with Njousi David Abang, Small Soppo Buea, 3 January 1998. He was an eye-witness and at the same time a student in ENS Bambili. This view was further confirmed by Yembe Faustina, Government High School Bokwango Interviewed, 3 February 1998.
6. President Babanki-Tungoh Cultural Association through the Sub-Divisional Officer Tubah Sub-Division to the governor of the North West Province, 28 May 1991. Emphasis are in the original.
7. Communique written by the Babanki-Tungoh community living in bambili to the Governor of the North West Province, 28 May 1991.

8. Chief of Bambili Developed Teaching Health Community living in bambili to the Governor of the North West Province, 28 May 1991.
9. Ibid.
10. Interview with John Kebeng, Babanki, 24 January 1998.
11. Interview with Tamgwa Helen, Nkwen, Bamenda 20 August, 1997. the informant's occupation is what is popularly called *bayam Sellam* and holds the view that whenever the boundary misunderstanding comes up, they always find it difficult transporting vegetables to the Nkwen and central Bamenda markets.
12. The use of the term "national income" is apt to suggest some association with the revenue of the government. It is important to guard against any confusion of this kind: the national income relates to the total income of the members of a community. The significance of the national income lies precisely in the fact that it is a measure of the economic wellbeing of the community. For more on national income, see Alec Caincross, *Introduction to Economics* (London: Butterworths, 1960), 392-415.
13. "North West (Bamenda Grassfields) why so many Inter-Tribal wars?" *Cameroon Tribune* No. 2468, 9 September 1996, 2.
14. District officer, Bamenda Central Sub-Division to the Senior Divisional Officer, 12 March 1970.
15. Senior Divisional Officer, Mezam Division, H.P. Sone to the Chief of Babanki-Tungoh 20 April 1971.
16. For the Divisional Officer and led by the Assistant Divisional Officer, W.W.L. Liteke, to the Fon of Babanki-Tungoh, 13 October 1980.
17. Ibid.
18. Senior Divisional Officer, Mezam Division H.P. Sone to the chief of Babanki-Tungoh, 20 April, 1971.
19. Divisional Officer, Bamenda Central, D.N.N. Pufong, to the Area Surveyor and Lands Officer Bamenda, 8 March 1972.
20. Ibid.
21. The Bafut Chiefs consisted of the Fons of Babanki-Tungoh, Bambili, Bafut, Mankon and Bafrend (Nkwen).

22. The five points of that meeting were:

Point I: That the area in dispute was allocated to Bambili following the Westmacott boundary of 1956.

Point II: That it is desirable for the Babanki-Tungoh people to have a market for their potatoes about this area, and so a piece of land should be sliced from the bambili land on this area and allocated to Babanki-Tungoh for this purpose. This piece of land will start from the present V.H.F. beacon to a point somewhat Westward to a point 10 meters away from the brick building now being constructed by one Babanki man somewhat Southwards into Bambili land. The rest of the boundary to follow the Westmacott demarcation towards its terminus.

Point III: Bambili and be known as Bambili people or to quit into Babanki-Tungoh. A statement to this effect was to be got from these men which will enable the administration and the Bambili village council to decide whether they should remain or quit.

Point IV: The Surveyor to be accompanied by four representatives of Bafut Clan Area drawn from Bafut West and Bafut East Constituencies. Stones were to be collected by both villages to pile up a various points on the boundary to be visible [sic] readily.

Point V: A copy of the amended Westmacott map with the statement as was agreed upon by the Bafut Clan Chiefs to be given to the chief of each of the two villages.

23. Ibid.

24. Prefectoral Field Inspection Notes Decision and Programme of 22 June 1971.

25. Ibid., (emphasis added).

26. Ibid.

27. By security here, the Area Surveyor meant that armed men and forces of law and order will be used to protect the survey team throughout the period of the demarcation.

28. Area Surveyor and lands Officer to the Senior Divisional Officer, 16 November 1971.

29. Area Surveyor and Lands Officer to the District lands and surveys Department, Buea 15 January 1971.

30. They were parliamentarians for their respective regions. While Mukong was MP for Babanki-Tungoh, Kindo was MP for Bambili.
31. Minutes of the traditional council meeting with Hon. Mukong and Hon. Kindo in the Chiefs Palace in Babanki-Tungoh to find out a peaceful solution to the Babanki-Tungoh/Bambili boundary dispute, 16 January 1972, 2-4.
32. Ibid., 3-4.
33. B.N. Mukong, through the Sub-Prefect, Bamenda to the Prefect, Mezam Division, 17 January 1972 (emphasis added).
34. The Bambili/Babanki-Tungoh *entente* signed by the Fons on 25 July 1973.
35. Oben Peter Shu to Ardo Jacky of Sabga; John Gwemo, Joseph Ngoh, Ndofor Mayeh, Francis Janga, Mathias Gwe, Sam Toh Ndong, Teku Ndong and Franices Aseheteh (all from Babanki-Tungoh), 18 September 1975.
36. Ibid.
37. One of the causes of the boundary dispute between Bambili/Babanki-Tungoh was the scarcity of arable land which has been taken over by the cattle graziers. If the S.D.O. for Mezam in 1975 inspected the area under dispute and attempted solving the problem, we could safely say that this was an attempt towards the resolution of this conflict.
38. (Emphases added). A report written by the S.D.O. Tubah, Tangwa Joseph on 19 February 1993.
39. Confidential note No. 00456/Ps/179 TA.1.
40. Ibid.
41. Amongst those who attended the meeting were: Divisional Officer Tubah, Tamandjo jeanneux, the Municipal Administrator, Tubah Rural Council, Nyamboli John Mfombe, Chairman Bambili Traditional Council, Awemo David Ndifor, Chairman Babanki-Tungoh Traditional Council, Loh mufi Emmanuel, the two traditional rulers of the belligerent villages; Notables from the two villages and a Technical Team in charge of the surveys exercise.
42. Report written by the Mezam Sub Technical Commission of 1994.
43. Ibid.

44. On the 25 of March 1970, the first attempted demarcation was carried out on this boundary by the civil administration, the second demarcation attempt took place on 3 April 1970, the third took place on 6 November 1971.

45. Director of Lands and Surveys, West Cameroon, A.L. Anyangwe to the Secretary General, Second attempt took place on 3 April 1970, the third took place on 16 November 1971.

46. Divisional Officer, D.N.N. Pufong to the Area Survey and Lands Officer, 8 March 1972.

47. Cited in a communiqué from the Rents Office, Kedjom Ketinguh, to the Chairman Bambili/Babanki-Tungoh Commission of inquiry, 27 July 1991.

48. Sub Divisional Officer to the Senior Divisional Officer of Mezam, Bamenda, 15 November 1995. (Translation is mine).

49. Chairman of Babanki-Tungoh to the Senior Divisional Officer, 19 April 1995. Interview with Lucas Atanga, Bamenda 14 December 1997. He works with the Provincial Delegation of Lands and Surveys and was present during the 1992 demarcation. He confirmed the view held by B.N. Mukong.

50. Ibid., (emphases added).

51. Area Surveyor and Lands Officer (North), Bamenda to the Director Lands and survey Department, Buea, 15 February 1972. (Emphasis added).

52. These two Commissions were the 1991 Commission and the 1994 Mezam Sub Technical Committee.

53. For more on boundary commission see Asiwaju, *Artificial Boundaries*,. 9.

54. Asiwaju, "The Global Perspective, Border management" in *partitioned Africans*, pp. 240-243, Boggs, *International Boundaries: A Study of Boundary*, cited in Asiwaju, *Artificial Boundaries*, 11.

55. Raymond W. Mack, *Race Class and Power* (New York: American Book company, 1963), 376, Asiwaju, "Problem Solving Along African Borders: The Nigerian-Benin Case" in Martinez Oscar J. (ed.) *Across Boundaries: Transborder Interaction in Camparative* perspectives (Texas, U.S.A.: University of Texas Press, 1986), 189.

56. [Jack Peter] *Land Tenure and State Lands* (Yaounde: Imprimerie Natioanle, 1981), 99.

57. Ibid., 34.

58. For more on how media could be used to resolve conflict see George Ngwane *Settling Disputes in Africa: Traditional bases for Conflict Resolution* (Yaounde: Bamukor, 1996), 34 - 35.

59. Ibid

60. By pastoral approach we mean a practical programme to meet with the defence of the value of the right to property - land, at the same time highlighting the moral dimensions of the choices that the faithful may follow to live in peace again within these communities. This approach might consist largely of instructions on church government and discipline. For more on pastoralism see R. Kucher "Pastoral Epistles" in *Catholic encyclopedia* (Vol. x, 1981), 1976 - 1084, Gam Chiatu Oliver, "A Pastoral Approach to Conflict Resolution" (Unpublished B.A. Degree (Theology) Dissertation, St. Thomas Aquinas Major Seminar Bambui - Cameroon (Affiliate of the Pontifical Urban University, Roma 1997), pp. 22 - 32, Yuntenwi Isidore, "The Inception and Growth of Christianity in Bambili village, 1 922 - 1 993" (Unpublished B.A. Degree (History) University of Buea, 1997), 21 -38.

Chapter Six
General Conclusion

Boundaries and borders are very much ubiquitous in our daily lives. More often than not we come across borders and sometimes we are either ignoring them or embracing them. Even in our houses there are boundaries; in classrooms; in churches and on highways. The Colonial frontiers were new in the sense that they came to bifurcate several common ethnic groups and were also determined by distant and sometimes ill-informed negotiators and in some cases settled by using a ruler and a compass alone. This laid the foundation of future problems with regard to African boundaries.

The boundaries were never adapted to the African needs. Even ethnic divisions appear to have exerted little influence on the colonial masters who were soaked in the ethic of superiority and felt that they were bringing civilization to a people who had been refused the gates of the Garden of Eden and who were best hewers of wood and drawers of water. Because of their imposing nature in Africa South of the Sahara, the Africans only stood up to discover that they were divided into two. For example, the Ewe people were divided between Gold Coast (Ghana) and Togo. Some Yorubas lived in Dahomey while the majority of their kinsmen lived in Nigeria. The partition of the indigenous groups has posed lots of problems in post independent Africa, some leading directly to boundary conflicts. Inside some of these states which have remained for most of the time fragile, there have been inter-ethnic boundaries. In Cameroon a classic example of an area that has been rife with inter boundary conflicts has been the North West Region of Cameroon popularly known in colonial historiographical parlance as the Bamenda Grassfields.

The historiography of the Bamenda Grassfields has been subjected to various types of studies. These studies include among others missionary, sociological, anthropological and historical. But very few have gone beyond hostile inter-chiefdom relations. This study has attempted to fill that gap. It has focused on boundary conflicts in Bamenda Grassfields in general and the Bambili and

Babanki-Tungoh boundary conflict from c.1955 to 2005 as a case study. Generally, the Bamenda Grassfields is mostly occupied by the set of people whose oral traditions traces them to have come from Ndobo in Northern Cameroon. They arrived in this region in waves following the Jihads of Uthman Dan Fodio which displaced them in Northern Cameroon.

By that fact we could say that most of the Bamenda Grassfields is inhabited by people of common origin although, and may be of different ancestry. In the 1990's a period of political liberalization and democratization in Cameroon and Africa at large, and also a period which the incumbent rulers of states were not anxious to lose power, the government apparently following the World Bank rhetoric of protecting minority peoples invented new forms of citizenship. In that light some people became known as the sons and daughters of the soil while others were branded as strangers even when they were all the citizens of the same country. In that scenario the whole political rigmarole of sons and daughters backfired in the Bamenda Grassfields. One of the ways in which there was this backfiring was reflected in the inter-societal cleavages which were exhibited in the boundary conflicts in the region. But what were the dynamics that ignited these boundary misunderstandings in the region?

The boundary conflicts in the Bamenda Grassfields are caused by geographical, political, social and economic factors. From the study, these causes reveal that the population of the ethnic groups in this region has increased considerably (and it is increasing) against the background of degenerating arable land. The situation is compounded and complicated by the arrival of the Fulanis and their cattle. The Fulani cattle needed grazing land but it has been unfortunate because the land has been limited and the graziers are always at daggers drawn with the indigenous population over arable land. The causes also reveal that boundary conflicts in this region are a product of the ever growing centralised state formation characterised by ambitious, expansionist and hegemonistic rulers. Finally, these causes explain why the Bamenda Grassfields is rife with boundary conflicts.

After situating the place and dynamics of the boundary conflict in the Bamenda Grassfields in general, the book took up the Bambili and Babanki Tungoh as a case study. If the region was made up of sons and daughters of the soil in a macro form, there was no other area in the region that was more of brothers and sisters historically than Bambili and Babanki Tugoh. Their only difference it would appear takes its rise from their common boundary which has preoccupied their relations for more than four decades. In the course of the research, it is evident from the work that the boundary conflict between the two villages stems, to a large degree, from economic imperatives. This is because of the fertility of the disputed piece of land, and secondly, the two villages carry out their daily economic activities in the disputed region.

Furthermore, the work envisaged to investigate who was the owner of the disputed area (land). The land under dispute has been claimed by the two warring villages. The Bambili claim that the land is theirs since they were the first to arrive in the area. On the other hand, the Babanki-Tungoh people claim the disputed land on the ground that the Bambili did not effectively occupy the land.[1] However, if it is accepted that the Bambili first arrived the disputed area it can be argued with a certain degree of probability that the land belongs to the Bambili. This could be valid if we take traditionally the way land ownership was carried out before colonialism. The advent of colonial administration gave a twist to land ownership and it would appear that colonial hangovers like the administrators has hung very tightly to the tail coats of colonial land ownership.

According to the colonial administration what could make the claims of Bambili and/or Babanki Tungoh authentic is the possession of a Land Certificate as spelt out in Decree No. 76/165 of 27 April 1976 which showed the conditions for obtaining Land certificates.[2] The land certificate, in Cameroon is the only document to claim land. It further stipulates that without a Land Certificate, the disputed land becomes state land. What is more with regard to the Babanki and Bambili conflict is their inability and/or unwillingness to produce a land certificate which can legally give them the land. It is therefore evident that none of the warring villages possesses a land certificate and consequently the disputed land should become state land.

The state (government) could use the land by planting forests, "natural forests" or open up an experimental farm which can remain an affiliate to the Regional School of Agriculture, Bambili or I.R.Z.

Bambui. If the government finds it impossible to plant the forests, it could apply what Boggs calls the "simplification of boundary function" which means that the boundary could be demarcated with possible adjustments. This is because there have been new developments in the disputed area since the conflict began in the 1950s. The work contends that to determine who owns the land it would be imperative for the traditional rulers to resort back to the traditional ways of settling boundary misunderstandings rather just becoming prisoners of colonial land certificates.

The work also set out to investigate who were the motivators of the boundary conflict between the Bambili and Babanki-Tungoh. It is evident from the work that the educated elite of the two villages have contributed to the outbreak of the conflict. Furthermore the work set out to answer the question: what made the two villages different? From the study, it is evident that from the beginning the two villages shared many common features and interacted in several domains-social and economic. The two villages intermarried and participated in cultural ceremonies. Economically, they shared the same treasury and market activities. Since they were dynamic societies, they were subjected to internal and external upheavals with the consequent periodic expansion of the territorial framework. This manifested itself in boundary conflicts which consequently made the two villages different.

Various attempts were made by various bodies to resolve the boundary conflict. Some of 'the bodies included amongst others colonial/civil administrators and legal experts. Some of the attempts included the creation of commissions, attempted demarcations and meetings convened by the civil administration, educated/traditional elite. These endeavours failed because of various reasons - the lack of consensus between the two villages, the difficulties in demarcating the disputed area, the lack of technocrats in the sphere of surveyor and the egoistic, expansionist and hegemonistic tendencies of the two villages and above all the different interpretations which the two communities attached to the Resident, judgment, Westmacott in 1958. Apparently at a tug of war situation the work has attempted to give some palliatives which if implemented the boundary conflict could be laid to rest.

It has therefore been suggested that the government could take the land as state land; secondly, settlement patterns could be investigated to better know who needs the disputed land most. To accomplish this suggestion, population statistics of the two warring villages could be compiled. Thirdly, the disputed area could be demarcated using Bogg's phrases of the "simplification of boundary function" or the government can forcibly demarcate the boundary according to her whims and caprices which will only enhance peace in the region. Fourthly, the commissions could be overhauled and endorsed in the state constitution. It could be directly placed under the Ministry of Territorial Administration. Finally, the pastoral approach could be used paying attention to justice and forgiveness. These and other suggestions could put an end to the long outstanding boundary conflict.

Understandably, the range, complexity, and nature of boundary misunderstandings in the Bamenda Grassfields have made it difficult if not impossible for any logical conclusions to be made because some of the actors were not there; some who were present were not willing to talk out the facts. Some of the key files were burnt at the orders of the Governor of the Northwest Province, Guillaume Nseke, in mid 1980s. What I have tried to do is to work dispassionately on the material available.

Man remains the architect of his destiny. The long outstanding boundary conflict that has rocked the belligerents since the 1950s and has led to enormous costs would have been resolved. Since naturally, man's activities are teleguided by greed and ambition, the boundary conflict is going on *ad nauseam*. History has revealed that boundary/land disputes have remained a thorny issue since time immemorial and the Bambili-Babanki-Tungoh boundary conflict is no exception.[4] This work has attempted to show a way by which the boundary conflict could be resolved. The work has also shown that even if people share the same characteristic features and come from the same place greed and competition over resources is likely to create everlasting conflict.

Finally, this study has been a prolegomenon, a preliminary observation and description, an invitation to a longer and nay, a tedious intellectual journey. May its substantive hypothesis be checked and expanded, boundary conflicts in itself be given closer scrutiny and a comparative approach undergone by other scholars elsewhere in the region. In other to do this I have suggested what I have not been able to finish within the time available at my disposal to which our attention must now turn.

The Unfinished Task and New Directions towards Research on the Subject under Study

As I indicated in the beginning, this work was an ambitious project. I started off by examining generally the boundary conflicts in the Bamenda Grassfields. It appeared that if I were to continue in that line the project would have gone on without an end. I decided to narrow the project to Babanki-Tungoh. The unfinished task therefore, which may interest others, is the study of boundary conflicts in zones to which I did not pay enough attention including: Nkwen and Bambili; Bali-Nyonga and Chomba and Widikum; Mbesa and Oku. An aspect of these conflicts not directly linked to boundaries is the hostile relations between the Bambui and the Funge. Rigorous empirical work is needed in these areas, including interviews with actors and actresses who lived the experiences and those who only heard about the events.

The National Archives in Buea as well as the Bamenda Provincial Archives are important stops for researchers. In addition, the archives in the Divisional offices contain copious and plenteous material relating to boundary conflicts. It is also incumbent on any researcher to locate human archives as much as possible. Such persons are fast becoming endangered species and it will do a lot of good for intellectual posterity if their stories are documented and kept.

Notes

1. Interview with Joseph Buteh, Bambili, 10 October 1997. Interview with Chumboin Pius, Babanki-Tungoh 23 December 1997. The two informants held divergent views with regard to who owns the piece of land. It was obvious because the two came from the two warring factions and as a result they will be supporting their various villages.

2. [Jack Peter] *Land Tenure and State Lands* (Yaounde: Imprimerie Nationale, 1981), 98.

3. Ibid.

4. Some of the outstanding boundary disputes that have affected societal relations include: The Mali-Burkina Faso border war over the mineral - rich gacher strip in 1985, the Lybya-Chad border armed conflict over the Aouzour strip in 1988, The Cameroon-Nigeria border dispute over the Bakassi Peninsula. For more see Asiwaju, *Artificial Boundaries*, p. 12, Jusful Wanandi "The International Implications of Third World Conflict: A Third world Perspective in Christoph Bertram (ed.) *Third World Conflict and International Security* (London: Macmillan, 1982), 17, Matinez (ed.) *Across Boundaries*

Appendices

Appendix I

TUBAH, le 26 FEV. 1996
Le Sous-préfet de l'Arrondissement de TUBAH
A
Monsieur le Préfet du
Département de la Mezam

-BAMENDA-

Ref.no.E29 01.2/10.55/215

OBJET: Conflit frontier Bambili-Babanki

J'ai l'honneur de vous rendre compte de ce que les Bambili et les Babanki s'affrontent depuis le week-end dernier sur le terrain qui fait l'objet de dispute entre les deux villages voisins. En dépit de des nombreuses actions menées pour essayer d'éviter tout affrontement arme, les deux ennemis traditionnels ont plutôt préférer la guerre. A l'heure qu.il est le bilan est a déjà triste: des morts et de nombreux blessé ont été enregistres de part et d'autre.

En effet, le Jeudi, 22 Février 1996, j'ai reçu à mon bureau deux émissaires dépêches par le Fon de Bambili pour m'informer que les Babanki ont attaque ses sujets et incendie 3 maisons dans la matinée de Jeudi. Pue de temps après le chef du quartier Chuku a Babanki nous rejoins et m'a rapport lui également que les Bambili les ont attaques dans le mâtiné et que un des leur a été sérieusement blessé.

Aux deux protagonistes, j'ai prêché la paix, et leur ai promis de faire une descente sur les lieux dans l'après-midi pour m'enguerir de la situation.

A 15 heures, je me suis rendu au village Chuku en compagnie du commandant de la Brigade de Gendarmerie de Tubah, de deux Gendarmes et d'un élément du commissariat Spécial. Sur notre chemin, nous sommes passes au Centre de santé de Bambili ou nous avons été informes que deux blesses ressortissants de Bambili, ont été transportes dans ledit établissement. Il s'agit des nommes Patrick Tanui et Wanki Awongu. Nous avons également trouve a 3 corners Bambili des émissaires du Fon qui venaient nous informer qu'un ressortissant Bambili, le nomme Nchumoh, notable la chefferie, a été fait prisonnier par les Babanki.

Arrive au village Chuku, nous avons tenu une séance de travail avec les chefs des quartiers Chuku et Kwighe et leur entourage. Nous avons plaide une fois de plus pour la paix et avons libéré le ressortissant Bambili fait prisonnier que nous avons ramené a Bambili. Nous avons rendu visite au ressortissant Babanki blesse dans la matinée, le nomme Aseh Francis, que se trouvait en traitement chez un guérisseur traditionnel et a qui nous avons conseille de se rendre plutôt a l'Hôpital.

Parallèlement, nous avons convoque les responsables des deux villages a une réunion le Vendredi a 14 heures, réunion qui a eu pour ordre du jour la recherché des voies et moyens consensuels pour parvenir a un arrêt des hostilités.

Au cours de cette rencontre j'ai essayes de persuader les deux parties sur le fait qu'au stade actuel de leur conflit, il était inutile de s'affronter car, le problème avait déjà connu un règlement au niveau de la justice et qu'il ne restait qu'a mettre en pratique la décision qui avait été arrêtée.

Il est apparu des interactions des uns et des autres que si tous reconnaissant que l'affaire a été réglée par un jugement rendu par Westmacott en 1958, chacun cependant a sa propre interprétation de cette décision de justice. D'où le conflit. Ils n'ont mêmes pas hésite à déclarer qu'il y aurait deux décisions de Westmacott.

J'ai assure les deux parties sur le fait qu'il ne saurait y avoir deux Westmacott, mais qu'il s'agirait plutôt d'une différence au niveau de l'interprétation. Je leur ai promis que l'Administration, comme par le passé, veillera a ce que cette décision soit appliquée et qu'elle s'impose a tous pour que ce vieux conflit puisse prendre fin. Je les ai invites à faire prévue de patience et de tolérance en attendant la matérialisation du jugement de Westmacott. J'ai demande a tous de garder le statuquo, et ai programme une descente sur les lieux avec les deux délégations le Lundi, 26 Février a 7h00. Le but était de voir les positions des uns et des autres sur le terrain, d'identifier les victimes et les dégâts subis lors des regrettables incidents des derniers jours, et d, appeler tout le monde a la tolérance mutuelle.

Toutes les deux parties, nous ont semble être détermines à tout faire pour que le calme revienne et rendez-vous a été pris pour Lundi matin a 7h00.

Mais fort curieusement, il m'a été rapport le Samedi matin à 8h00 qu'au petit matin, les Babanki ont encore incendie quelques maisons des Bambili situées très loin de la zone dite litigieuse. L'informateur qui était un émissaire du Fon de Bambili a plaide pour une descente urgent sur les lieux afin d'éviter une riposte de la part des Bambili. J'ai ors réuni mon état-major et a 11 heures nous nous mis en route pour ces lieux en passant par Banja. Nous avons constate trios cases incendiées, toutes situées sur la zone qui avait était le terrain de bataille la fois passé. A distance nous avons vu las Babanki de leur cote armes. Ils ont fait partir quelques coups de feu a notre arrive, en signe d, alerte, et tous ont replie.

De retour de la, j'ai demande au Fon de Bambili de continuer à calmer ses populations afin que nous puissions éviter un affrontement. On n'avait jusque la enregistre aucun dégât corporel, ni perte en vies humaines, car les cases incendiées n'étaient pas habitués. J'ai promis que tout sera mis en œuvre pour une intervention rapide des forces de l'ordre pour neutraliser les deux camps.

Mais contre toute attente, j'ai été informe a 20 heures, que l'hôpital d, Arrondissement de Tubah avait reçu cinq blesses originaires de Bambili dont un décès constate un décès.

Je me suis aussitôt rendu a L'Hôpital pour me rendre compte, qu'après avoir quitte les lieux vers 14h30, les Bambili ne s'étaient pas croises les bras La guerre s'était au contraire déclenchée, et se poursuit jusqu'ici. Le bilan s'alourdit chaque jour avantage.

La réunion prévue ce jour à 7h00 n'a pas eu lieu faute de participants. En ce qui concerne les victimes du coté des Babanki, il ne nous est pas possible d'en avoir une idée. La communication n'est pas possible d'en avoir une idée. La communication n'est pas possible avec eux. La route Bambili- Ndop est barrée toutes les nuits et un contrôle strict y a cours afin d'empêcher les Babanki résident en ville ou Big Babanki à monter pour donner le renfort. Toutefois les informations obtenues font état de plusieurs blesses et déjà deux mortes.

La vie a Bambili à cesse depuis d'être normale. On est en état guerre. A three corners le War office a été à ménage. Toutes les boutiques sont fermes. Toutes les mondes est appelles a soutenir l'effort de guerre allogènes comme autochtones. Les quêtes sont organisées, et les paniers vont de port à porte. Les étudiants en souffrente, car même les restaurants ne sont pas epergnes. C'est la mobilisation générale il doit en être de même du cite Babanki, bien que n'ayons pas assez d'informations. C'est donc la guerre ouverte entre les Bambili et les Babanki a l'heure qu'il est.

Il m'apparait urgent d'organise rune intervention des forces de l'ordre sur les lieux. Pour ce qui est des moyens nécessaires, j'ai eu à poser le problème au chairman Traditional Council de Bambili ainsi qu'a une élite de Babanki résident en ville. Leur réaction est donc attendue. Une telle intervention doit avoir lieu le plus tôt possible pour éviter la catastrophe.

Je vous saurai gré des dispositions que vous jugerez utiles de prendre à cet effet.

Compte vous sera rendu le plus tôt possible de toute évolution de la situation. /-

Appendix II

ARRETE
No.00210/A/MINAT/DOT/ADOA/SCA
Portant approbation du procès-verbal du 9 mai 2000 de la Commission Nationale pour le règlement du litige de Limites Territoriales entre les Communautés BAMBILI et BABANKI-TUNGOH (Département de la MEZAM)

LE MINISTRE DE L.ADMINISTRATION TERRITORIALE,

VU la Constitution;

VU le Décret No. 72/349 du 24 juillet 1972 portant Organisation Administrative de la République du Cameroun et ses modificatifs subséquent;

VU le Décret No.78/322 du 3 aout 1978 portant institution des commissions pour le règlement des litiges relatives aux limites des circonscriptions administrative et des unités de commandement traditionnel

VU le Décret No.97/205 du 7 décembre 1997 portant organisation du Gouvernement;

VU le Décret No.97/207 du 7 décembre 1997 portant formation du Gouvernement, modifie par le Décret No.2000/51 du 18 Mars 2000;

VU le Décret 98/147 du 17 juillet 1998 portant organisation du Ministère de l'Administration Territoriale;

VU le Procès verbal du 9 mai 2000 de la commission Nationale pour le règlement du litige de limites territorial entre les Communautés BAMBILI Et BABANKI-TUNGOH, Département de la MEZAM

VU les nécessités de maintien de l'ordre

ARRETE:

ARTICLE 1er-Est approuve le procès verbal du 9 mai 2000 de la Commission Nationale pour le règlement du litige de limites territoriales entre les Communautés BAMBILI et BABANKI-TUNGOH.

ARTICLE 2- La limite entre les Communautés BAMBILI et BABANKI-TUNGOH est sur les points litigieux, précise ainsi qu'il suit:

Le point de base et situe sur le Pic entre le Lac BAMBILI et le Lac DESSECHE, point 1 de coordonnées X =0637898;Y=0655627; Z=2494.

Du point 1, la limite suit la ligne traversant une plantation d, Eucalyptus, propriété privée de Monsieur NSE jusqu'a point BL 7 situe au début du talus (falaise) point 2 de coordonnes X=0640611; Y=0660814; Z1974.

Du point 2, la limite suit la falaise jusqu'a sa fin point BKT6/BL 8, POINT 3 de coordonnées X=0641473; Y=0661556; Z=1988.

Du point 3 la limite suit la ligne droite jusqu'a BL 11/BKT 9 sur la route allant de BAMENDA a KUMBO, point de coordonnées X=0643105;Y=0664627; Z=1841

Le document utilise est la Carte dessinée par le Service Département du Cadastre de la MEZAM a BAMENDA, plan No. MZ 2365 échelle 1/15000 des 6 et 7 juin 1996 par NDIP Andrew.

ARTICLE 3- LES exploitations situées sur la zone litigieuse restent la propriété de leurs légitimes détenteurs indépendamment de la trace de la limite. Toutefois, les exploitants dont la propriété viendrait à passer sous le contrôle du groupement voisin doivent accepter l'autorité du Chef de Groupement territorialement compétent, lequel est tenu pour sa part de respecter et protéger leur droit de propriété

ARTICLE 4- les contrevenants aux dispositions de la présente arête seront sanctionnes conformément aux textes en vaguer.

ARTICLE 5-Le préfet du Département de la MEZAM, et le Sous-préfet de l'Arrondissement de TUBAH sont charges, chacun en ce qui le concerne, de l'application de la présente arête qui sera enregistre, publie et communiqué partout ou besoin sera/-

YAOUNDE, le 16 AOUT 2000
Ferdinand KOUNGOU EDIMA

AMPLIATIONS:
PRC
PM
MINAGRI
MINUH (Dir.Domaines)
MINUH (Dir.Cadastre)
GOUVERNEUR NORD-OUEST/ BAMENDA
PREFECTURE DE LA MEZAM
PARTIES INTERESSEES
CHRONO
ARCHIVES

APPENDIX III

Fon's Palace, Kedjom Ketinguh
Tubah Sub Division
26-08-2000

The District Officer,
Tubah Sub Division.

Sir,

INJUNCTION ORDER ON CHURCH CONSTRUCTION SITE IN KEJOM KETINGUH

With reference to your injunction Order No. 18, 2005 of 4th July 2005 stopping further work on a Presbyterian Church house being constructed in my village, I want to state as follows:

1) The injunction order is at the request of the Fon of Bambili who had earlier placed a traditional injunction on the said plot he claims (I guess) should be on Bambili land.

2) It may have been necessary for the D.O to visit the site before taking a decision. Things may have been a lot different.

3) A church building just as the MTN and Orange antennae are public utilities and I consider that these do not need to be identified

as belonging to X or Y. This explains why I did not register any protest when the antennae were planted though both of them are in Kejom Ketinguh village (land)

4) The church house under construction is at last 1 km away from the Kejom Ketinguh Kiephen market and about the same distance from Mr. Ngahbuen's land (towards Bambili) and which was demarcated by your office and approved to be on Kejom Ketinguh land. I now find it difficult to understand the imaginary boundary line between our two villages.

5) Mr. Abety Peter is building presently on disputed land while the Bambili people are building a market on the same disputed area. Why have these two projects not been stopped? It is but just fair that injunction orders from your very office be put on these 2 projects being carried out by the Bambili people.

Finally, Mr. District Officer, I pray you to evoke the injunction order so that work can continue on God's House. After all, the said piece of land is right inside Kejom Ketinguh village. I continue to state emphatically that my people are peace loving and law abiding and hate anything that will interfere with the peace that now reigns between our two neighbouring villages. As I have seen elsewhere, a stitch in time saves nine.

It is also necessary to remind you here that when the Prime Minister last visited the North West Province, the Fons of the Province unanimously decided that all land disputes in the Province be settled using only colonial maps. For your information, my people have all along respected the Westmacott decision, copies of which are in both villages and in your office. An agreement was even signed to that effect and I here furnish you with a photocopy. If my brothers of Bambili village want to turn their backs on this agreement, then there is no option other than to revert to the 1913 map that clearly defines the boundary between the two villages.

Signed,
Fon Viyouh Nelson Sheteh
(Fon Kejom Ketinguh)

Cc
The S.D.O. for Mezam
For information and intervention

Appendix IV

BAMBILI-BABANKI TUNGO LAND DISPUTE AN AGREEMENT SIGNED ON 25TH JULY 1973

WE the undersigned Fons of Bambili and Babanki-Tungo do hereby accept the Westmacott Decision on our existing land dispute as being the only and authentic administrative decision that can put to an end our long standing dispute.

-WE are fully prepared to collaborate with the team of surveyors that will be sent by the Administration to trace and define the boundary between our people. Our people will carry stones and send for the successful accomplishment of this task.

-IN addition we will accept the technical advice that will be given us by the surveyors to demarcate the boundary. We will collaborate with the Native Authority surveyor who drew the maps which are now in our possession.

-FINALLY we are going to request our people to refrain from carrying out any activities on the supposed disputed area until the final demarcation is made by the Survey team. Any person encroaching on this disputed area will be penalised by the Administration. We are fully prepared to maintain peace and respect each other's interest on this area until the final demarcation of this boundary.

Dated at BAMENDA this 25th DAY OF JULY, 1973

Signed:

Chief of Bambili	Chief of Babanki-Tungoh
Witness: Lands Officer	Witness: NGONGE SONE
	For Administration
Witness: S.N.KINDO	Witness: B.N.MUKONG

Appendix V

Ref. No.E29.03/165/503,
Divisional Office, Tubah Sub Division,
Mezam Division,
10 April 2007.

The Senior Divisional Officer, Mezam Division-BAMENDA

Subject: **IMPLEMENTATION OF MINISTERIAL ARRETE NO.00210/A/MINAT/DOT/SDOA/SCA OF 6/8/00 FOR THE DEMARCATION OF THE BOUNDARY BETWEEN BAMBILI AND BABANKI TUNGOH**

I have the honour to transmit to you for your perusal and further necessary action, Letter dated 25th March 2007 from the Fon of Bambili on the subject matter above.

Cognizant of the recent happenings in Bali and Bawok, it would be very timely if the boundary between Bambili and Babanki Tungo is finally actualized as per the Ministerial Arrete quoted in the above letter in a bid to pre-empt any skirmishes between these two villages.

DIVISIONAL OFFICER-TUBAH
Nkwenti Jacob Musima

Cc
-The Fon of Bambili

Appendix VI

THE BAMENDA-BABANKI-TUNGOH LAND DISPUTE THE SUBMISSIONS OF THE BAMBILI DELEGATION TO THE NATIONAL COMMISSION CHARGED WITH THE SETTLEMENT OF INTER-VILLAGE DISPUTE ON 23 FEBRUARY 2000 AT BAMENDA.

Your Excellency The Hon Minister of Territorial Administration
Your Excellency The Governor of the North-West Province
The Senior Divisional Officer, Mezam
The Divisional Officer, Tubah Subdivision
Members of the national commission charged with the settlement of inter-village Dispute
The Forces of Law and Order
The Fon of Babanki-Tungo
Distinguished Ladies and Gentlemen

Brief History

1)the present inhabitants of Babanki-Tungoh broke off from the present Big Babanki and is one of the most recent migration because of a chieftaincy succession dispute between two princes. The break away faction wandered about without a home. The Fon of Bambili and the Fon of Bamessing took pity on them and each village ceded land to allow them settle. Little did our fon know that he was creating a future problem for his successors and his people. There was no intension at the time either expressed or implied that the Fon of Bambili intended to continually cede land as the new settlers need and population increased. This would have been impossible since land is limited. Soon after the Babanki Tungo settled they started expanding very rapidly and soon exceeded the limits which had been allocated to them by the Fon of Bambili. They also expanded to other directions and started having problems with other neighbouring villages e.g. Bamessing, Balikumbat, Bambui.

Resort to Peaceful Settlement of The Dispute

2) Our Fon being a peace-lover, took the matter to the Customary courts (Lower and Appeal Courts) and then to the Administration. The then Colonial Divisional Officer, Mr. R.C. Ward decided the matter following natural features, namely Tuentueng stream which the Bambili people reluctantly accepted.

3) The Babanki Tungoh people however appealed against the decision of Mr. R.C. Ward to Resident Mr. Westmacott (the equivalent of governor now) who reviewed the matter and even though he agreed with R.C.Ward, he was sympathetic with the Babanki-Tungoh who had illegally occupied Bambili land and would have been ordered to move to their side or stay and pay their taxes to the Fon of Bambili, only on the grounds that whereas some Babanki Tungoh people would be affected, no single Bambili person would be required to make a choice.

One of the reasons why the Babanki Tungo people have continued to violate all injunction orders put in place by the administration and the Christian Justice and Peace favour. Your Excellencies, if you will be able to visit the disputed area, you will be able to see for yourselves that the Babanki Tungo people have carried out extensive farming on the disputed area. We pray you, Your excellencies, that they should not be rewarded a second time for their stubbornness.

4) The Fon of Bambili appealed against the decision of the Resident Mr.A.B.Westmacott to the commissioner of the then Southern Cameroon; but lost to be precise, the commissioner ruled that the government could not interfere with the Resident's judgement. Not being able to go any further, the Fon of Bambili accepted the decision of Resident A.B. Westmacott an in 1973, he signed an agreement with the Fon of Babanki Tungo: by which agreement, both parties accepted to abide by the Westmacott decision. This agreement was witnessed by the administration and the lands officer. The Babanki-Tungo people were later on to repudiate this agreement which has been one of the causes of the recent conflicts between the two villages.

The Intervention Of The Christian Justice And Peace Commission

5) Shortly after the most recent conflict which took place in January 1996, the Babanki-Tungo Catholic church Parish Council by a letter dated 1st April 1996, requested the Parish Councils and the Christian community of Babanki Tungo and Bambui Parishes to form a Christian Justice and Peace Commission to look into the matter with a view of having a permanent solution to the problem.

6) The Christian Justice and Peace Commission painstakingly and judiciously studied the problem and carried out detailed investigation for over three years (April 1996 to June 1999) and came out with a report which confirmed the Westmacott's Decision. The Bambili people therefore accepted the report for the following reasons:

> a) The Christian Justice and Peace Commission had painstakingly and judiciously studied the matter for over three years.
>
> b) The commission sought and obtained documents from appropriate sources to support their decisions.
>
> c) The operating tool in the commission's arbitration is peace based on justice.
>
> d) The commission's decision as to the boundary between Bambili and Babanki Tungo is in line with the Letter and spirit of the Westmacott,s decision accepted by both parties in 1973.
>
> e) For too long we have been fighting, feuding and hating each other and it was our ardent wish to put this longstanding dispute behind us once and for all.
>
> f) Without peace, there has been little or no development in our two villages. In fact the developments which have been carried out by both villages have been largely destroyed by the intervillage conflict over the years.

References to the Christian Justice and Peace Commission

7) We understand that a copy of the Final Findings and resolutions of the Bambili-Babanki Tungo Boundary Dispute arrived at by the Christian Justice and Peace Commission was handed to members of the National Commission that came here last year. Consequently we shall not bore you with many details. We will therefore simply refer you to some pages of the document which we are attaching here as appendices

> a) The Decision of Divisional Officer, Mr. R.C. Ward of 08/09/56 gave Bambili some of the Bambili land which the Babanki Tungo had illegally acquired and directing the Babanki Tungo people who were on Bambili side to stay if they wished but will have to pay their taxes to the Fon of Bambili.

> b) Decision of Resident A.B. Westmacott of 15/05/58 which modified R.C.Ward's decision only on the grounds that it was one sided in view of the fact that whereas some Babanki-Tungo people would be affected, no single Bambili person would be required to make the choice.

> c) An agreement between the Fons of Bambili and Babanki Tungo dated 25/05/1973 and witnessed by the Lands Officer, the Administration and one notable each from Bambili (S.N. Kindo) and Babanki Tungo (B.N.Mukong). This agreement stipulated that both villages accepted the Westmacott Decision on their existing land dispute. We will like note to be taken of the fact that the Babanki-Tungo people now deny that the Westmacott Decision was accompanied by a map. It is clear from the last sentence of paragraph 3 of the agreement that the parties had maps in their possessions. Furthermore, the map which the Christian Justice and Peace Commission retrieved from the archives of the Bamenda Provincial Surveys with transfer reference from Provincial Survey Buea agrees with the map produced by the Fon of Bambili.

Appendices

Instances of Violation of Injunction Orders by the Babanki Tungo People

8)
a) It is on record that the Babanki Tungo people stubbornly built a market on Bambili land and when ordered by the administration to dismantle it, they failed to do so and so the administration gave instructions to the forces of law and order to burn it down. This happened in 1961.Theyhave rebuilt this market. Your commission will be able to see things for themselves if you go on the field.

b) The Babanki Tungo people have repeatedly failed to respect injunction orders issued by the administration and by the Christian Justice and Peace Commission as they continue to farm and carry out other developments.

Efforts in the Settlement of the Dispute.

9) (i)Government:
a)The destruction in 1961 of the Babanki Tungo market built on Bambili land was a demonstration by the government that the land belonged to Bambili.

b)As stated above, the Westmacott decision was accompanied by a map and each village was given a copy. The Babanki Tungo people have never accepted having been given a copy, neither have they accepted the copy given to the Fon of Bambili. This is the reason why Senior Divisional Officer, Mezam (late Sufor) resorted to going to the National institute of Geography, Yaounde for a team surveyors who together with him went to the field and traced the boundary and planted six pillars which were immediately destroyed by the Babanki Tungo people. Their ring leaders were arrested and detained for fifty-six (56) days.

It should be noted that the Christian Justice and Peace Commission (CJPC) finally sorted out a copy of the map mentioned above from the lands and surveys, Buea. This is a clear proof that the Babanki-Tungo community is only out to distort facts and caused problems.

A decision of Westmacott in this respect is as follows:
"*After carefully inspecting the land (3 days) I have decided that Babanki Tungo should remain in possession of the land which they now occupy but that all the grazing land on the Bambili side which is now unoccupied-with the exception of three Babanki houses with several Fulani rugers-should be confirmed as belonging to Bambili. Starting from Bambili lake, the boundary will be as decided by the appeal court until it approaches the footpath running from Babanki Tungo to Bamenda. It will then bear almost due north from this point along a grassy spur until it reaches a rocky outcrop on the steep escarpment defining the valley. It will run along the edge of this escarpment until the cliff feature ends and the land becomes rolling down land. The boundary will then follow the line as defined by cairns until it reaches the main Bamenda-Kumbo Nkambe road (the ring road) at the sharp corner just beyond mile post 13. The village head of Bambili to have the right to carry out sacrifices at the spot in the valley now on Babanki land as heretofore. Each party is to be supplied with the copy of the map showing the boundary*"

ii) The Christian Justice and Peace Commission reaffirmed the Westmacott Decision. The Resolutions of the Christian Justice and Peace Commission were as follows:

> "From all our findings above and working with impartialility, honesty and objectivity expected of such a justice and peace commission we have come out with Bambili-Babanki-Tungo boundary as follows:
>
>> The boundary starts at the high point separating the dry Awing lake and lake Bambili (See what Westmacott said) "starting from Bambili lake" Also see the declaration of the Fon of Awing lastly the technical and logical advice of the surveyors. The boundary starting here would include all the lake and its crater in Bambili land.

From the boundary moves straight towards the direction of the footpath up to a point 100m away from the source of the first tributary of the outlet (to the right facing the footpath). This is the point that initiate an angle from where the boundary shoots straight taking an average of the high knolls to the right flank of the high peak over looking the footpath. Here the boundary passes on the right flank of the new road on the foot of that hill. From here it follows the new road for 100m and moves right from some 50m and shoots straight along the grassy spur till a heavy rocky outcrop with a fig tree is reached. This is as described by Westmacott, shown by surveyors and confirmed by the members of the commission.

After the rocky outcrop the boundary moves along the cliff top edge over looking Babanki Tungo built up area to the right in the valley. Westmacott had sett aside SDO Ward's Decision because it puts too many Babanki Tungo people on Bambili side needing displacement and this boundary was at Tuentueng stream down the valley. Westmacott also saw all the grazing land on the Bambili side which is now occupied with the exception of three Babanki Tungo houses and several Fulani rugars should be confirmed as belonging to Bambili.

At the end of the escarpment the boundary follows a line below the knoll to the end. (This point is in a valley and there is a small footpath moving up there). This area is the rolling down lands. From here the boundary shoots straight to the foot of the highest conical hill recently excavated for laterite and over looking the road of Babanki village and below which there are some small streams.

From the base of this hill a straight line moves towards the mile post 13. Over the Babanki Tungo market on the right side of the road going to the Babanki Tungo village there is a tree which marks another point. From that tree the boundary shoots straight splitting the Babanki Tungo market into two and ending at the sharp bend beyond mile post 13. All these spots were identified and to be showed the two villages in the field. Remember the description is from the Bambili lake through the famous footpath to mile post 13 area. We understand there are many similar geographical features in the area. Sequence of their occurrence has helped us a lot. The fact that no original boundary claim was ever accepted and that no decision ever used the lake outlet as boundary; we stand by this decision which ties with our appendices A and H. This adopted Babanki Tungo Bambili boundary by the CJPC is shown below.

We the members of the commission understand it is long time (40 years) since this boundary was made. Much development has taken place in the disputed area; sometimes with the thinking that such effective occupation would yield the area in the long run to the developer. The commission frowns at this. Yet such a development is bound to attract sympathies would come up on both sides but advise that it is left to you the Bambili and Babanki-Tungo brothers and sisters to willingly put your heads and hearts together and talk to one another on these areas of sympathies. That will be left to you people. We may only be of assistance if requested. Our reference was the Westmacott boundary of 1958 between Bambili and Babanki-Tungo and that is just what we have done and is the end of the commission,s work"

BAMENDA 23RD February 2000

Signed————————————————————

HRN AWEMO 11(*Fon of Bambili*)

Appendix VII

REPUBLIQUE DU CAMEROUN REPUBLIC OF CAMEROUN
Paix- Travail-Patrie   Peace-Work-Fatherland
Province du Nord Ouest   North-West Province
Départment de la Mezam   Mezam Division
Arrondissement de Tubah   Tubah Sub Division
Sous Prefecture de Tubah   Sub Divisional Office Tubah
Ref.No.E29-03/165/.3336   Tubah, le 15 September 1999
            Le Sous Prefet de l'Arrondisment de Tubah
            The Divisional Officer Tubah Sub Division

To: The Fons of Bambili and Kejom Ketinguh;
      —The Chairman, Christian Justice and Peace Commission

Objet: BAMBILI- KEDJOMKETINGUH
         BOUNDARY DISPUTE.

Despite several attempts made by the Administration and, of recent, by the Clergy of Tubah Subdivision, the old boundary dispute between Bambili and Kedjom Ketinguh village is yet to be settled. We all placed our hopes on the venture of the Christian Justice and Peace Commission, but it couldn't succeed to bring the two parties to a compromise. All the same, a great step has been made forward, towards the final solution of the dispute.

The findings and resolutions of the Commission are certainly going to be of great help to the National Commission, which is now handling the matter. Let's hope that its decision will not delay any longer.

But in the meantime, we should not relent our efforts in maintaining the peace between the two belligerent communities. The relative peace prevailing since 1996 has to be preserved, and this will require our joint efforts.

Presently, the situation is not encouraging as the administrative injunction order prohibiting farming activities on the disputed area is being grossly violated and most especially by some farmers of Kedjom Ketinguh origin. It should be understood that such attitude of the farmers constitutes a serious threat to peace, and therefore can no longer be tolerated.

The Administration is determined to ensure the strict respect of the injunction order by all, but this cannot be possible without the full cooperation of the Traditional Authorities and the Clergy.

It is my appeal to Clergy to continue, through the Christian Justice and Peace Commission, to educate the both communities as they did during the past three years.

As concerning the two Traditional Authorities, they should, each in his own capacity, take all necessary measures to see to it that all illegal occupants withdraw from the disputed area immediately. They must start from now to warn these defaulters, and should report all cases of resistances to the Administration for exemplary punitive measures to be taken against recalcitrant one.

I count very much on your usual cooperation, for peace to reign between Bambili and Kejom Ketinguh pending the final decision on the boundary dispute opposing the two villages./-

C.c
-S.D.O./ Mezam
-FLO/Tubah
-Concerned
-File

Appendix VIII

FON'S PALACE
BAMBILI, The 16th July 1996

His Excellency,
The President of the Republic of Cameroon, Yaounde
The Hon. Vice Prime Minister in charge of Territorial Administration Yaounde
Through
His Excellency,
The Governor,
North West Province.

SUBJECT: APPEAL FOR THE EFFECTIVE IMPLEMENTATION OF THE WESTMACOTT DECISION OVER THE BAMBILI-BABANKI-TUNGOH BOUNDARY DISPUTE.

On behalf of the Bambili people, I have the honour to appeal that you kindly take steps to implement the 1958 decision taken by residence Westmacott over the Bambili-Babanki-Tungo boundary dispute.

First of all, I wish to make the point that the Bambili community had appeal against the Westmacott decision because it awarded Bambili land to the Babanki-Tungo people on the basis of their effective though unlawful occupation of the land. Unfortunately the commissioner of Southern Cameroons on behalf of the Government, to whom this appeal was directed for redress, confirmed the Westmacott decision giving room for no other avenue for appeal in consequence.

Over the years, the both communities have accepted the Westmacott decision as the only medium to resolve this dispute. Unfortunately successive administration has failed to implement this decision on the field, though they have constantly referred to it.

The Bambili people totally and fully reject the present line of action being taken by his Excellency, the Governor of the Northwest Province which is out to create a new boundary ignoring the Westmacott Decision.

He is in effect awarding Bambili and Babanki-Tungo people under the pretext of effective occupation of land and mutual agreement by both communities which is not the case.

For example, in 1965 the Senior Divisional Officer, for the Bamenda Division, basing his action on the interpretation of the Westmacott Decision ordered the destruction of the Babanki-TungoMarket because it was built on the Bambili land. In effect, the market was officially burnt down by a detachment of the police force. It has since again been unlawfully and stubbornly rebuilt by the Babanki-Tungo People. The present proposal of the Governor of the North West Province awards the same area which the market has been rebuilt to the Babanki Tungo people on the whimsical grounds of their effective occupation of the land thereby condoning their unlawful act of occupying Bambili land. It also shows that the administration is contracting itself by going forward and backward on its decisions.

Recently, the Senior Divisional Officer, Mezam, after long research and deep consultation with both communities undertook an Interpretation and Implementation of the Westmacott but was rudely interrupted in his endeavours by the Babanki Tungo who illegally dug out the boundary pillars and sued the S.D.O. to court for wrong interpretations but the court upheld his action. Again, the Governor's action is in direct contradiction with the decision of his S.D.O and thereby confirms the illegal action of the Babanki-Tungo people.

We therefore appeal to his Excellency, the President of the Republic, to insure the effective implementation of the Westmacott Decision on the field based on an official objective interpretation of the said decision.

Documents attached:
1) A copy of the Westmacott Decision
2) A copy of the Westmacott Map
3) A copy of the 1973 Pact
4) A reply of the petition written to the Government of Southern Cameroon by the Fon of Bambili.

Cc
-The Divisional Officer, Tubah
-The Senior Divisional Officer, Mezam
-The Right Honourable Prime Minister, Head of Government, Yaounde

Appendix IX
THE BAMBILI FONDOM
C/O Bambili Fon's Palace,
Tubah Sub-Division
Mezam Division
10th March, 2003

The Divisional Officer,
Tubah Subdivision,
Subdivision Office, Tubah.

Dear Sir,

The Demarcation of the Boundary between Bambili and Babanki Tungo.

On 5th March 2003 you invited the Fon of Babanki Tungo and the chairman of his Village Council and myself and the Chairman of the Bambili Village Council to your office. We were very happy about this invitation and were looking forward to agreeing on the work plan for building the boundary pillars on the four locations already shown to the two villages by the technicians of the commission charged with the said duty. Naturally we were surprised when you instead invited all four of us to state our positions regarding the boundary dispute between our two villages. Both my village council chairman and myself left you in no doubt as to our surprises to the question you posed and went on to state our positions which we now summarise hereunder.

Firstly we are attaching a copy of the submissions which we made to the National Commission charged with the Settlement of Inter-Village Dispute at the Governor's office, Bamenda on the 23rd

February 2000. On this occasion the Babanki-Tungos also made a submission which we are sure is available in your office. Please kindly note that this event took during the time of your immediate predecessor. We will like you to kindly note carefully the opening paragraph on brief history at page 1 of our attached submissions of 23/02/2000.

After listening to these submissions, the National Commission, personally headed by the Minister of Territorial Administration in his capacity as Chairman of the National Commission for the Settlement of Inter-Village Disputes visited the disputed site and after further briefing by the technicians, the National Commission determined the present boundary, which largely followed the Westmacott decision taken by Resident A.B. Westmacott on the 15 May 1958.

Please kindly note that following this Westmacott decision, the Fon of Bambili appealed against it to the Commissioner of the then Southern Cameroons. The appeal was rejected by the Commissioner of Southern Cameroons. (see letter referenced 36 (569)/T/19 dated 8th July 1959 attached to the submissions of the Bambili Delegation as Appendix B. please kindly note furthermore that an agreement was subsequently signed by the two fons on 25th July 1973 agreeing to abide by the Westmacott decision.

The national Commission subsequently issued Ministerial Arrete No. 00210/A/MINAT/DOT/SDOA/SCA dated 16th August 2000 which is attached to this letter. Following this Ministerial Arrete, the Senior Divisional Officer for Mezam convened a meeting at his office on the 14th November 2000 as well as many other meetings. Most of them were boycotted by the Babanki-Tungos. However, on the 14th June 2001, the Senior Divisional Officer for Mezam convened another meeting of the technical commission to see about the practical implementation of the Ministerial Arrete for erecting the boundary cairns. He handed copies of the Arrete which we have just quoted above to the two Fons. He informed both villages that no petitions will be entertained since the Mezam administration was only executing the decision of National Commission. At this particular meeting the Divisional Delegate of Surveys stated that the Babanki-Tungo people had accused him of corruption but on the contrary he stated that it was the Babanki-Tungo people who had attempted in vain to bribe him to make an incorrect technical report. He had been so disturbed by the accusation of the Babanki-Tungo people that he broke down in tears and was unable to continue with his report which was then continued by the Divisional Delegate of Town Planning and Housing. The Senior Divisional Officer had to stand up and to hold and calm him down. Finally the Senior Divisional Officer instructed that the technical committee should meet on the 25th June 2001 in the office of the Divisional Officer, Tubah, to draw up their programme of work. The meeting took place with the representatives of the two villages and the full technical commission present and the programme of work was drawn up. The programme was followed on the first and second day with both villages present then boycotted on the third day by the Babanki-Tungos. On the fourth day (9 July 2001) the technical team was surrounded assaulted and held hostage by the Babanki Tungo people and the materials brought by the technical team seized (spades, iron rods, boxes, buckets). On this occasion, you, our Divisional Officer, and Head of State's Representatives was verbally assaulted. The boundary cairn built on that day was destroyed by the Babanki Tungo people on the same night and the materials carried away. Subsequently, the Tubah administration assessed the damage and the Babanki Tungo people asked to pay. This has never been done.

Following this incident the Senior Divisional Officer in his letter No. 390/L/29/PS of the 1st August 2001 again invited the two villages and the technical commission to his office on the 7th August 2001 and severely warned the Babanki Tungoh people about the consequence of their action in holding the technical team hostage, threatening their lives and destroying the boundary cairns, built with state funds. He told them that by boycotting a meeting called by the Tubah administration is contempt of authority and is punishable. He told that their attitude in the matter could no longer be tolerated and that the administration could have taken very drastic action to impose state authority. However, he was giving them a last chance because he believes in dialogue and concertation. He reminded them that the National Commission charged with the settlement of inter-village disputes whose decision he was executing is the supreme authority and its decision is final given the fact that all land is state land. Despite these warnings by the Senior Divisional Officer for

Mezam, the Babanki Tungo people still went on the 10th September 2001, to interrupt the work of planting the cairns by the technical team For on the 3rd September you did convene a meeting in your office in which it was agreed by all parties including the technicians that two trips will be made on the 10 and 12 September 2001 to complete the planting of the four cairns whose exact positions had already been determined by the technicians and shown to the Bambilis and the Babanki Tungos. However, on the 10th September 2001, to surprise of yourself, the two Gendarmerie Officers who accompanied you, the commissioner of Special Branch and the work was not to continue unless a 1913 map which they produced was used. You will recall that you detained the Fon of Babanki and his five delegates at the gendarmerie office, Tubah, but they were later transferred to Bamenda and released by the S.D.O Neither at the meeting with the Minister of Territorial Administration (as chairman of the National Commission of the Settlement of Inter-Village dispute) held on the 23rd February 2000 at the Governor's conference hall referred to above nor at any other meetings before then had the Babanki-Tungos make any reference to a 1913 map. In any case we do not think that any person is competent to raise a belated objection to the decision of the highest competent authority on the matter. It is also necessary to note that the Westmacott decision was taken in 1958, that is 45 years after 1913. The two Fons also signed an agreement in 1973 to abide by the Westmacott decision. Again in August 2000 the highest competent authority of the land issued Ministerial Arrete No.00210/A/MINAT/DOT/SDOA/SCA spelling out precisely the demarcation of the boundary between Bambili and Babanki Tungo. The Divisional Officer of Tubah Subdivision, as the direct representative of the Head of State and of the Minister of Territorial Administration may not review that decision. His job is to enforce that decision.

We are therefore appealing to you to enforce that decision and have the cairns planted now before the rains set in. When you opened discussions at your office on the 5th of March 2003, you stated that since you have been the Divisional Officer of Tubah Subdivision, there has been no conflict between Bambili and Babanki Tungoh but you are certainly aware that peace has persisted because we have used all traditional means to keep the Bambili people from reacting to the constant and persistent provocations of the Babanki-Tungo people. These provocations also amounted to a challenge of state authority. We list only a few of them as follows:

i) Babanki-Tungo people have violated with impunity all administrative injunction orders placed over the disputed area. A visit to the site will show anyone that the Babanki Tungo people are farming on the disputed area.

ii) Earlier cairns built by the administration were destroyed by the Babanki Tungo people. Although some of their ring leaders were arrested and detained, they were later released and no further action was taken against them.

iii) Most administrative meetings convened by both the SDO Mezam and D.O. Tubah were boycotted by the Babanki Tungo people.

iv) Cairns erected by the Technical committee on the 9th July 2001 were again destroyed by the Babanki Tungo people, the technical team held hostage and the material purchased with state fonds(sic) taken away and no punitive action has been taken against them

v) On the 10th September 2001 when the technical committee went to the field to continue its work, the Babanki Tungo people perturbed the work by introducing a map which they claimed was drawn in 1913 and insisted that the work could not continue unless this map is followed, thereby instructing the administration on what to do.

vi) In the light of the above the sovereignty of the state is being seriously challenged by a village (Babanki Tungo). We draw attention to the provision of article 4 Ministerial Arrete No. 00210/A/MINAT/DOT/SDOA/SCA of 16th August (already referred to above) which stipulates for sanctions against any person contravening the terms of the Arrete in accordance with the laws in force.

Finally we wish to restate our commitment to justice and peace and look forward to your administrative authority, to settle this matter in the spirit of peace and justice

Yours Respectfully,

HRN Awemo 11
Fon of Bambili

Appendix X

Traditional Council,
Babanki Tungo
Bafut Area
Mezam Division
7th November 1971

The Sub District Officer,
Bamenda Central,
Mezam Division.

Sir,

PETITION: REFERENCE TO SURVEYOR,S LETTER

We have received a letter from the Area Surveyor Bamenda dated 3rd November 1971 in respect of Babanki Tungo vs Bambili Boundary dispute which he proposes to commence work on the survey and Demarcation of Babanki Tungo/Bmabili boundary on the 9th Nove. 1971. The surveyor quotes his authority being the decision reached by the Senior Divisional Officers team of inspection on 22nd June 1971.
 We will like to know from you if this directive was issued to the Area.
 Surveyor by you to commence work on the 9th November 1971 on the Disputed Area. We will also be very grateful if you will give us a copy of the decision reached by the Senior Divisional Officer's team of inspection of the 22nd June 1971 to enable us studies this decision before taking a decision on this matter.

Appendix XI

THE DIVISIONAL OFFICER
TUBAH SUB DIVISION   OFFICE OF THE FON,

KEDJOM KETINGUH,
TUBAH SUB DIVISION,
9TH OCTOBER 1995.

Sir,

UNATHORISED ACTIVITIES AT THE DISPUTED AREA BETWEEN BAMBILI / KEDJOM KETINGUH.

With reference to your letter No.E29 01.2/165/299 of 28/09/95,I wish to inform you that there is nothing like disputed area between Bambili and Kedjom Ketinguh.

Once more, be informed that this disputed was settled by West macott Vide his decision dated 15/05/ 58 and in the contrary it was the Kedjom Ketinguh people who were not satisfied and later paid in the sum of 138.400 Francs on the 26/7/67 as deposit for appeal against part of the boundary but unfortunately this appeal was never heard.

Furthermore, on the 18/09/75 Mr. Oben Ashu, the Present Governor of the South West Province, who was then the Divisional Officer Bamenda Central Sub Division, after inspecting the place on the 26/6/75 did issued letter No.ABA.23/681 of 18th September 1975, giving directives to Ardo Jacky of Sabga Babanki Tungo and the Farmers of Chuku Babanki Tungo, how and what to do before farming on that area.

The Bambili people accepted the West-Macott Decision and have all along respected that decision till about 1991 when they started their Criminal activities perhaps being supported by some administrative authorities, to be naming some area in Kedjom Ketinguh as "Disputed Land"

I wish to state further that, this matter was disposed by the High Court of Bamenda holding on the 3rd day of July 1995, Ref. Suit No.HCB/28/95

If the Bambili people or the administration is not satisfied with the decisions taken so far, they may take further action to the proper authorities than going through Criminal ways of which we are not afraid.

I sincerely appeal to you to ask the Bambili people in the name of peace to immediately stop any trespass into Kedjom Ketinguh Land.

Yours Faithfully,
The Chairman K.K.V.T.

CC
-The S.D.O. Mezam
-The Brigade Commander Gendarmerie
-The Commissioner of Special Branch, Tubah

Appendix XII

Office of the Chairman
Kedjom Ketingo Village Traditional Council
Kedjom Ketinguh
19th April 1995.

The Senior Divisional Officer
For Mezam

Sir,

PETITION AGAINST THE SO-CALLED DEMARCATION OF THE BOUNDARY BETWEEN BAMBILI AND BABANKI TUNGO ACCORDING TO THE WESTMACOTT DECISION BY THE SO-CALLED EXPERTS FROM YAOUNDE

We the people of Kedjom Ketinguh (Babanki Tungoh) would like to express our objection to the work that was started yesterday 18th April 1995 by the so-called experts from Yaounde and to point out to the S.D.O. that what they are doing does not in the least come close to the dictates of the Westmacott decision of 1958 which the public media advertised that the S.D.O. had decided was going to be used to retrace and demarcate the boundary between Bambili and Kedjom Ketinguh.

Sir, we would like to register that all efforts made y our delegation in your office on 17 April 1995 to have the commission made up of five delegates each from Bambili and Kedjom Ketinguh, prior to going to the field ensure that the experts were going to interpret the Westmacott decision and not impose a boundary fabricated in Yaounde were shouted down. We were told that the interpretation will be done on the field but when we requested on 18 April 1995 on the field that the commission talk with experts before the retracing took off, the S.D.O. refused and to our utter dismay, the expert pulled out from his bag a map displaying an ink demarcation line and told us he had his directives from Yaounde. (One would have expected the said expert to know his bearings, but he was not ashamed to ask where the lake was.)

Our first reaction was not to be party to the masquerade that was not in the least going to solve the unfortunate conflict that has cost our two villages too much in human life and property, but we decided to give the said experts a chance and follow them to the lake where the Westmacott decision of 1958, page two, paragraph five, line six clearly states where the boundary starts from, but the experts and the S.D.O.'s party went parallel to and far beyond the lake to take their bearing and from there descended, rather embarrassingly, into the Kedjom Tinguh village where people lived long before the Westmacott decision of 1958.

Sir, we would like to call your attention to the following facts:

1. The S.D.O. for Mezam had previously told us that he was going to bring 1,000 gendarmes and impose a boundary irrespective of what we thought.

2. We have not been given an opportunity to listen to the experts, tell us what portion of the Westmacott they are implementing.

3. The experts we were told, did their interpretation in Yaounde and came to implement it.

4. The Westmacott decision reviews
   a) The Native Court judgement of suit No.23/53 of 1953

   b) Native Court Appeal Judgement dated the 15th July 1955 and

   c) District Officer's review judgement dated the 18th September 1956 and clearly says in paragraph three on page two of the decision that it sets aside the District Officer's decision

5) Westmacott,s decision is stated in paragraph five on page two of the said decision.

6) The Westmacott decision, the Appeal Court sketch map, a copy of which we obtained from the Native Court archives in Tubah, must be used to retrace the boundary from the lake up to the footpath as mentioned in the Westmacott decision.

7) The Westmacott decision accepts the Appeal Court decision starting from the Bambili lake until it approaches the footpath running from Babanki Tungo to Bamenda

8) The boundary that was being traced by the S.D.O.'s experts on 18th April 1995 dangerously violates the reasons for which Resident Westmacott set aside D.O. Ward's decision in 1958.

9) Boundaries are best trace by people on the spot and there are competent surveyors of lands in Bamenda who have, in fact carried out studies of the disputed land, but their reports have never been released to our commission. If experts are brought from Yaounde, then there is reason to believe that it is a design to impose a boundary from Yaounde

10) The Bambili and Babanki-Tungo people have both respected the Westmacott decision since 1958. It is enough to retrace it.

Sir, we find it extremely objectionable and futile to be party to an exercise that is at best a masquerade and that can only intensify the conflict between our peoples and cause them to continue to destroy themselves and their property.

We pray to with hold our participation in the demarcation exercise until such a time that the parties concerned will understand the Westmacot decision. To continue in the exercise is to be party to the imminent aggravation of the existing conflict and its attendant consequences.

THE CHAIRMAN
KEDJOM KETINGUH VILLAGE
TRADITIONAL COUNCIL

CC:
-The Hon. Prime Minister
-The Vice Prime Minister of Territorial Administration
-The Governor of the N.W. Province
-The Sub Divisional Officer, Tubah

Appendix XIII

TRADITIONAL COUNCIL MEETING WITH HON.MUNKONG AND HON. KINDO ON THE 16-1-72 IN THE CHIEF,S PALACE IN BABANKI-TUNGOH TO FIND OUT A PEACEFUL SOLUTION TO THE BABANKI-TUNGOH/BAMBILI BOUNDARY DISPUTE.

At about 2:30 p.m. Hon. B.N.Mukong, in the presence of the chief, Traditional Council members and a host of other Babanki-Tungo people introduced the Hon. S.N. Kindo and the topic of his visit. In his brief introduction, Hon. Mukong told the house that on the 13th January, 1972, Hon. Kindo, the District Officer, Mezam, the Surveyor and himself went to the disputed boundary, and saw things for themselves. He then told the Babanki Tungo people that as the leaders of the area and also sons of the two villages had deemed it expedient to address the two villages in order to seek ways and means by which they could and the long standing boundary dispute between the two villages. He then concluded by saying that, that was the reason why they were in the palace that day. He declared the floor opened for Kindo to speak to the people of Babanki Tungo.

Having addressed the Chief, His Council and the people, Hon.S.N.Kindo told the house that the boundary dispute between the two villages was one of a long distance. He went on to say that, they the Parliamentarians of the area had come to seek from the people ways by which the matter could be ended. He pointed out that Parliamentarians come and go, and that they could leave Parliament tomorrow. Continuing, he said that since they were the children of the two villages, they were out to find a suitable solution to the dispute. He added that if they are changed or leave Parliament next day, new persons coming might not all the time be children from Babanki Tungo and Bambili, and as such might not know the problems of the people very well, and consequently might not tender the right cure to their problems.

Kindo Hon., said that in the multiparty days there was a lot of enmity, nepotism and tribalism among people but today under the C.N.U. Government peace and security are the only media of solving disputes. We went to the boundary site, on. Kindo went on and saw that one village claims land and never puts it into effective use, but on the contrary the other village claims land and never puts it into use at all. He said that he was not going to call the spade a spade. Kindo pointed out that it is the rule of the Government to make the best use of the land they have and not to allow it stand wasted. Hon.Kindo appealed to the house to think constructively and to resolve at a peaceful and lasting solution to the boundary issue. As an eye witness of the boundary from start to the finish Hon. Kindo observed:

a) That one village is claiming land and using it, while the other is not doing so

b) That in certain place on the boundary as shown by Westmarcout Babanki Tungo had trespassed into Bambili land and Bambili had done vice versa

c) That when he first came into parliament he was received in Buea by Babanki elements and that Mukong and himself were not well loved by all in the two villages. He then revealed that the hatred for them cannot make Mukong give part of Babanki land to Bambilinor claim part of Bambili and give to Babanki, likewise himself.

d) That in certain places on the boundary site, he took to himself the powers of the D.O. to suggest to the surveyor to change the boundary so as to avoid problems from either villages

e) That the deposits given by the two villages calling on the land Tribunal was not to be returned and that it was small, and should be increased so as to meet up with the cost of stones, sand, and labour in the construction of a permanent boundary between Babanki-Tungo and Bambili.

f) That he Kindo was free of blames in Babanki Tungo because if he knew of any cause to be blamed he would not have come to address the Babanki Tungo people without fear. He then opened room for questions from the people.

Appendix XIV

Catholic Mission Bambui
Tubah Sub Division
P.O.Box 56, Bamenda
18th June 1998.

Through the D.O. Tubah Sub Division,
To: The Senior D.O. Mezam

Sirs,

Topic: AN APPEAL FOR THE SERVICES OF SURVEYORS TO PINPOINT SOME OUTSTANDING POINTS ON BABANKI-TUNGAW/BAMBILI AS DESCRIBED BY WESTMACOTT BOUNDARY DECISION OF 1958.

I have the honour to request for surveyors to accompany the CHRISTIAN JUSTICE AND PEACE COMMISSION TUBAH(a joint venture by the major Christian churches and communities in Tubah Subdivision formed some 20 months ago with the main objective of seeking a Christian solution to the numerous wars and conflicts plaguing the area) which has been working on the Babanki/ Bambili land dispute to locate some strategic points on the Westmacott decision (sic) boundary which has been accepted by both villages as the only authentic and working document.

For twenty months the commission made up of the clergy and lay gentlemen, had 12 main commission meetings, 4 visits to the disputed area, acquired and studied, relevant court judgement, pacts, agreements, maps, sketch maps, interviews and other investigations. 4 shuttle visits, 2 each chiefdom, to meet the fons and their people were made.

Both villages accept the commission,s project to end the dispute. They promised to assist the commission for the final solution and wished the commission to end the work with the government administration together with both villages putting in place a final boundary.

Sir, the final issue now is to determine two points for clarification. These are:

1) The point linking the footpath to the lake as endorsed by Westmacott

2) The point from the rolling down land to sharp corner just beyond Mile Post 13 on the Bamenda Banso part of the Ring Road.

So, only a surveyor can help us here.

The commission should be very grateful if the Senior Divisional Officer would help us help these people.

Thanks Rev.Fr. Henry Mesue(Parish Priest Bambui)

Appendix XV

BAMENDA HIGH COURT JUDGEMENT OF BAMBUI/FINGE CASE, 1954-1988 IN THE HIGH COURT OF MEZAM DIVISION HOLDEN AT BAMENDA

Another very serious but very little studied conflict in the Bamenda Grassfields has been the Bambui-Finge conflict. Unlike most conflicts in the region which are centred on the boundaries and land that conflict is centred on the Finge people fighting for their autonomy from Bambui since 1954. The Finge people are exiles from Kom who were hosted by the Bambui people. As time went on the Finge developed their own socio-political institutions. One of these institutions was the Kwifoyn which placed them now at par with their host. The Bambui could never sit to watch Finge gain their autonomy. In 1988 the struggle for autonomy by the Finge reached fever heat and the only way to resolve the problem was to go to court. This appendix has reproduced that judgment in full and is meant for any person who is interested in carrying out research in this thorny but yet very interesting subject.

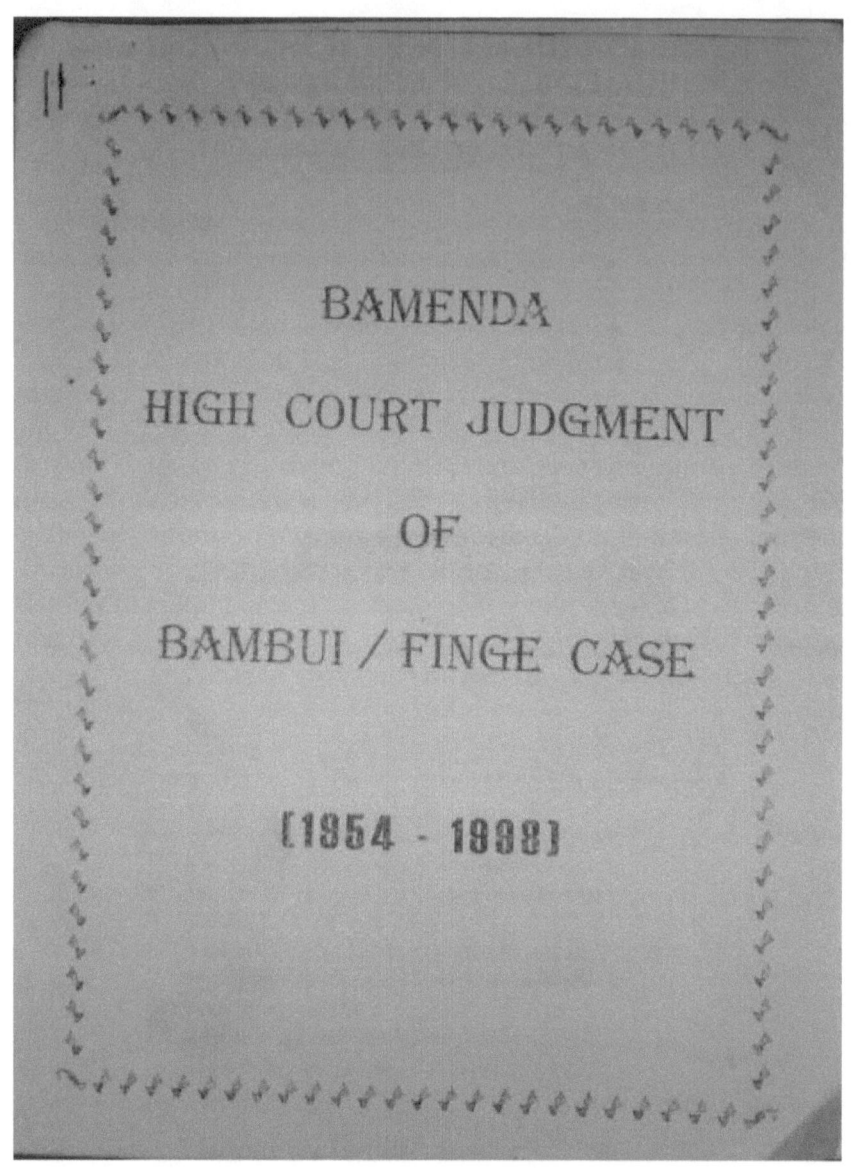

Appendix XII

IN THE HIGH COURFT OF MEZAM DIVISION
HOLDEN AT BAMENDA

BEFORE HIS LORDSHIP MR. JUSTICE M. C. MOMA - JUDGE
THIS MONDAY THE 12TH DAY OF DEC. 98

BETWEEN   SUIT NO. HCB/35/97

THE PEOPLE OF BAMBUI (BEING REPRESENTED BY
ANGAFOR MOMBO-III (FON OF BAMBUI)   ..   ..   PLAINTIFF

AND

THE PEOPLE OF FINGE (BEING REPRESENTED BY
NCHI ERIC LOBTI II (SUB CHIEF OF FINGE)   ..   ..   DEFENDANTS

Plaintiff present.
Defendant present.

APPEARANCES:
Mr. Tafah and Ndamaba for the plaintiff. Mr. Njamnsi for the defenfant.

"REPUBLIC OF CAMEROON".
"IN THE NAME OF THE PEOPLE OF CAMEROON"
=JUDGMENT=

By this originating summons the plaintiff seeks this court to construe the following instruments.

(1) Judgment of the customary court Tubah in Civil Suit No. 65/54 between Mbengwi V. H. of Bafinge and Amungwafor V. H. of Bambui delivered on the 2/6/54.

(2) Judgment in civil appeal No. 29/54 of 12/10/54 between Mbengwi V. H of Bafinge and Amungwafor V. H. of Bambui.

(3) Judgment in civil suit No. 81/54 between Bambui and Bafinge of 22/5/54.

(4) Judgment in civil appeal No. 80/54 against judgment in civil suit No. 81/54 between Tifinge of Bambui appellant and Amungwafor V. H. of Bambui respondent of 14/7/54.

(5) Minutes of the settlement of the Dispute between Bambui and Finge people by the premier Hon. J. N. Foncha at Tubah, Bambui on the 23rd January 1960.

(6) Southern Cameroons High Court Judgment No. SC/6A/1960 of the 25/1/61 between Finge and Bambui.
(7) Minutes of the reconciliatory meeting of Bambui/Finge long standing dispute held in the Sub-Divisional Office Bamenda on Friday May 23 1980.
(8) Minutes of the concertation meeting relating to the bloody clashes between Bambui and Finge held in the conference hall of the Sub-Divisional Office Tubah on the 29/4/96.
(9) Minutes of the meeting presided over by His Excellency the Governor of the North West Province in his cabinet on the 21/8/96 relating to the Bambui Finge conflict.

In support of the documents sought to be construed Counsel for the plaintiff filed a 44 paragraph affidavit to which is attached 17 annextures and a furthercounter affidavit and two further affidavits. In reply defendant counsel filed a 44 paragraph counter affidavit to which is annexed 7 annextures and a counter affidavit to the further affidavit.

What is germane in this judgment is the construction that the court will place on the documents it is called upon to interpret. Consequently it will be bootless to delve into the history or background of things leading to the decisions in the documents. The court is called upon to place a construction, having said so the affidavit and further affidavit, were unnecessary. All counsel for the plaintiff would have done was only to invite the court to interpret the documents named in the originating summons. Having said so the court will restrict itself to providing an interpretation of the documents which are annexed to the affidavit. The interesting thing I have realised in all the documents is that the answers are provided in the document the court is invited to construe. I shall now take the documents seriatim and give an interpretation to each.

(1) In Civil Suit No. 65/54 that is between Mbengwi V. H. of Bafinge and Amungwafor V. H. of Bambui the judgment of the court was very clear and unambiguous. This is what the judges said: "Obviously the plaintiff is a quarter head or sub town to defendant. Bafinge is a sub town to Bambui. Therefore it is impossible keeping a boundary between the plaintiff and deft. Since they are from the same village and plaintiff is subordinate to defendant Verdict Case dismissed".

(2) In Civil Appeal No. 25/54 of the 12/10/54 between Mbengwi V. H. and Amungwafor V. H. of Bambui the judgment in Civil Suit No. 65/54 was confirmed. This is the conclusion of the court." The question of land cannot arise between Bambui and Bafinge the plaintiff says Bambui people have entered his land and claiming his economic crops, if that is true he should sue those people in court, then suing the village Head of Bambui. However we advice the Chief of Bambui to call the Bafinge Chief and make peace. Anyway we accept the lower court judgment. On appeal, judgment upheld".

(3) In Civil Suit No. 81/54 of the 22/5/54 between Bambui and Bafinge and this was a review judgment of Civil appeal No. 29/54 of the 12/10/54. This is what the trial judge said." I consider the present claim to be entirely justified. Bafinge people have received considerable assistance and concessions from the Bambuis and I must warn them against any further attempt to abuse these concessions. The claims put forward by the deft. are in my view both incorrect and can only lead to bad feelings between peoples, the majority of whom live and work in harmony. I uphold the judgment of the lower courts with costs.

"Signed K. C. Shaddack"
22/5/54"

(4) In the judgment in civil appeal No. 80/54 which was an appeal in the civil suit No. 81/54, this is what the judge said "Court: Defendant did not participate in the land dispute between Big Babanki and Bambui and the boundary is known as between Bambui and Big Babanki. Defendant has no right over kola trees bushes"

"On appeal Lower Court judgment upheld" and this judgment was signed by Chief Njoya.

(5) With regard to the settlement of the dispute on the 23rd of January 1960 between Bambui and Finge people which was chairmaned or presided over by the Hon. J. N. Foncha this is what the Premier told the SDO Bamenda Mr. J. Smith, the Fon of Bafut Achirimbi II and the Five Chiefs who were in attendance, the Finge leader and the Chief's councillors: This is what the Prime Minister in paragraph 3 said "Continuing the Premier reminded the chiefs that the case between the disputants had been decided in court several

times and that on each occasion the court had found itself unable to accept the claims of the finge people. He said that different Senior District Officers in Bamenda had on different occasions decided the case in favour of the Bambuis who own the land. There were seven chiefs in bafut clan Area, he said, and the Government had no intention of recognising an eighth chief. He said the finge leader should be informed in the plainest language that he could not be made chief.

At the same time the premier continued, the Chief of Bambui should be represented to accept the Finge leader as a sub chief entitled to enjoying the same privilege as other sub-chiefs in Bambui". In paragraph 17 of the said settlement this is what the premier said: "Regarding the clapping of hands, the premier said that the Finge leader could have to pay the same respect to the Chief of Bambui as is the case with the rest of the sub-chiefs. In this respect, it would be necessary for the chiefs of the Bafut clan to meet as soon as possible in the palace of the Chief of Bambui to finalise the decision on the clapping of hands. This was agreed to by all the chiefs and councillors present and the meeting closed."

(5) With regard to the High Court judgment No. SC/6.A/1960 of 25th January 1961 - that is between Tifinge of Finge (defendant/appellant Vs Chief Amungwafor, village head of Bambui) I say that this judgment is clear, lucid, visible and to me it settled all the problems involving Finge and Bambui, consequently there is nothing by way of interpretation that I can add to this judgment. For the purpose of this judgment I shall reproduce the judgment here in its entirety.

"Concluded judgment: It must have been made plain to the defendants/ Appellant by his counsel and from what I said at the December session that he has lost his Appeal. I gave my detailed grounds then and there is little for me to add to them. This matter was put back for the assessment of general damages as cases such as these are affected by the question as to whether there is continuing challenge by the losing party to the rights-vested in the successful party.

I have said that it has been held by the native court that the defendant appellant is sub chief under the respondent Chief Amungwafor, the village head of Bambui. There is no separate village of which the appellant can be chief himself except as sub-chief to the Bambui village head. Those findings of the native court have been upheld upon review and it is plain that those findings had the support of the court headed by the Fon of Bafut and had the agreement of the district officer upon review.

There are no grounds upon which I am prepared to upset the decision of the learned Magistrate. It is possible that had some indication been given that the appellant did in fact accept the findings of the Native Court I could have held that the matter in dispute had been reduced and it would be justifiable to reduce the amount of general damages, and that might have been reflected in the costs awarded. There can be no question of that now, but I would like to thank Mr. Kubenje and Mr. Ogwo for their efforts to assist the court in trying to arrive at a compromise."

"I have to dismiss the appeal. The respondent must have his costs of these appeal which I assess at twelve guineas".

"I still hope that this is some chance of the parties coming together and accepting the present position for the sake of future peace. I have pronounced the opinion of the High Court of this territory and I think the appelant, a man of mature years, would be wise to counsel his followers to accept it and to accept it himself. It will be enforced, but unless he is prepared to accept it now as final he will only bring unhappiness to his people."

Signed: A. H. Sainbury
Judge."

(7) With regard to the minutes of the reconciliatory meeting of Bambui/Finge which was held in the sub divisional office Bamenda on Friday the 23rd of May 1980 the decision of this meeting can be found in the chairman's remarks. This is what the chairman said".

The Chairman after listening to the contestants lengthy representation pointed out to the parties that Government policy is aimed at bringing good understanding, peace and concord among its people. He blamed the sub chief of Finge for his complete failure to respect decisions of constituted authorities. He warned the sub chief to refrain from his poor behaviour towards the Fon of Bambui and warned in strong terms that he would entertain no further complaint on the issue. If thed sub chief of Finge was not prepared to obey all the decisions contained in the documents presented and hold himself out as a chief independent of the Fon of Bambui, the Divisional officer will cause his arrest for impersonation which was a crime punishable by the Penal Code."

5   From the minutes of the concertation meeting relating to the Bloody clashes between Bambui and Finge it is very clear from these minutes that only four main villages, to wit, Bambui, Bambili, Kedjom Keku and Kedjom Ketingoh make up Tubah Sub Division. Concerning the minutes of the meeting of the 21/8/96 presided by the Governor of the North West Province relating to the conflict
10 between Bambui and Finge conflict the decision that was taken can be found in the Governor's advice. I reproduce it hereunder:

"Then came the final remarks and recommendations of the Governor on this conflict. He first asked the two traditional rulers if they really wanted peace. Each of them answered yes. He then advised them to have first the goodwill to
15 leave in peace. He said from the documents on the issue and the discussions of this meeting, it is clear that the Bambui people came first in that area and the Finge people settled there later on. He stressed that the Finge people cannot leave the area where they are living now. The decision is that decree No. 77/245 of 15/7/1977 shall be implemented. The Finge people will remain under Bambui"
20 Chiefdom as a third class chiefdom. With the collaboration of the Fon of Bambui, the Senior Divisional Officer, for Mezam will take a prefectorial Order and demarcate the boundary of Finge not as an autonomous village but as a quarter inside Bambui village".

25 I have taken the pains to reproduce the various decision of the courts and ministers so that when I am giving my conclusions from all of them it should not be a surprise to anybody. As aforesaid also in this judgment the documents presented for the court's interpretation speak for themselves. There is no ambiguity in them that will require any other interpretation. Nonetheless from all
30 these documents the following simple construction, interpretation or conclusion can be given.

(1) That there is no village known as Finge in Tubah Sub-Division.
(2) That Finge is merely a quarter in Bambui village
(3) That the leader of the Finge people is a third class chief under the Chief of Bambui.

(4) That being under the Fon of Bambui, the sub chief of Finge should pay allegiance to the Fon of Bambui.

From the above findings all the questions contained in 2(a) to (d) of the originating summons have been answered.

With regard to paragraph 3 (a) to 3 (b) of the originating summons the plaintiff should bring a proper action for the court's determination.

"WHEREFORE, THE PRESIDENT OF THE REPUBLIC OF CAMEROON COMMANDS AND ENJOINS ALL BAILIFFS AND PROCESS SERVERS TO ENFORCE THIS RULING, THE PROCUREUR GENERAL AND THE STATE COUNSEL TO GIVE THEM SUPPORT AND ALL COMMANDERS AND OFFICERS OF THE ARMED FORCES AND POLICE FORCE TO GIVE THEM ASSISTANCE WHEN SO REQUIRED BY LAW."

IN WITNESS WHEREOF THE PRESENT JUDGMENT HAS BEEN SIGNED BY THE PRESIDENT/JUDGE AND THE REGISTRAR OF THE COURT.

REGISTRAR-IN-CHIEF

M. C. MOMA
JUDGE.

Notes on Sources

1) Oral Tradition

The area of research which comprised the Bambili and Babanki Tungo communities were semi-literate communities. As a consequence the sources of these works were largely drawn from Oral Tradition- information received from various peoples at different times about their histories. For convenience sake I can distinguish between two broad categories which were systematically used during the field work: firstly, recordings of Oral Tradition or testimony made from people who were contemporary to the events they described and, secondly, recordings from those who only heard the accounts as handed form one generation to the other. It was interesting to note that contemporary oral tradition was recorded in the mid nineteenth century by European visitors who published reports on their ethnographic travels and experiences amongst the people whom they lived with.

It would also appear that the bulk of the contemporary oral tradition was recorded in the first three decades of the twentieth century at the instigation of European officials who desperately needed the information to facilitate their administration. To that effect these reports were largely recorded in pieces of administrative reports, Annual and Intelligence reports. A cursory peruse of the documents shows that the administrators were faced with insurmountable methodological and psychological problems in the collection of the tradition, but however, in the whole their reports remain one of the foundational basis for further research. The importance of these sources as well as archival repositories, for historical construction cannot be underscored. According to the Hiatian scholar, Michel-Rolph Trouillot, in his book, *Silencing the Past: Power and the Production of History*, (1995:52)"archives are institutions that organize facts and sources and condition the possibility of existence of historical statements. Archival power determines the difference between a historian, amateur or professional, and a charlatan". Trouillot continued by saying that, "...archives assembly and their assembly work is not limited to a more or less passive act of collecting. Rather, it is an active act of production that prepares facts for historical intelligibility. Archives set up both the substantive and formal elements of the narrative. They are the institutionalised sites of mediation between the socio historical process and the narrative about the process. They enforce the constraints on debatability and convey authority and set the rules of credibility and inter dependence; they help select the stories that matter".

Although Trouiilot did not pay attention to the other side of the archives it is worth saying here that historical sources cannot be taken uncritically. *Ipso facto*, the archival data that was used in this book were critically interrogated.

Not coming from neither Bambili nor Babanki Tungoh I found it very imperative to used interpreters since I was from the onset handicapped by language. My interpreters were mostly men who commanded local trust and were rooted in the society and its customs as well. Their presence at my side always bridged an essential psychological gap that existed, seemingly, between me and my informants. My principal informants whom I visited both at home-the communities which I was studying and abroad were those known as "historians". The best informed men were those who were nearest the events and as I moved from one place to the other I cross-checked information about one place which I had heard from another.

There was random sampling of the informants whom I visited. I gave no preference to the groups that I interviewed. At times I even had no control over my informants as I was often directed to meet the informants by a notable in the community.

In conclusion I will say like Martin Zachary Njeuma, my history teacher from 1994 to 1998 at the University of Buea, Cameroon, "… success in the collection of historical data from Oral traditions depend upon a number of general rules, but even more so on the personal qualities of the researcher, the time of his visit, the time at his disposal and above all, luck and common sense". It was only in combining all of these qualities that I came out with this volume.

List of Some Principal Informants
(Interviewed between October 1997 and 2006)

Atanga, Lucas. Bamenda, North West Province. Interview 24 August 1997 and 14 December 1997. He has been working with the Lands and Surveys Department, Bamenda since 1975. He also witnessed attempted demarcations of the disputed area in 1995 which led to the dragging of the Divisional Officer to the Bamenda High Court, Bamenda.

Beng, Ambrose. Njinikom, Boyo Division, North West Province. Interview 10 August 1997. On this date he was 90 years being the oldest informant I met on the field. He supplied valuable information with regards the origins and migration of the Kom people.

Benjamin, Aseh. Babanki-Tubgoh North West Province. Interview 20th August 1997 and 2006. The memories of the wars and resultant effects on his uncle and brother were still very fresh in his mind.

Bekeng, Francis. Bambili. N.W. Province. Interview 22nd August 1997. He had been to the war front twice to fight and defend the land of his forefathers as he firmly believed. He was from Babanki-Tungoh.

Besaka, Thomas. Bamenda Town N.W. Province, Interview 26th August 1997.

David, Shomboin. Bambili, Tubah Sub Division, North West Province. Interview 20 August and 28 December 1997. He is a "Chamberlain" of the Bambili palace.

Emmanuel, Yenshu, Department of Anthropology and Sociology, University of Buea, Interview 10 July 1997. He comes from big Babanki and shares the view that Babanki-Tungoh settled in their present site after Bambili.

Faustina, Yembe (Mrs) Great Soppo, Buea, South West Province. Interview 3 February 1998. She was an eye witness to the destruction of Babanki-Tungoh people's property and the disturbing of students.

Helen, Tamgwa. Nkwen Market, Bamenda, North West Province. Interview 20 August 1997. She is popularly known as "Bayam Sellam" and trades in huckleberry cultivated from the disputed area. She maintains that whenever the boundary dispute flared up, the supply of "jamajama" was not constant.

Innocent, Akuli Nkwen, Bamenda, North West Province. Interview 10 November and 17 December 1997. He is a retired police officer and comes from Babanki-Tungoh. He is one of the elite in "diaspora" that contributed in kind towards the sustenance of the war effort.

Joseph, Buteh. Bambili, Mezam Division, North West Province. Interview 8 August and 22 December 1997 and 10 March 2006. He is one of the Bambili educated elite.

Kebeng, John. Small Soppo Buea, South West Province. Interview 24 January 1998. He is one of the Babanki-Tungoh educated elite in "diaspora".

Kohfor, James Bambili, Mezam Division, North West Province. Interview 24 December 1997. He is one of the traditional elite of Bambili (Quarter Head of Membi).

Mbain, Henry. Buea Town, South West Province. Interview 18 August 1997. He is a prince of Kom Fondom and the son of the Kom oral historian, Jinobo II.

Ngong, Julius. Great Soppo Buea, South West Province. Interview 10 December 1997. Being a police officer he enlightened the researcher on what qualifies a Cameroonian to possess arms. He also maintained that people have illegal ways of possessing guns which the government might not know.

Njoussi, David Abang. Small Soppo, Buea, South West Province. Interview 3 January 1998. He was a student in E.N.S. Bambili when his Babanki-Tungoh colleagues were disturbed from writing their examination. In 2007 when I met him again he could vividly remember the names of his classmates who were victimized during the 1991 clashed. I crosschecked the names with the least I had and he was right.

Pius, Chumboin. Buea, South West Province, Interview 25 August, 19 November, 31 November and 24 December 1997. A Babanki-Tungoh elite who strongly holds the view that the disputed territory belongs to Babanki-Tungoh. Unfortunately, they do not possess any land certificate. I later on met him in Bamenda in 2004 but he had not changed his mind from his previous ideas.

Takwifon, Fidelis. Bambili, N.W. Province. Interview 30th August 1997. He had witnessed the attempted demarcation in 1992, 1995 and still holds very strongly that the two communities must hold on to the Westmacott decision of 1958.

Tingum, Edward Ndi. Buea, South West Province. Interview 8 January 1998. He is the Director of Lands and Surveys Department, Bamenda. I later met him again on 13 September 2001 and gathered fresh information on government's attitude towards land ownership in Cameroon.

Voyuoh, Nelson. Babanki. N.W. Province. Interview 8 September 1997.

2) National Archives Buea
i) Assessment Reports

Cantle, L.L. Assessment Report on the Wum Native-Authority of the Bamenda Division, 1932.

Evans, G.V. An Assessment Report on the Kom (Bikom) Clan, 1926. Georges, E.H.F. An Assessment Report on the Kake-Ntem Area, 1932.

Gregg, C.J.A. Assessment Report on the Meta Clan of the Bamenda Division, 1924.

Hawkesworth, E.G. Assessment Report on the Bafut Tribal Area of the Bamenda Division, 1926.

_____, Assessment Report on the Banso District, 1922.

_____, Assessment Report on the Nsungli Clan, 1924.

_____, Assessment Report on the Bafut and Babanki, Bamenda Division, 1931.

Hunt, W.E. Assessment Report on the Bali Clan of Bamenda Division, 1925.

Pollock, J.H.H. An Assessment Report on the Bum Area, 1927. Smith, J.S. Fongom District Assessment Report, 1929.

William, G.S. An Assessment Report on the Ngunu and Neighbouring Villages, 1926.

Ab 20 Assessment Report on Moghamo and Ngemba, Bamenda Division, 1926.

Ab 22 Assessment Report on bandop Area, Bamenda Division , 1924.

Ac 9 The Mbembe Assessment Report, Bamenda Division, 1926.

ii) Intelligence Reports

Carpenter, F.W. Intelligence Report on Nsungli Clans, Bamenda Division 1934.

_____, Intelligence Report on the Mbaw Mbem and Nfumte areas, Bamenda Division, 1935.

Croasdale, C.H. Intelligence Report on Moghamo Speaking Families of the Widekum Tribe in Bamenda Division, 1933.

Hook, R.J. An Intelligence Report on the Associated Village Groups occupying the Bafut Native Authority area of Bamenda Division, 1933.

_____, Intelligence Report on the Ngie Clan, Bamenda Division, 1933.

Johnson, V.K. Intelligence Report on the Meta Clan in the Bamenda Division, 1935.

_____, Intelligence Report on the Fungom Area, Bamenda Division, 1936.

Newton R. Report on the Re-Organisation of the Wum, Befang, and Beba Tribes in the Wum Native Authority Area, Bamenda Division, 1934.

_____, Intelligence and re-assessment Report on the Ngemba Area, Bamenda Division, 1934.

File No. 596 Handing Over Notes Bamenda Division, 11, November 1941.

File No. 596 Handing Over Notes for Bamenda Division, 16 April 1946.

File No. 1441 Minutes of the third Conference of Chiefs and Natural Rulers, Bamenda Province, held at Ball on November 10, 1954.

File No. NW/1974/1, Social, cultural and Land Conflicts in the North West Province, 197461984.

3) Published Sources
I. Articles

Adadevoh, I.O. "Ethnicism and the Democratization of Civil Society: Envisioning Changes in the Proximal and Causal Ideologies of Marginality in Africa and America" *Afrika Zamani*, Nos. 9 and 10, 2001-2002: 1-18.

Asiwaju, A. I. "Towards an Ethnohistory of African State Boundaries" (Paper for UNESCO Seminar on Methodology of Contemporary History Of Africa, Ouagadougou, May 1979).

_____, The Concept of Frontier in the Setting of State in pre-Colonial Africa." *Presence Africaine*, Special ness 32/34, 1983.

_____. "Problem Solving Along African Borders: The Nigeria-Benin Case Since 1989" in Oscar J. Martinez (ed). *Across Boundaries: Transborder Interaction in Comparative perspective*. Texas, U.S.A. University of Texas Press, 1986.

Raymond, W. Mack and Richard, C. Snyder "The Analysis of Social Conflict: Towards an Overview and Synthesis". *The Journal of Conflict Resolution*, 1957, 1:121- 248.

Touval, S. "The Organisation of African Unity of African Unity and African Borders" *International Organisation.*^^ 1, 1967.

_____. "Africa's Frontiers: Reactions to a Colonial Legacy" *International Affairs,* 4, 1996, pp. 641 -651.

_____. "Treaties Borders and the Partition of Africa," *Journal of African History* VII, 1996, pp. 641-651.

Wallerstein, I., "Ethnicity and National Integration in West Africa" *Cahiers d'Etudes Africaines, 3 October 1960pp; 129 — 39.*

Zartman, I.W. "The Politics of Boundaries in North and West Africa" *Journal of Modern African Studies,* III, 2.73.

II Books

Ajayi, J,F. Ade and Crowder, Michael, (eds.) *History of West Africa. 2* Vols. London: Longman, 1976.

Anene J.C. *The International Boundaries of Nigeria : The Framework of an emergent African Nation.* London: Longman, 1970.

_____, and Brown Godfrey, (eds). *African in the Nineteenth and Twentieth Centuries.* Ibadan, Nigeria: Ibadan University Press, 1966.

Assefa, H. *Peace and Reconciliation as a Paradigm.* Nairobi: Nairobi Peace Initiative Monographs Series, 1993.

Asiwaju, A.I. (ed). *Partitioned Africans: Ethnic Relations Across Africa's International Boundaries, 1884 - 1984.* Lagos, Nigeria: Lagos University Press, 1985.

_____. *Borderlands Research: A Comparative Perspective.* Texas, U.S.A: Border Perspective Monograph Series, Center for Inter-American and Border Studies, University of Texas et El Paso, 1983.

_____. *Artificial Boundaries.* New York: Civilities International, 1990.

Barth, F. (ed.) *Ethnic Groups and Boundaries.* Bergen, Oslo: Universities - Forlaget, 1969.

Bertram, Christoph (ed). *Third World Conflict and International Security.* London: Macmillan, &9_e.

Bleisem, J. Van. *A Geography of West Cameroon.* Buea: Government Printing Press, 1967.

Boggs, S.W. *International Boundaries: A Study of Boundary Functions.* New York: Academic Press, 1940.

Bohannan, Paul. *Africa and Africans.* New York: the Natural History Press, 1964.

Boutros-Ghali, B. *Les Conflits des frontiers en Afrique.* Paris : Etudes et documents, 1973.

Brownlie, I. *African Boundaries: A Legal and Diplomatic Encyclopedia.* London: C. Hurst, 1972.

Chilver, E.M. and Kaberry. P.M. *Traditional Bamenda. Vol 1: Pre-Colonial History and Ethnography of the Bamenda Grassfields.* Buea: Government Printing Press, 1967.

Clark, Colin. *Population Growth and Land Use.* London: Macmillan, 1967.

Cook, Chris. *Dictionary of Historical Terms.* New York: Peter Bedrick Book, 1989.

Collins, Robert O. (ed). *Problems in African History.* New Jersey, U.S.A.: Englewood Cliffs, 1968.

Curtin, Philipe, Feierman, Steven, Thompson, Leonard, and Vansina, Jan. *African History.* London: Longman, 1978.

Davidson, Basil with Buah F.K. *The Growth of African Civilization: A History of West Africa 1000 - 1800.* NOP.., N.D.

Davidson, Basil *Old Africa Rediscovered.* London: Longman, 1989.

_____, *Which Way Africa? The Search for A New Society.* London: Penguin Books, 1964.

Dillon, Richard G. *Notes on the Pre-Colonial History and Ethnology of Meta.* Paris: Les Editions Internationales, 1973.

_____. *Violent Conflict in Meta Society.* Paris: Les Editions Internationales, 1980.

Douglas, Mary; Barry, Gerald ; Bronowski, J ; and Fisher, James S. *Man in society: patterns of Human Organisation.* New York, U.S.A.: Doubledey and Co. Inc. 1964.

Duignan, P. and Gann, L.H. *Colonialism in Africa, 1870 - 1970, 5 Vols:* The Politics and economics of Colonialism. Cambridge: Cambridge University Press, 1975.

East, Gordon W. *An Historical Geography of Europe.* London: Metheun&Co.Ltd., 1948.

Espie, Ian and Ade, J.F. *A Thousand Years of West African History.* Ibadan, Nigeria: Ibadan University Press, 1965.

Eyongetah, Tambi and Brian, Robert. *A History of the Cameroon.* London: Longman, 1974.

Ezenwe, Uka. *ECOWAS and the Economic integration of West Africa.* Ibadan, Nigeria: West Books Publishers, 1984.

Page, J.D. *A History of West Africa.* Cambridge: Cambridge University Press, 1969.

Fanso, V.G. *Cameroon History for Secondary Schools and Colleges Vol; I. Prehistoric Times to the nineteenth century.* London: Macmillan, 1989.

_____. *Cameroon History for Secondary Schools and Colleges Vol. 2. From Colonial and Post-Colonial Periods.* London: Macmillan, 1989.

Fardon, R.O. *Raiders and Refugees in Chamba Political Development 1750-1950.* Washington, D.C.: Smithsonian Institution Press, 1988.

Forde, Daryll and Kaberry, P.M. (eds). *West African Kingdoms in the nineteenth century.* Oxford: Oxford University Press, 1967.

Fortes S.M. and Evans-Pritchard. *African Political Systems.* London: Longman, 1940.

Fowler, Ian and Zeitlyn. *African Crossroads: Intersections between History and Anthropology in Cameroon.* 2 Vols. Oxford: Berghan Books Providence, 1996.

Fukui, Katsuyoshi and Markakis, John (eds). *Ethnicity and Conflcit in the Horn of Africa.* Athens: Ohio University Press, 1993.

Gann, L.H. and Duignan, Peter. *The rulers of German Africa, 1884 -1914.* Cambridge: Cambridge University Press, 1977.

Genove, S. Satiago. *Is Peace Inevitable: Aggression Evolution and Human Destiny.* New York, U.S.A.: Walker and Co., 1970.

Gescheire, P. and Nyamnjoh, Francis B. "Capitalism and Autochthony: The Seesaw of Mobility and Belonging. *Public Culture* 12 (2): 143-52.

Gould, J. and Kolb, W.L. (eds). *Dictionary of Social Science.* Glencoe: Free Press, 1965.

Hagget, Peter. *Geography: A Modern Synthesis.* London: Harper and Fro w Publishers, 1972.

Hargreaves, J.D. *Prelude to the Partition of West Africa*. London: Macmillan, 1963.

Harthshorne, L. *A Study of the Boundary Problems of Europe*. Cambridge: Cambridge University Press, 1938.

Hatch, John. *A History of Post War Africa*. New York, U.S.A.: Praeger, 1965.

Hazlewood, Arthur (ed). *African Integration and Disintegration*. Oxford: Oxford University Press, 1967.

Holdich, T.H. *Political Frontiers and Boundary Making*. London: Longman, 1916.

Jones, S.B. *Boundary Making: A Handbook for Statesmen, Treaty editors and Boundary Commissioners*. Washington D.C.: Carnegie Endowment, 1945.

Karp, Mark. *African Dimensions: Essays in Honour of William Brown*. Boston: Boston University Press, 1975.

King, Grace E. *Conflict and Harmony*. London: George Philip Ltd. 1972.

Lugard, Sir F. D. *The dual Mandate in British Tropical Africa*. London: Longman, 1923.

Mack, Raymond W. *Race and Power*. New York, U.S.A.: American Book Co. 1963.

Malthus, Thomas Robert. *An Essay on Population*. 2 Vols. London: J.M. Dent, 1958.

Martinez, Oscar J. (ed). *Across Boundaries: Transborder Interaction in Comparative Perspective*. Texas, U.S.A: University of Texas Press, 1986.

Mazrui, Ali I. A. *The Africans. A Triple Heritage*. London: BBC Publications, 1986.

McEwen, A.C. *International Boundaries of East Africa*. Oxford University Press, 1971.

Money, D.C. *Patterns of Settlement: Human Geography in Colour*. London: Evans Brothers Ltd., 1972.

Murdock, G. *Africa: Its Peoples and Culture History*. New York: McGraw Hill, 1959.

Mveng, Engelbert. *Histoire du Cameroun*. Yaounde, Cameroun: CEPER, 1984.

Nelson, Harold D., Dobert, Margarita, McDonald, Gordon C., Laughlin, James Mc., Marvin, Barbara and Moeller, Phillippe W. *An Area Handbook for the United Republic of Cameroon*. Wisconsin, U.S.A.: Wisconsin University Press, 1974.

Ngwane, George. *Settling Disputes in Africa: Traditional bases for Conflcit Resolution*. Yaounde: Buma Kor House, 1996.

Ngoh, Victor J. *Cameroon since 1800*. Limbe: Presbook Ltd. 1996.

Njeuma, Martin Zachary. *Fulani Hegemony in Yola (Old Adamawa) 1809-1902*. Yaounde, Cameroon: CEPER 1978.

Nkwi, P. N. *Traditional Diplomacy: A Study of Inter-Chiefdom Relations in the Western Grassfields, North West Province of Cameroon*. Yaounde: Department of Sociology, 1987.

_____. *Traditional Government and Social Change: a study of the Political Institutions among the Kom of the Cameroon Grassfields*. Switzerland: University of Fribourg Press, 1976.

_____, and Warmer, J.P. *Elements for a History of the Western Grassfields*. Yaounde: SOPECAM, 1982.

Nkwi, Walter Gam, "Elites, Ethno-regional competition in Cameroon, and the Southwest elites association (SWELA), 1991-1997" *Africa Study Monographs*, 27, (3) (October 2006):123-143.

_____, "Boundary Conflicts in Africa: A Case Study of Bambili and Babanki Tungoh (North West Province of Cameroon), c.1950-1995" *Journal of Applied Social Sciences: A Multidisciplinary Journal of the Faculty of Social and Management Sciences*, vol.6, No.1and 2 (2007):6-41.

Nyamnjoh, Francis B. *Insiders and Outsiders: Citizenship and Xenophobia in Contemporary Southern Africa*. London: Zed Press, 2006.

_____*Africa, s Media: Democracy and the Politics of Belonging*. London and New York: Zed Books, 2005.

_____ "Ethical Challenges and Responsibilities in Social Research: An Introductory Essay" n.d.: n.p.

Paden, John N. and Soja, Edward W. (eds.) *The African Experience*. 2 Vols. London: Heinemann Educational Books, 1970.

Palmer, Alan. *The Penguin Dictionary of Modern History, 1789 - 1945*. London: Penguin Books, 1989.

Presscott, J.R.V. *The Evolution of Nigeria's International and Regional Boundaries, 1861-1671.* Vancouver: Tantalus Research, 1971.

_____. *The Geography of Frontiers and Boundaries.* London: Hutchinson University Library, 1965.

_____. The Evolution of Anglo-French Inter-*Cameroons* Boundary. Paris. C.N.R.S., 1975.

Robinson, Kennedy and Madden, Federick A. (eds). *Essay in Imperial Government presented to Magery Preham.* Oxford: basil Blackwell, 1963.

Rosen, Steven and Jones, Walter. *The Logic of International Relations.* Massachusetts: Withrop Publishers, 1974.

Rubin, Neville. *Cameroon: An African Federation.* London: Prager, 1971.

Rudin, H.R. *Germans in the Cameroons 1884-191: A Study of Modern Imperialism.* New York, U.S.A.: Yale University Press, 1938.

Sertillanges, A.D. *Foundations of Thomistic Philosophy.* London: Northumberland Press, 1931.

Stamp, Sir Dudley (ed.) *A Glossary of Geographical Terms.* London: Longman, 1966.

Sullivan, Michael P; *International Relations: Theories and evidence.* New Jersey" Prentice-Hall Inc, 1976.

Truillot, Michel-Rolph. *Silencing the Past: Power and Production of History.* Boston, Massachusset: Beacon Press, 1995.

Turabian, Kate L. *A Manual for Writers of Term Papers, theses and Dissertation.* Chicago: University of Chicago Press, 1967.

Warnier, J.P. *Pre-Colonial Mankon: The Development of Cameroon Chiefdom in its regional Setting.* Pennsylvania, U.S.A. University of Pennsylvania Press, 1975.

Whynne-Hammond, Charles. *Elements of Human Geography.* London: UnwinHyman, 1985.

Widstrand, C.G. (ed.) *African Boundary Problems.* Uppsala: Nordiska Afrikainstulet, 1969.

4) Unpublished Sources
Long Essays, Theses and Dissertations

Isidore, Yuntenwi. "The Inception and Growth of Christianity in Bambili Village, 1922-1993". B.A. dissertation, University of Buea, 1997.

Lima, Pascal Valondeng. "Babanki-Bambili Relations, 1958-1995" B.A. Long Essay, University of Buea, 1996.

Mambego, Ngwefimi Alfred. "The Tikari Fondom of Bafanji since 1800" B.A. Dissertation, University of Buea, 1997.

Mbutruh, Nyiwatumi Eric. "The Economy and Society of Southern Cameroons Under British Colonial domination, c. 1916 - 1961: A Case study of the Impact of British Imperialism on Bamenda Division". M.A. Thesis, Ahmadu Bello University Zaria, 1995.

Minang, J.W. "The Bambili Chiefdom and its Institutions". Post-graduate Teachers Diploma, E.NS. Yaounde, 1986.

Oliver, Gam Chiati, "A Pastorial Approach to Conflcit Resolution" B.A. dissertation (Theology) St. Thomas Aquinas' Major Seminary Bambui - Affiliate of the Pontifical urban University, Rome, 1997.

Simo, Mope J.A., "Gender, Agro-Pastoral Production and class Formation in Bamunka, North West Cameroon" PhD Dissertation, University of East Anglia, 1991.

Sango, Ndeh Martin: "The Bali-Batibo Conflict 1930 6 19523 B.A. Long Essay, University of Buea, 1996.

Tembi, Njong Paul. "The Mengen-Bali Dispute 1891 - 1982" B.A. Long Essay, University of Buea, 1996.

Wombong, Befika Christopher. "Tribal Wars in Ndop (Ngoketunjia-division) 1955-1995: Causes and Consequences. B.A. Long Essay, University of Buea, 1996.

Che-Mfombong, Walters. "Bamenda Division Under British Administration 1916 - 1961: From native Administration to Local Government" M.A. Thesis, University of Yaounde, 1980.

Fanso, V.G. "Trans Frontier Relations and Resistance to Cameroon-Nigeria Colonial Boundaries, 1916 - 1945", Doctoral d'état, University of Yaounde.

George, Atem. "Cameroon-Nigeria Relations, 1884 - 1960". Ph. D. Dissertation, University of Calabar, 1984.

Nzume, Anastasia Nlende. "The Colonial Frontier and Bilingualism in Cameroon: The Case Study of the Bakossi, 1936 - 1961". Doctorat de 3eme Cycle, University of Yaounde, 1988.

Newspapers and Journals
Newspaper

The Herald

Cameroon Tribune

Le Messenger

Cameroon Post

www.ingramcontent.com/pod-product-compliance
Lightning Source LLC
Chambersburg PA
CBHW031549300426
44111CB00006BA/231